HERE
NOT
THERE

Trek through Italy's Adamello-
Brenta Nature Park for
breathtaking views (page 132).

HERE NOT THERE

100 UNEXPECTED TRAVEL DESTINATIONS

Andrew Nelson

NATIONAL GEOGRAPHIC

Washington, D.C.

Indonesia is home to Borobudur,
the world's largest Buddhist temple
(page 196).

Contents

Front cover: This may look like Hawaii, but it's actually a pathway on Portugal's Azores.
Back cover (clockwise from top left): Visit Riga, Latvia, rather than popular Prague, Czechia; see Alaska's big five in Denali National Park & Preserve instead of Africa's big five; take in the Pont de Grenelle Statue of Liberty in Paris as an alternative to New York's Lady Liberty; go bird-watching on California's Channel Islands rather than on Ecuador's Galápagos Islands; see mosaics in Philadelphia that rival well-known art installations in Brooklyn; kayak around Detroit's Belle Isle rather than Biscayne Bay in Miami.

Introduction

Where are we going to go next? After the turbulence of the past few years, with travelers confronting every frustration from inflation to canceled flights to jam-packed destinations, this question elicits consternation as much as it does anticipation. And a decision is not made easier by a rush of often conflicting suggestions coming from your well-meaning family and friends: *What about Yellowstone? Bora-Bora? Turks and Caicos? Austin?* Confusion reigns. Meanwhile, on your feeds and screens the media happily promote "top 10" lists for just about every conceivable kind of vacation, while scrolls through Instagram and TikTok show breathless travel influencers hyping destinations such as Iceland's hot springs, Sicilian hill towns, or the temples of Cambodia's Angkor Wat as the #MostAmazing spot to visit now. The result? In some of the planet's most inspiring places, visitors are confronted with long waits, short tempers, and costly stays.

Travelers' aggravations span the globe. The best time to see Rome's Trevi Fountain is now 7:30 a.m. In Kenya's Masai Mara National Reserve, there are more jeep sightings than lions. And Amsterdam is running online ads to *discourage* people from visiting. No one can blame the Dutch city. A tsunami of sightseers is not just a passing irritant; too

The Fontes Windmill overlooks the lush meadows of Graciosa Island in the Azores (page 238).

Walk beneath the falls in
Nantahala National Forest in
North Carolina (page 72).

For a less crowded light show, head down under for Tasmania's aurora australis (page 54).

many visitors can be an existential threat to a destination itself. Overtourism and its attendant environmental degradations overwhelm even our most treasured places: Bali must fight a tide of plastic on its beaches. Crowds overwhelm the resources of Florence. Short-term rentals are pushing out lifelong New Orleanians from the places where they once danced, played music, and cooked up a storm. Sadly, we have discovered, we can love a place to death.

Consider *Here Not There* a modest proposal to help with all that. Use it as a tool to help decide where you're going to go and a compendium of truly interesting places frequently overlooked by the FOMO crowd. The following pages present 100 alternatives to the usual traveler's bucket-list destinations you've always heard about. First, however, let's be clear about one thing: I'm not suggesting you avoid visiting the classic destinations for which I've provided an equally appealing alternative. Far from it. Humphrey Bogart was right when he told Ingrid Bergman in the classic 1942 film *Casablanca*, "We'll always have Paris." We will. As well as Buenos Aires, the Everglades, and the Taj Mahal. Such places will be forever part of our shared cultural heritage—and worthy of our visits and our wonder. So I present these 100 new destinations with the assumption that travelers will, at some point in their lives, see the classic landmarks. Instead, *Here Not There* offers a suggestion that there are some new ones to visit as well.

Inside you'll discover a raft of imaginative destinations (Here) that possess some of the same attributes we love about iconic places (There) but without the same costs or the hassles that can afflict more popular spots. For example: The Smoky Mountains are often jammed with lines of cars, but just a hop away, the Cumberland Gap (page 122) offers a similar national park without the gridlock. Feeling the need to celebrate amid vivid local color? Consider San Antonio for Fiesta (page 18) instead of Venice for Carnival. How about Tasmania (page 54) to see the southern lights (aurora australis) instead of Scandinavia to view the northern ones? You might even see a wallaby or a kangaroo. Or head to Alaska's Denali National Park and Preserve (page 78) for its version of a "big five" photo safari instead of South Africa. Explore the Azores (page 238) if Hawaii seems too far or too familiar. And if you do happen to make it to the

A mural commemorates where Washington, D.C., native and jazz pioneer Duke Ellington held his first paid performance (page 313).

Aloha State, don't just hit Diamond Head or drive the Hana Highway, add a visit to the island of Molokai (page 262) for a taste of authentic Hawaii long vanished from the beach at Waikiki. Then there are the usual tourist magnets: The great cities are still great, but instead of a repeat visit to London, how about trying Manchester (page 16), two zippy hours away by train? Art lovers may come back to Santa Fe's galleries, but they should also check out the art in Asheville (page 94), aka "Santa Fe East," and make a plan to revisit New Mexico's capital for Zozobra (page 298), a family-friendly version of Burning Man that's decades older. Something new is waiting for your discovery.

Start with short trips. Should you only have a three-day weekend to explore a new part of the United States, why not visit Indianapolis (page 166) to explore its canals and urban biking culture instead of Amsterdam? If you're on business in a familiar city, uncover what's unfamiliar there: Try swapping East Los Angeles for West Los Angeles (page 330), taking a break from Washington, D.C.'s many museums to walk around the District's historic African American Shaw neighborhood (page 312), or stepping away from San Diego's beaches to shop and wander in the city's historic Latino community Barrio Logan (page 316).

Of course, this doesn't mean you'll have these places exclusively to yourself. Many of these suggestions are also popular with residents, but mixing it up with the locals carries positive benefits itself. Such encounters offer you a chance to dive deeper into culture and community and forge authentic connections between visitors and residents.

Take in the colorful buildings along historic Calle La Ronda in Quito, Ecuador (page 32).

Some suggestions will surprise: Travel to the Netherlands instead of Montana to encounter a wild buffalo herd? They're there (page 70). And some may even startle: Cleveland's theater scene and not New York's (page 164)? The city's theater district, Playhouse Square, is the largest performance art center in the United States west of the Hudson River. So, why not?

My hope is that this new bucket list prompts you to think out of the box for your next trip, and even the one after that. These suggestions often come with the added bonus of fewer people and lower cost. So settle into a comfortable chair, open your mind, and turn the pages to find adventure, history, and wonder *here*—not there.

More than 150 feral horses inhabit the sandy shores of Cumberland Island, Georgia (page 248).

CHAPTER 1

NEW ICONS

Napa and Venice are legends, but crowded ones—as any traveler stuck in a Wine Country traffic jam or shoulder to shoulder in a swarm on the Piazza San Marco knows. The world is full of these iconic tourist attractions. Here are 10 alternatives in unexpected locales that range from Southeast Asia to a reborn Alamo.

Watch the sun sink into the Atlantic from Montevideo's Pocitos Beach (page 26).

For Authentic Southeast Asian Street Life
George Town, Malaysia

Instead of Singapore

Inside Pinang Peranakan Mansion, marvel at more than 1,000 antiques and collectibles.

Singapore's modernity dazzles. The rich Southeast Asian city-state with a futuristic skyline and high-tech infrastructure marches forward, but at a cost. Much of its old heritage vanished as redevelopment transformed the formerly low-rise city into a new-age metropolis. If you miss the old Singapore (or never knew it to begin with), there's another Asian port city that has preserved much of its past. The city of George Town in Malaysia's state of Penang has kept the 21st century at arm's length to better protect its low-rise, old-fashioned charm. George Town's diversity—a blend of Chinese, Indian, and Malay cultures—is similar to that of skyscraping Singapore, but the city's noisy, vibrant neighborhoods are a portal to another time.

George Town is the state capital of Penang, which lies on Malaysia's west coast along the Strait of Malacca, 370 miles (595 km) northwest of Singapore. Founded by the British, who ruled it for 150 years, George Town was built by the sweat and ingenuity of its Native Malays as well as other Asian immigrants who labored here. As a free port, George Town prospered by trading Southeast Asia's riches, including cinnamon, peppers, nutmeg, and silks—items still for sale today beneath its colonnaded arcades.

Today the heart of George Town's old city is preserved as a 64-acre (26 ha) UNESCO World Heritage site. The tightly packed and steamy streets offer surprises on every corner, including splashes of modernity in the guise of colorful, **city-sponsored murals**. There are also numerous walking tours, including several self-guided ones. The Penang Heritage Trust, a nonprofit historical organization, is a good place to discover the best routes.

Traders of every nationality set up small businesses in George Town and midwifed its signature

Take a pedicab around George Town in search of the city-sponsored murals.

architecture—the narrow two- and three-story town houses called shop-houses. The buildings usually featured small retailers such as grocers, tailors, and barbers at street level, while families lived on the floors above. Shaded walkways kept pedestrians out of the sun and rain, and colorful and decorative tiles marked the floors and walls. The tiles are George Town's signature. Called Peranakan tiles, they were named after the pioneering South Chinese migrants who settled in the ports along the Strait of Malacca. On Church Street the **Pinang Peranakan Mansion**, the former home of a 19th-century trading tycoon, illuminates the history of this influential community.

George Town's ethnic kaleidoscope finds expression in a mix of Taoist, Hindu, Christian, and Muslim holy sites tucked behind hidden courtyards or shoehorned between ordinary homes. Visitors can call on the Chinese **Goddess of Mercy Temple**, an 18th-century Taoist complex on Pitt Street, and the colorful **Sri Maha Mariamman Temple**, the oldest Hindu sanctuary in **Little India**, a section of town known for its aromatic shops selling curry powders and spices, garlands of flowers, and saris of every color. Traces of British rule remain on view as well. Atop a plinth near the old colonial **Fort Cornwallis** stands **a statue of a homesick-looking Queen Victoria**, forever peering toward England.

As might be expected, hotels in George Town are also historic in nature. Many of the accommodations are in restored shophouses, each one seemingly more evocative than the next. Then there's the **Eastern & Oriental**, a grand wedding cake of a hotel built during British rule that sprawls like a Victorian garden party along the water. There's no better end to a day spent exploring this fascinating city's streets than gathering poolside beneath the E&O's palms to watch the sun drop into the sea.

Penang's Street Food

The same multicultural mixture found along George Town streets is found on its cooktops and stoves. The local cuisine is a mix of spice, heat, and flavors that reflects the city's diversity. A traditional Penang breakfast might include a plate of *roti canai*, a rolled pancake served with various sauces, or another Malaysian favorite, *nasi lemak*, a mound of white rice soaked in coconut milk and accompanied by roasted peanuts or dried anchovies.

For a midmorning snack, order *roti bakar*—essentially two slices of grilled toast with your choice of sweet or savory filling. Visit Little India to sample samosas and dosas sold on the street, or have a sit-down meal at one of the neighborhood's many vegetarian restaurants. Try *nasi kandar*, a fiery rice-and-curry halal dish traditionally made by Indian and Malay Muslims. For dinner head to the harbor for *koay teow th'ng*—flat rice noodles in a savory, clear soup served with bits of chicken or duck or fish balls.

Given this variety of tastes and dishes, myriad food tours here specialize in various kinds of meals, such as traditional breakfasts, dinners, or street fare.

For a Buzzy, Busy English City
Manchester, England, U.K.

Instead of London, England, U.K.

Everyone needs to visit London before they die—but there's more to British urbanity than Notting Hill Gate or Piccadilly Circus. Manchester's got the verve to elbow aside other cities in a bid for an alternative to another London pub crawl. Travelers will find this northwest English city, only a two-hour train ride from the British capital, to be an energetic, diverse place with a rich past and legendary pop music.

Manchester claims suffragette Emmeline "Deeds Not Words" Pankhurst, Harry Styles, and a club scene made famous by the film *24 Hour Party People*. Its downtown will seem familiar to North American visitors with its mix of Victorian brick and terra-cotta buildings interspersed with glassy skyscrapers such as the skinny 47-story **Beetham Tower**. The mix of old and new has attracted many filmmakers: **Dale Street**, in the city's North Quarter neighborhood, has served as the cinematic body double for New York City and other locales in action films such as *Captain America: The First Avenger*. But Manchester forged deep links to the United States way before Hollywood, as its statue of Abraham Lincoln attests. During the Civil War the U.S. president thanked Mancunians for their refusal to handle Southern cotton in the city's textile mills. Manchester, in turn, honored him with a statue.

As a center of the industrial revolution, Manchester was known as the "shock city of the new." Celebrity tourists from Charles Dickens to Karl Marx flocked there to gawp at the latest technological advances. Visitors today can have fun exploring its **system of canals** that once transported goods and raw materials beneath riveted steel bridges and past enormous brick warehouses and cast-iron buildings that resemble a steampunk Venice. To learn about the machines and their impact, visit Manchester's newly expanded **Science and Industry**

Opened January 1, 1900, the John Rylands Research Institute and Library houses much of the University of Manchester's special collections.

The Manchester skyline showcases the Beetham Tower (center left) and a cluster of four buildings that make up Deansgate Square (center right).

Museum and clamber up nearby **Castlefield Viaduct**—an enormous railroad trestle with its new High Line–style gardens—and gaze down on the ruins left by the Romans who established the city. Also visit Britain's **National Football Museum**, unsurprisingly located in the home of Manchester United, the city's world-famous soccer team.

Manchester's Gilded Age tycoons built imposing monuments such as the great neo-Gothic **John Rylands Research Institute and Library**—allegedly the inspiration for Harry Potter's Hogwarts—and the **Manchester Art Gallery**, noted for its collection of pre-Raphaelite paintings. They left the city with a grandeur that survived its decline after World War II. Manchester's 21st-century revival attracted thousands of new residents to its urban core, drawn by cutting-edge cultural institutions such as **Factory International**, which opened in 2023, a futuristic performance space built on the site of an old TV studio.

Two places to stay include **Native Manchester**, a former 19th-century warehouse with an industrial lobby sporting an enormous bar, and the **Dakota Manchester**, part of a boutique British chain. Both are in the Piccadilly East neighborhood.

BBC radio broadcaster Mark Radcliffe once described Manchester as "a city that thinks a table is for dancing on." That's true, especially on weekends when music spills onto the streets outside downtown dance clubs and entertainment complexes such as **Escape to Freight Island**, housed in an abandoned railway freight depot, or **Mackie Mayor**, a food hall in a Victorian-era building. Nightlife focal points are the **Gay Village** on Canal Street—the heart of the LGBTQIA+ community—and the **Northern Quarter**. Such exuberance stems partly from being home to four major universities and more than 100,000 college students, ensuring Manchester will remain "Madchester," a lively, boisterous town well worth discovering.

Manchester's Big Noise

London may have fostered the Swinging Sixties, but younger fans who are still old enough to remember disco, new wave, or the explosion of 1990s dance and trance beats will appreciate the impact of Manchester's storied pop music and cultural scene. The city that raised up the Bee Gees (the lyricists behind "Stayin' Alive" and "Night Fever" relocated to Australia in their teens) became a musical powerhouse in the 1980s and '90s, birthing legendary bands such as Joy Division, the Smiths, and Oasis. Not to mention New Order and the Stone Roses. Their successes established Manchester as a music history mecca, says local authority and writer Jonathan Schofield, who, among other tours, conducts a detailed musical walk of his city, complete with a playlist of Manchester hits. The meandering tour takes visitors into the city's nooks, crannies, and neighborhoods. It includes iconic site visits to landmarks such as the **Salford Lads Club**, a youth and recreational hall that appeared on a famous Smiths album cover; the famed **Factory Records** offices, now a nightclub; **The Hacienda**, a popular 1980s and '90s music venue and now apartments, at 15 Whitworth Street West; and **The Boardwalk**, a venue on Little Peter Street where Oasis got its start. The Edwardian Manchester hotel on Peter Street stands at the site of the old **Lesser Free Trade Hall**, where the Sex Pistols performed the "gig that changed the world," a seminal 1976 concert.

Stroll San Antonio's River Walk or hop on a river barge for a guided tour.

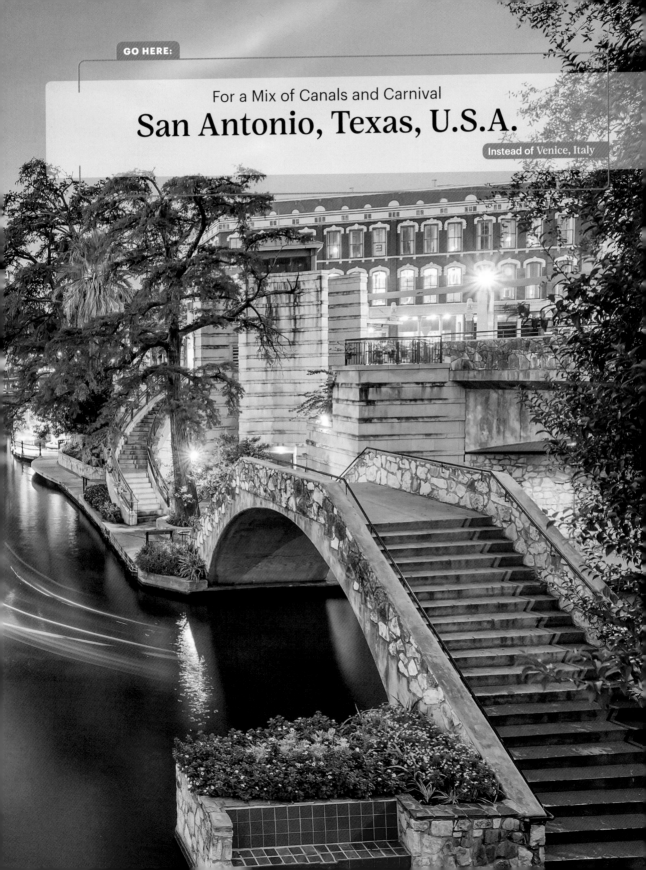

For a Mix of Canals and Carnival

San Antonio, Texas, U.S.A.

Instead of Venice, Italy

Imagine a city of colonnades and canals distinctly *not* Venice. That Italian city, celebrated for its gondolas and atmospheric architecture, fosters a sense of both intimacy and history, but there's a North American city also graced with a watery downtown where residents know how to party as exuberantly as any masked reveler on the Piazza San Marco. San Antonio, deep in the heart of Texas, is a place full of traditions as colorful as those along the Grand Canal and home to a party called Fiesta, which is filled with as much music, costumes, and color as the Venetian Carnival.

More than 300 years old, San Antonio is perhaps the most soulful city in Texas—a place of historic battles ("Remember the Alamo!") and multicultural firsts. The city's heritage is a tangle of Black, Mexican, German, and Czechian roots that's fostered musical traditions, such as mariachi, Tejano, and polka, as well as edible ones. San Antonio—one of the progenitors of what came to be called Tex-Mex cuisine—has fused the food traditions of its original settlers as a host of new chefs reinvent dishes, such as Texas quail and schnitzel and donuts drizzled with green jalapeño syrup. In 2017 San Antonio was named a UNESCO Creative City of Gastronomy, one of the first in North America, and it hosts one of only four campuses of the Culinary Institute of America.

Many of the ornate houses of the King William Historic District were constructed in the mid to late 19th century.

Like Venice, San Antonio's distinguishing feature is the urban waterways that snake through the heart of the city. An early 20th–century effort to control floods on the San Antonio River led to the linear park, called the **River Walk**, that now weaves through the downtown with landscaped walkways below the street level. The River Walk now extends 15.2 miles (24.4 km) in either direction. Head north to the **San Antonio Museum of Art** and the **Witte Museum**. The River Walk reestablished the river's riparian woodlands while connecting four **Spanish colonial missions**, all UNESCO World Heritage sites.

For the past decade San Antonio has worked hard to expand its urban amenities. It has reimagined its 1968 World's Fair site, spending $400 million to create the urban **Hemisfair Park**, which boasts artworks, playgrounds, restaurants, and even a *paleteria*, or Mexican frozen treat shop. At its most famous landmark, the **Alamo**, there's a new pedestrian mall and museum filled with some $15 million worth of historic artifacts donated by rock musician Phil Collins. Visitors can use augmented reality on their smartphones to learn the story of America's most famous fort.

Close to the River Walk are several downtown neighborhoods worth exploring, such as the historic, bungalow-filled **King William community**; **Lavaca**, a traditional Latino neighborhood; and the **Pearl District**. A former industrial zone, Pearl is now the focus of San Antonio's nightlife and home to hip restaurants, stores, and the **Hotel Emma**. The former brewery turned hotel mixes existing factory parts with a glamour vibe that's more Beyoncé than Laverne and Shirley, with dozens of Instagram-ready displays and flower arrangements. Another downtown hostelry worth checking out is the **Hotel Havana**. The 27-room boutique hotel exudes a Spanish Caribbean flavor. Havana's decor somehow jibes perfectly with San Antonio's eclectic and welcoming cultural mash-up.

Dine at a student-run restaurant or take a cooking class at San Antonio's Culinary Institute of America campus.

San Antonio's Fiesta

Like Venice, San Antonio is known for an annual party: an 11-day celebration called **Fiesta**. Though not held at the same time as the Italian city's Lenten celebration of Carnival, San Antonio's Fiesta also focuses on hijinks and renewal, but with a charitable underpinning: Money is raised during the event for community causes. Like Carnival, the Texas city's celebration involves revelry, with plenty of dancing, music, and bright costumes. There are torchlit parades on barges floating down the San Antonio River, "royal" courts packed with locally prominent celebrants, and invitation-only balls and masquerades—but that shouldn't discourage visitors from joining in the festivities. Fiesta is, at its heart, a celebration open to all. Look for the beribboned medals pinned on shirts and blouses. With new designs each year, they are Fiesta's version of Mardi Gras beads. Also watch for *cascarones*—hollow eggs filled with confetti that are cracked over heads. In a link to Italy, the tradition is believed to have originated with Venetian Marco Polo, who brought the custom from China. It arrived in the Americas via Spain.

For Surfing
Southwestern France

Instead of Southern California, U.S.A.

A sunny day at Biarritz's Grande
Plage is an ocean lover's paradise.

Originally a Hawaiian sport, surfing blossomed along California's Pacific beaches from San Diego to Santa Barbara after World War II. With their Beach Boys anthems, popular slang, and flip-flops and board shorts, surfers defined the endless California summer. But there's another coast—on a different continent—where the sport is pursued with equal fervor. France's Atlantic beaches hold a string of communities that welcome surfers of every age and type. If you're an absolute beginner, competitive pro, or just a fan of French culture, cuisine, and joie de vivre, head to southwestern France's coastline, not Southern California, for *le surf*.

Legend dates surfing's arrival in France to 1957 when a Californian friend of screenwriter Peter Viertel, who was working on a movie in Biarritz, lugged his board there. From that humble start, a French surf culture spread along the country's Atlantic coast from the Côte de Lumière, or Coast of Light, to Saint-Gilles-Croix-de-Vie near Nantes in the north to Les Sables-d'Olonne in the south. The Côte d'Argent, or Silver Coast, begins at Soulac-sur-Mer near Bordeaux and heads south to the Adour River and Basque country. The beaches of the Côte de Lumière are recognized as good spots for beginners and dabblers, while the Côte d'Argent is considered the more challenging coastline, producing the bigger swells that attract the pros. Surf schools and rental shops are found along both.

Tranquil Marais Poitevin, a regional park in Coulon, sports houses along the riverfront.

OPPOSITE: A surfer carves through a wave at a competition in Hossegor, France.

But whether feet are planted on a surfboard or beneath a café table, there's no mistaking where you are. This is France with its chic beachside resorts, important regional and national parks, stone farmhouses, and charming villages. There are plenty of things to slide into besides a wet suit. The Côte de Lumière offers sandy beaches in which to scrunch your toes while **Nantes**, with its famous cathedral, busy shops, and restaurants, is the nearest big city. Farther south is the **Vendée**, a region known as one of France's sunniest destinations (second only to the French Riviera), the islands of **Yeu** and **Noirmoutier**, and the **Marais Poitevin**, a regional natural park with wetlands, dunes, and forests.

The Silver Coast begins near the Gironde estuary, where the sandy beaches and pine forests unspool along the coast. The Gironde region is probably best known for **Bordeaux**, both the ancient city and its legendary wine. Don't miss sampling the **Bordeaux blanc**, an underappreciated white wine unique to the area. Bordeaux, just an hour south of the birthplace of oceanic explorer Jacques-Yves Cousteau, has deep ties to the sea. The nearby coast is a popular weekend destination for the Bordelais, as residents are called, who have a reputation for enjoying life. "Bordeaux is a merchant city. It's got money and a cool vibe. Call it 'preppy meets the coast,'" says wine importer Devon Magee, who surfs at **Lacanau**, a short drive west of town. The area is famed for its beaches, including the two-mile-long (3.2 km) **Pilat sand dune**, Europe's highest, near Arcachon Bay.

Farther south in Landes is the coast's biggest surfing town. **Hossegor** is home to the French Surf Federation and world-class breaks at **La Gravière** and **La Nord**. Just 25 miles (40 km) farther south is the famous and wealthy resort town of **Biarritz**, where it all began. Remember that France's southwestern coast, like the Côte d'Azur, is one of the country's most popular holiday destinations. Come August, the traditional French vacation month, it can get crowded, and campgrounds quickly fill up.

Boards and Bees

France's southwestern coast isn't the only French-speaking ocean-front where surfers can shred *les vagues*, or waves. In Africa, Morocco—with its 1,140-mile-long (1,835 km) coastline—has developed a surprising reputation as an up-and-coming surfing destination. Some 300 miles (480 km) south of Casablanca, the Atlantic Ocean village of **Taghazout** has drawn an international collection of surfers and digital nomads with its souk-to-surf vibe and beaches dotted with clusters of sky blue wooden fishing boats, plus the occasional camel or two. Hotel developers have followed. In 2021 Fairmount opened a 127-room resort called **Taghazout Bay**, equipped with four villas and a hammam, or steam bath.

Visitors to the town can book surf lessons and honey-tasting expeditions, as Taghazout is also close to the hill town of **Imouzzer**, a center for Moroccan honey production. As wine is to France, honey is to Morocco. It's a source of pride and a key ingredient in Moroccan cuisine. Considered on par with the world's best honey, like the United States' tupelo or New Zealand's manuka, Morocco's output is harvested in different regions, from the deserts to the Atlas Mountains. Each locale produces its own sweet varietal. Also try *amlou*, a peanut butter–like spread made of honey, almonds, and argan oil used in local cuisine. The region is dotted with fig, walnut, and banana groves, and features a series of rock pools fed by the Tamraght River that are perfect places to splash around.

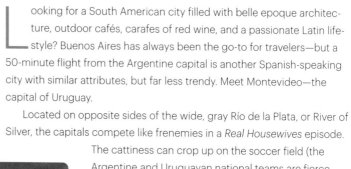

For Boulevards, Cafés, and Red Wine
Montevideo, Uruguay

Instead of Buenos Aires, Argentina

ooking for a South American city filled with belle epoque architecture, outdoor cafés, carafes of red wine, and a passionate Latin lifestyle? Buenos Aires has always been the go-to for travelers—but a 50-minute flight from the Argentine capital is another Spanish-speaking city with similar attributes, but far less trendy. Meet Montevideo—the capital of Uruguay.

Located on opposite sides of the wide, gray Río de la Plata, or River of Silver, the capitals compete like frenemies in a *Real Housewives* episode.

The sun sets behind the Palacio Salvo, with a monument honoring revolutionary hero José Gervasio Artigas in Plaza Independencia in the foreground.

The cattiness can crop up on the soccer field (the Argentine and Uruguayan national teams are fierce rivals) but also in jokes and insults. Good-natured ribbing aside, the citizens of both countries move back and forth with relative ease. Around 120,000 Uruguayans live in Argentina. Recently more Argentines have moved to Uruguay, attracted by lower taxes.

One-third of all Uruguayans live in the capital city, Montevideo (population 1.32 million), which for visitors can feel like Chicago, New York, and Washington, D.C., all rolled into one. (Uruguay's Miami is the resort town of Punta del Este, 80 miles [130 km] away, on the Atlantic Ocean, which can make for a pleasant excursion during the Southern Hemisphere's summer months.) The Uruguayan capital's vibe is relaxed, unlike the rush of its larger Argentine neighbor. And for a relatively traditional part of the world, Montevideo is a tolerant town. Marijuana consumption is legal, and the city has been named a top gay-friendly destination (Uruguay decriminalized homosexuality in 1934). The annual **September pride parade** is one of the largest events held in Montevideo.

It's a strollable city, too. Montevideo's **La Rambla** is a beachfront promenade that locals insist is the world's

Musicians march through the streets during Las Llamadas, a pair of parades held during Uruguay's 40-day Carnival.

longest sidewalk at 13.7 miles (22 km). The expansive boardwalk is open to bikers and runners, and is fringed by apartment buildings, casinos, and hotels. A memorial to the Holocaust is a reminder of the town's extensive Jewish roots—Montevideo welcomed Jewish emigrants during World War II, many settling or doing business in the **Barrio de los Judíos**. Montevideo's **Ciudad Viejo** (Old Town) dates from 1724 when Spain established a fortress on the river estuary. Today the blocks of colonial buildings, with their wrought iron balconies, attract both artists and expats.

Should you grow an appetite, Montevideo's many restaurants will certainly feed it. Vegetarians be warned: In carnivorous Uruguay, it's meat, meat, and more meat on the menu. Protein on the hoof is dished up in a seemingly infinite number of ways and is accompanied by the sensory pleasures of sizzling grills and the smoky smell of the *carne*. Try a *parrillada*, a steak or barbecue joint that specializes in grilling mountains of meat as well as side dishes of sweet peppers and potatoes. Or, if you prefer, try a *chivito*—a stuffed beef sandwich. You certainly won't leave the table hungry. Though maté—the ubiquitous caffeinated tea—is a revered institution, the drink is an acquired taste for many travelers. It's certainly worth trying to see if you become a devotee of the beverage.

To walk off your meal, take a pleasant stroll in **Plaza Independencia**, Montevideo's main square. The plaza is surrounded by some remarkable buildings, like the **Palacio Salvo**, a fantastical 27-story 1928 skyscraper designed by Mario Palanti in a bowerbird's nest of architectural styles. One of the world's most eccentric skyscrapers, it's matched only by its fraternal twin, Palanti's Palacio Barolo, in Buenos Aires. That building, to Montevideans' constant delight, is shorter than their own.

Big Bird

Travelers taking day trips outside Montevideo will see broad savannas dotted with cattle. Explorers are frequently wowed by the enormous brownish-gray birds pecking contentedly in the grass. Meet the greater rhea, a large flightless relative of the ostrich and emu and a Uruguayan native that graces the nation's five-peso coin. Rheas, called *nandus* in Uruguay, are about five feet (1.5 m) tall and weigh 33 to 66 pounds (15 to 30 kg). A second species, the Darwin's or lesser rhea, can be found in Bolivia, Peru, and Argentina. The birds live on plants, seeds, and fruit, plus the occasional snack of a lizard or other small animal. Rheas are polygamous, with the male of the species acting as the caregiver—tending to nests of up to seven clutches of eggs laid by different females. The Uruguayan rhea population is considered "near threatened," but the big birds have proven quite adaptable. There is a thriving population of more than 500 feral rhea in northeastern Germany, all descended from seven birds that escaped from a private enclosure.

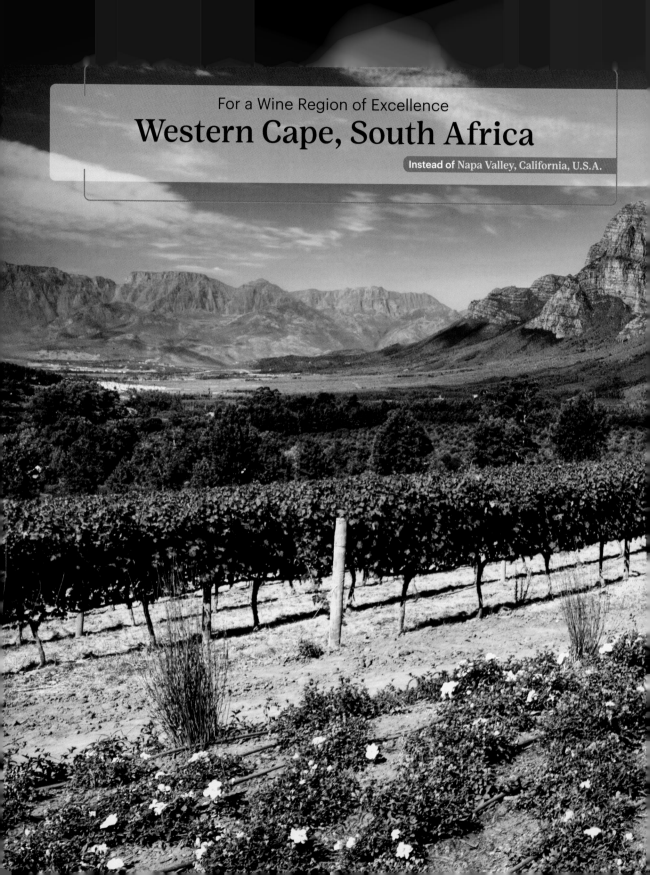

For a Wine Region of Excellence

Western Cape, South Africa

Instead of Napa Valley, California, U.S.A.

Simonsberg Mountain rises above vineyards in the Western Cape's Stellenbosch district.

"Napa" has been synonymous with "wine vacation" since at least 1976 when the Northern California county's vintages walloped French ones in a historic blind-tasting competition. Napa went on to define a lifestyle beyond the grapes, centered on cuisine and cultural activities set in a landscape warmed by both the sun and a tourist industry eager to cash in on the visiting crush. But there are other worthy wine regions beyond Napa, France, or Italy. Look to South Africa's Western Cape Province to explore a wine country eager to reveal its vintages, vineyards, and bucolic landscapes. And just like Napa and Sonoma, the Western Cape lies within a stone's throw of one of the most diverse cities in the world.

As wine regions elsewhere hike their prices, South Africa's wineries remain celebrated for their unpretentiousness and value. South Africa's wine-making tradition is not new. It dates back to 1659 when Jan van Riebeeck, the Dutch explorer who established a fort at Cape Town, recorded the first grape harvest. The Western Cape's soil and its Mediterranean climate proved excellent for viticulture, with landscapes full of dramatic mountain ranges, granite boulders, and rolling hills on which rows of vines crest and break like ocean surf—a compelling backdrop few visitors can resist. The region is not only accessible to travelers (it is only a 30- to 40-minute drive from Cape Town) but also an easy experience in other ways. Many of the vineyards are

Sip on opulent reds and crisp whites at Lanzerac Wine Estate in Stellenbosch.

OPPOSITE: Babylonstoren, a historic farm in Paarl, showcases classic elements of Cape Dutch architecture.

family owned and operated, creating a casual, laid-back atmosphere that makes the wineries feel less like businesses and more like a passion.

The Western Cape contains five major wine regions, further broken down into more than 20 districts. Two of the oldest and best known regions are Stellenbosch and Franschhoek; think of them as Africa's Napa and Sonoma, thanks to their proximity to Cape Town, the city that plays San Francisco to the Cape's vineyards. **Franschhoek** (Afrikaans for "French Corner"), founded by French Huguenots seeking a religious refuge, is noted for its rolling vineyards, good restaurants, and comfortable inns and B&Bs. **Stellenbosch**, with its white-washed thatch-roofed cottages, is surrounded by mountains. Other noted wine centers include **Paarl**, or Pearl; **Constantia**; and **Durbanville**. These can also be reached in reasonable time from Cape Town.

Winery tours are easy to arrange from either Cape Town or within the regions themselves. In Franschhoek, there is even the **Wine Tram**, which features vintage street cars that allow you to hop on and off along one of four routes. Independent-minded travelers can arrange things easily on their own by renting a car, though keep in mind driving in South Africa is, like in Britain, on the left, and driving while intoxicated is forbidden.

The Cape wine regions' inns and hotels are integral to the experience. Properties, many built in the vernacular Cape Dutch style, compete with the best in terms of amenities. Some worth investigating include **7 Koppies**—set on a private hill, or kopje, overlooking the Franschhoek Valley and Simonsberg Mountain—or **Babylonstoren**, a conservation-focused estate nestled on one of the oldest Cape Dutch farms in the valley, with a garden featuring more than 300 medicinal or edible plants. The **Lanzerac Wine Estate** hotel and spa in Stellenbosch is one of the finest examples of Cape Dutch architecture, with grounds dating from 1692.

Raise a glass to the Western Cape.

Diversity of Cape Town

Travelers visiting Cape Town sometimes call it the "African San Francisco" for its spectacular setting and diverse assemblage of cultures and lifestyles. The city drew waves of settlers, including Africans, Europeans—notably Afrikaners and the British—and South Asians. Together they created a cultural mixture as diverse as San Fran's. Travelers can taste Cape Town's diversity in the food and drink along the **Victoria and Alfred (V&A) Waterfront**, where the views of the Atlantic Ocean and Table Mountain are as delicious as the array of global offerings on restaurant menus. The neighborhood serves as the embarkation point for **Robben Island**, a onetime leper colony turned prison where South Africa's revered leader Nelson Mandela was jailed by the apartheid government. Today you can visit his cell and learn more about the history of apartheid in South Africa. Also nearby is **Green Point**, a community known for its nightlife and LGBTQIA+ attractions. The **Bo-Kaap** neighborhood is celebrated for its historic pastel-colored houses, mosques, and vaunted Cape Malay cuisine—a mix of Dutch, Southeast Asian, and Middle Eastern cooking. Much of the eastern part of Cape Town is protected by **Table Mountain National Park**, which offers visitors the chance to swim with penguins at Boulders Beach and stand at Africa's southernmost tip, the place where the Indian and Atlantic Oceans merge—another mash-up in a city celebrated for them.

For Charm, Cuisine, and Culture
Quito, Ecuador

Lima, Peru, with its history and cuisine, has proved a popular travel destination. But there's another South American city that possesses similar treasures from the days of Spanish colonial rule. For a Latin city with verve and charm—and a popular jumping-off point for the Galápagos Islands—consider Quito, Ecuador's capital, for a unique and easy getaway just four hours from Miami (with direct flights from Houston and Atlanta as well).

Quito's old town boasts exquisite architecture and colonial-style indoor courtyards.

Quito is not as well known as Lima, the Peruvian capital, or its ceviches and pisco sours. However, the Ecuadorian capital possesses a magical old town neighborhood replete with grand white churches, graceful buildings, thick cobblestones, and colorful markets selling quinoa and other whole grains that outshine even the selection at Whole Foods. Quito is set in the Andes some 9,300 feet (2,835 m) above sea level and surrounded by several active volcanoes (thanks to the high altitude, it's recommended travelers take a day or so to acclimate to the thin air).

Like most big Latin American cities, modern Quito is busy and noisy with a lot of glass-faced high-rises and a newly completed metro system (2022). But much of the 21st century vanishes when you amble across the **Plaza Grande**, or Grand Plaza, which contains the **presidential and municipal palaces,** and stroll into Quito's old town, one of the first city centers in the world to be named a UNESCO World Heritage site, an honor bestowed in 1978. The city is proud of that distinction.

There's good reason for that. In the first place, Quito is old—founded in 1534 by Spanish settlers on the ruins of an Inca town. Today the **Centro Histórico,** or Historic Center, features more than

The Mitad del Mundo monument is meant to mark the "center of the world."

5,000 buildings that date to the colonial era, earning Quito the nickname "Florence of the Americas" for the red-tiled roofs and many graceful buildings. Many of the most eye-catching ones are churches constructed in an architectural style known as the baroque school of Quito. Inside the glories are to God but it's the mammon that strikes visitors: Interiors including altarpieces, paintings, and sculptures drip with gold and other precious materials from the Inca mines. None appears more gilded than the **Iglesia de la Compañía de Jesús**. Construction began in 1586 and took 160 years to complete. Covered with gold leaf, the building is a visual tour de force.

Beyond the colonial center, take a trip to the top of **El Panecillo**, a strategically located hill and former site of an Inca temple, now topped by a 147-foot-tall (45 m) Madonna and offering panoramic views of the city. At its base is **Calle La Ronda**, a street lined with colonial houses and private courtyards that attracted bohemians in the 20th century and today is filled with boutiques and restaurants catering to tourists. Farther afield, take a day trip to **Cotopaxi National Park**, site of the world's highest live volcano, which you can climb—or circumnavigate the base.

Another big tourist attraction lies just outside town: the earnest **Ciudad Mitad del Mundo** (Center of the World City), built in the 1970s. Its monument marking the site of the Equator, from which Ecuador derives its name, is topped with what could be a disco ball from that decade. Visitors take great delight in taking selfies straddling a yellow line delineating the divide between the Northern and Southern Hemispheres. But it might be a miscalculation: Some GPS readings suggest the actual equatorial line is about 780 feet (240 m) away. No one really cares. It's a fun day out.

Dollar Economy

New travelers to Ecuador are first mystified, then pleased, upon discovering the U.S. dollar is the official currency of this independent South American country. U.S. citizens can dispense with currency exchanges and their commissions, conversion rates, and phone calculators. Why does Ecuador use the dollar? Economics. Thanks to the United States' superpower status, the dollar is held throughout the world as a reserve currency, but only seven countries other than the United States—El Salvador, the Marshall Islands, Micronesia, Palau, East Timor, Zimbabwe, and Ecuador—consider greenbacks legal tender within their borders. In 2000 a financial crisis caused Ecuador's then currency, called the sucre, to collapse. During the collapse, many Ecuadorians sought out dollars as a financial life preserver. The government acknowledged the reality and "dollarized" Ecuador's economy. Since then, tourism and other services have benefited from the easily convertible dollar. There is some criticism, however, that dollarization hurts Ecuador's more traditional village economies.

Downtown Burlington and Lake Champlain sit beneath the Green Mountains.

For a Lakeside City With Mountain Views

Burlington, Vermont, U.S.A.

Instead of Geneva, Switzerland

Take a sunset sail past the Burlington Breakwater South Lighthouse in Lake Champlain.

OPPOSITE: Church Street Marketplace houses more than 100 shops and restaurants, including a Ben & Jerry's outpost.

How does a laid-back town in New England serve as a stand-in for Geneva, one of the wealthiest spots on the planet? The mountains rising snowcapped and unchallenged across the waters of Lake Geneva offer an inspiring tableau. Lakeside grandeur is also what you will find in Burlington, Vermont, where Adirondack High Peaks rise precipitously above Lake Champlain. Geneva is walkable and filled with shops and restaurants in its medieval quarter. Burlington isn't as old, but it too is walkable, between its numerous historic neighborhoods and downtown's four-block-long pedestrian mall, **Church Street Marketplace**, which is punctuated with outdoor cafés, small boutiques, and vibrant street life. Lake. Mountains. Town. A perfect combination whether in Switzerland or the Green Mountain State.

Burlington, which began life as a lumber town, has always been a feisty place. Its small size—the 2020 census counts its population at just 45,743—belies a reputation for rethinking urban planning and sustainability. Home to the **University of Vermont**, the city is full of students and progressives with a passion for green causes—so much so that in 2015 Burlington became the first city in America to run totally on renewable energy. Visitors will notice its commitment to sustainability first on their menus. Many of Burlington's restaurants and microbreweries are committed to farm-to-table practices, using locally sourced food, from fresh vegetables to dairy products to free-ranging chickens. The **Burlington Farmers Market**, bustling with local farmers, bakers, specialty food producers, and artisanal craft makers, is a necessary stop if only to sample the fresh cheese, fruit, meat, cider, and beer. Saturday's market is the largest, and there's a midweek version on Thursdays in **Wehmhoff Square**.

Burlington isn't known as a center of chocolate making, like its Swiss counterpart. It's better known for another dairy treat, being the birthplace of **Ben & Jerry's ice cream**. The original store opened in 1978 in a gas station at St. Paul and College Streets. That's vanished, except for a commemorative plaque, but tours of the company's ice-cream factory in nearby **Waterbury** are available. Free samples are included.

Burlington also possesses a unique sense of humor. It proudly boasts the **"world's tallest file cabinet,"** a 34-file-tall tourist attraction built to protest slow-moving government bureaucracies. During the summer, consider the annual family-friendly **Festival of Fools**, which draws buskers, musicians, comics, and acrobats from across the country to perform for huge crowds, or gather lakeside to watch the **Dragon Boat Festival**, in which more than 75 teams compete for charity. There's also a drag troupe, **The House of LeMay**, that's been performing around Burlington for 25 years.

Consider departing Burlington by water on the car ferry, if open, across **Lake Champlain** for a 10-mile (16 km) trip to Port Kent, New York. If closed, try the ferry from Charlotte, Vermont, to Essex, New York. The **Adirondacks** may not be as tall as the Alps, but their High Peaks offer a spectacular backdrop as the ferry chugs across Lake Champlain's cool expanse. On a hot and sunny August day there are few things better for the spirit than a lake breeze on your face and a green and forested mountain rising up to greet you.

See the Shelburne Museum

Burlington is Vermont's big city, but the state is best known for its rural character, summarized by its Green Mountain chain, red barns, and white farmhouses. For an opportunity to explore and learn about life as it was once lived in rural New England, the Shelburne Museum and its collection of old-school Americana make for a day well spent. The museum, seven miles (11 km) south of Burlington, is spread across 45 acres (18 ha). Its 39 buildings, many of historical importance, date from the 18th and 19th centuries and were hauled here from various sites across New England and upstate New York.

There's a little bit of everything, including lilac gardens, a picture-perfect covered bridge, an old steamboat, and a carousel. Visitors can tour old barns, including a rare round barn dating from 1901, an 1840s general store, and an apothecary shop displaying 2,000 patent medicines and medical instruments. The collections include 500 quilts, 225 horse-drawn vehicles, and 1,000 farm implements—a tally that doesn't include the museum's 5,000 handheld tools such as those found in a blacksmith's shop, where smithies conduct daily demonstrations of this traditional craft. When they've seen enough agricultural artifacts, visitors can rest their eyes exploring the Shelburne's surprising art collection, which includes Impressionist prints and paintings by Mary Cassatt, Claude Monet, and Edgar Degas.

For a European Mountain Getaway
Transylvania, Romania

Everybody enjoys an Alp or two on vacation. Germany's southern state of Bavaria is, of course, famous for such snowy peaks, along with beer steins, BMWs, and fairy-tale castles like Neuschwanstein, the reputed model for Sleeping Beauty's digs at Disneyland. But there's another region where the landscape is just as majestic, the buildings as charming, and the people as welcoming: Transylvania and the Carpathian Mountains. First, however, we need to shoo the bats from its belfry.

Bran Castle, also known as Dracula's Castle, is said to have inspired Bram Stoker's tale.

The Romanian region, made notorious as Dracula's home by Irish author Bram Stoker (who never actually visited the place), has often been entangled in the count's legend. Transylvania's spooky branding is unfortunate, as it obscures the region's amazing heritage and natural beauty. Bordered to the south and east by the Carpathian Mountains, Transylvania, Latin for "land beyond the forest," has been fought over for centuries. Romans, Turks, Hungarians, and Germans have all battled for its fertile farmlands and forested mountains. And each left their own imprint, visible today to travelers in Transylvania's colorful architecture (the region counts more than 100 castles, a figure sure to impress in both Munich and Anaheim), cuisine, dress, music, and legends.

Transylvanian cities are postcard picturesque. Places like **Sighișoara** and **Cluj-Napoca** are filled with pastel-colored baroque churches, red-tile-roofed palaces, and art nouveau–style town houses that would look right at home in Vienna or Prague. The old town of **Brașov** is, in fact, one of the best preserved medieval towns in Europe. Less developed than Germany, Romania can be a lot less expensive, another discovery to please inflation-weary travelers.

The Maria Magdalena Waterfall flows from the Retezat Mountains, the highest peaks in Romania, into the Pietrele River.

Perhaps the most striking aspect of Transylvania is its natural beauty, blanketed by fields and forests, and bear-hugged by the Carpathian Mountains. Romania possesses one of Europe's largest populations of large carnivores, including 6,000 brown bears and 2,000 wolves. Other unique mammal species include red deer, lynx, and wisent, or European bison. While illegal logging is a problem, much of Transylvania's forests are protected as part of the country's park system. Wild places to visit include the caves and karsts of the **Munţii Apuseni**. The **Scărişoara Ice Cave**, a Romanian national monument, protects an underground glacier with icy stalactites and stalagmites. **Retezat National Park**, a UNESCO biosphere reserve, counts more than 60 peaks over 7,500 feet (2,286 m) tall, 80 glacial lakes, and one of Europe's last old-growth forests. **Piatra Craiului National Park** might look familiar with its picaresque forests and white limestone ridges; it was the location of Nicole Kidman and Jude Law's Civil War epic *Cold Mountain*. Trekking across its spectacular landscapes and through its traditional villages is a popular excursion.

And finally, there is Dracula's Castle. Though the vampire isn't real, Stoker based him on the historic figure of Vlad III, a Wallachian king also known as Vlad the Impaler because of his bloodthirsty habit of skewering enemies. The ruins of Vlad's home, **Poenari Castle**, high above the Argeş River, are considered one of Stoker's inspirations for Dracula's abode. However, the romantic and intact **Bran Castle**, near Braşov, is also linked to the fictional count. The latter's turrets and towers are perched on a 200-foot-tall (60 m) rock, the site of a Teutonic Knights' fortress. Plus, its 60 rooms are filled with medieval armor, furniture, and weapons, making it a more entertaining visit, if not a scary one.

Braşov

The well-preserved medieval town of Braşov is a standout for travelers. Situated between central Europe and the Ottoman East, Braşov became a fixture on trade routes and a place where Saxon merchants, Hungarians, and Bulgarians settled and prospered. Many of Braşov's old walls and towers were constructed as protection against the Turks between the 13th and 15th centuries. Called Kronstadt, or "crown city," in German, Braşov's old town consists of ancient buildings with red-tiled roofs lining narrow streets, including four-foot-wide (1.2 m) **Rope Street**, one of the most claustrophobic alleys in the world. Among the number of baroque and Gothic landmarks is the **Biserica Neagrǎ**, or Black Church, the largest Gothic church in Romania. Dating back to 1477, its exterior was sooted by a 1689 fire that destroyed most of the city. Braşov's 15th-century **Old Town Hall**, now a museum, features the **Trumpeter's Tower**, where the hour was announced with a blowing horn. Today costumed figures appear at midday to do likewise in a colorful ceremony.

For an Offbeat Small Town
Bisbee, Arizona, U.S.A.

Instead of Key West, Florida, U.S.A.

The quaint streets of Bisbee offer unexpected public art installations.

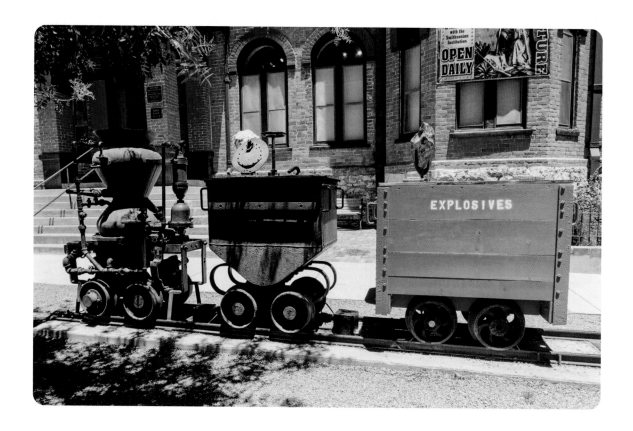

Visit the Bisbee Mining & Historical Museum to learn about the boomtown's history of copper mining.

OPPOSITE: Fine art galleries, cafés, and shops line Bisbee's eclectic Main Street.

If curmudgeonly iconoclasm makes for an interesting town to visit, that may explain why Key West is always so crowded. The Florida redoubt is famous for its unconventionality, but Hemingway's hideaway is not the only U.S. town in a remote setting that enjoys telling the outside world to go pound sand. Like its Gulf Stream counterpart, Bisbee, Arizona (population 4,923), has both a unique setting—in the Mule Mountains, just 11 miles (18 km) north of the Mexican border—and a character that's colorful, blunt, and charming.

Incorporated in 1902, when Arizona was still a territory, in its early years Bisbee was rough and tumble, filled with sudden fortunes, labor strikes, and riots centered around its principal source of money: copper mining. The metal boom gave the town its life—and its flash points—before dwindling away as its high-quality copper veins were exhausted. Bisbee's independent streak stems in part from its free-thinking nature. During World War I, residents resisted efforts to conscript 1,000 men, and the Industrial Workers of the World labor union organized a 1917 copper miners' strike to protest the war. Ultimately, mine owners suppressed the strike, but the efforts of the strikers lived on as a symbol of Bisbee's independence, which continues today. In 2013 the town defied its state government by becoming the first Arizona municipality to authorize same-sex unions.

Today travelers can experience what that frontier mining town felt like in its heyday. Bisbee is about an hour and a half drive from Tucson, and arriving visitors will want to head straight for its historic district. Called **Old Bisbee**, it's clustered in a narrow valley where Victorian houses rise along the steep hills surrounding Main Street. The neighborhood is compact, walkable, and fun to explore with a historic library atop a post office where townspeople still come to collect their mail. First revived in the 1970s when hippies and urban refugees arrived bringing art galleries and cafés, Old Bisbee has seen more development with new breweries and shops.

The abandoned **Copper Queen Mine** has been transformed into a tourist attraction, with retired miners taking visitors 1,500 feet (460 m) underground to tell them how the wealth was extracted. The vast **Lavender Pit** outside town shows visitors what open-pit mining looks like. More such stories, along with exhibits, are found at the **Bisbee Mining & Historical Museum**. There's also a quirky tribute to the mineral: the 1935 **Copper Miner**, a copper-covered statue of a valiant miner standing across from Bisbee's art deco–style courthouse. Bisbee's **Warren Ballpark** dates from 1909, making it one of the nation's oldest baseball stadiums.

Two very local places to stay are the **Shady Dell Vintage Trailer Court**, comprising a 1950s-style Airstream and other antique trailers, and, in town, the **Copper Queen Hotel**, which serves as both vintage accommodation and town watering hole. Designed as an Italianate villa, the landmark is celebrated for its rich architectural details. Open since 1902, it is Arizona's longest continuously operated hotel. Perch atop a barstool and order a pint or two of cold microbrew and you may be treated to colorful commentary from locals. Bisbee is a place where opinions are freely shared, even when, or perhaps especially when, they go against whatever the prevailing wisdom might be.

Hummingbirds

Like Bisbee's humans, the 15 species of hummingbirds flitting around southeastern Arizona's Huachuca Mountains are isolated—and they're just as happy about it. The region, where the ecosystems of the Sonoran and Chihuahuan Deserts, Rocky Mountains, and Sierra Madre Occidental all meet, creates a rich natural diversity that supports a multitude of wildlife, including the largest concentration of hummingbirds in the United States.

Only a 30-minute drive from Bisbee, the town of Sierra Vista is the official hummingbird capital of Arizona and the jumping-off point for birding expeditions to a particular gem: **Ramsey Canyon**, located in the Upper San Pedro River Basin. Here high walls and a spring-fed stream keep the region cool deep within the Huachucas. Protected by the nonprofit Nature Conservancy, the canyon's distinct setting creates a unique habitat that fosters exceptional biodiversity within groves of maples and columbines to be found alongside cacti and agaves.

For bird-watchers and hummingbird fans, the best months for hummingbird sightings are from April to October, when the tiny fliers migrate to and from Mexico. Two species to look out for are Rivoli's hummingbird and Anna's hummingbird. The latter, with its purple-pink head and stocky body, is a Pacific coast favorite, while the former is resplendent with iridescent green and purple Mardi Gras markings.

At Denali National Park and
Preserve, Dall sheep inhabit the
Alaska Range (page 78).

CHAPTER 2

NONTRADITIONAL NATURAL WONDERS

The past 100 years presented a paradox for conservation. Nations rushed to protect their natural wonders and scenic landscapes but simultaneously publicized them as tourist attractions. The latter strategy worked all too well. With famous parks both overcrowded and overly familiar, the following collection of nontraditional wonders sends you packing for places with fewer fellow travelers and unsung natural beauty.

For Fall Colors
West Virginia, U.S.A.

What could possibly spoil a leisurely drive through the gold and scarlet splendor of New England's autumn leaves? Gridlock. New Hampshire's famous Franconia Notch frequently sees bumper-to-bumper cars on the weekends when leaf-peeping is at its height. To beat the crowds and see less traffic and more leaves when they are at their peak colors, consider the hollows and mountains of West Virginia, which possess similar autumn foliage without the feeding frenzy that overtakes New England's two-lane roads. A three- to four-hour drive west of Washington, D.C., you'll find plenty of attractions to explore along the way, including one of America's newest national parks. It's time to take the family to West Virginia for an October surprise. The mostly rural and mountainous state makes a perfect fall canvas.

Travelers can kick off a leaf-watching amble by stopping at **Hanging Rock Raptor Observatory**'s fire tower for an eagle's-eye view of the autumnal color in **Jefferson National Forest**. It's a mile (1.6 km) hike to the crest of Peters Mountain and the fire tower, but the site is one of the nation's best perches from which to spot birds of prey such as hawks, falcons, and osprey. A clamber up the tower will put visitors at the same height as the soaring raptors, while enjoying the 360-degree view of the surrounding autumn hues.

Stretch your legs in **Lewisburg**, named for colonial founder Andrew Lewis, a comrade-in-arms of George Washington during the French and Indian War. The historic town in the Greenbrier Valley features numerous shops and restaurants as well as accommodations including the **General Lewis Inn**, now a boutique hotel.

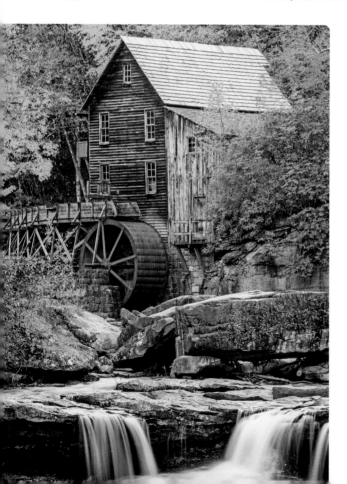

Visit the Glade Creek Grist Mill in West Virginia's Babcock State Park during peak autumn hues.

The Dolly Sods Wilderness in the Allegheny Mountains

The Victorian-era railroad town of **Hinton** on the **New River**—actually one of the world's oldest waterways—is known for its historic district featuring antique stores, galleries, and hotels. Hinton forms the southern entrance to one of America's newest national parks, **New River Gorge National Park and Preserve**. Established in 2020, the park protects more than 70,000 acres (28,325 ha) of mostly forested land along a 53-mile-long (85 km) stretch of the New River. Besides providing spectacular leaf-watching, New River Gorge is also filled with cultural and natural history as well as numerous recreational opportunities, including an easy hike to **Sandstone Falls**. The largest waterfall on the New River, Sandstone plunges some 25 feet (7.5 m). A short, quarter-mile (0.4 km) accessible boardwalk leads to an observation deck offering great views of the cascade. The road to the falls is lined with numerous access points, scenic overlooks, and campgrounds.

The park's northern entrance is at **Fayetteville** and includes a pass over U.S. Route 19's dizzying **New River Gorge Bridge**. The longest steel span in the Western Hemisphere, the bridge is the site of an annual fall festival. On the third Saturday in October the bridge is closed to motor traffic and pedestrians take over to celebrate **Bridge Day**, complete with 300 or more BASE jumpers whose derring-do draws both applause and alarm.

To descend to the river without a parachute, drive **Fayette Station Road**, a hundred-year-old thoroughfare with hairpin turns twisting down to the bottom of the gorge, past abandoned coal towns, across a narrow bridge, and up the other side again. Along the drive are gorgeous vistas of the river, train tracks and bridges, and the surrounding hardwood forests reclaiming the abandoned land and ablaze with fall colors.

Scottish Fall

Scotland doesn't usually bring leaf-peeping to mind, but the country was once home to the great Caledonian Forest, where pine, rowan, and oak grew in abundance before being clear-cut centuries ago. The surviving Scottish forests offer a colorful panorama between September and November. Sites to explore include **Loch Lomond and the Trossachs National Park**, Scotland's first, established in 2002 and filled with lakes and hiking trails. The woods and dells of **Perthshire** along the border between England and Scotland are also full of fall foliage. Visit the **Hermitage**, the former property of the Dukes of Atholl, for sweeping views or embark on the five-mile-long (8 km) Lady Mary's Walk on the River Earn. Hikers can stop at the **Glenturret Distillery**—Scotland's oldest working distillery. Future Scottish falls will be even more spectacular as the nation embarks on a rewilding effort. Above Inverness, the 23,000-acre (9,300 ha) Alladale Wilderness Reserve has already planted one million trees, and the Affric Highlands Project will start rewilding 500,000 acres (202,300 ha).

For Dramatic Fjords

Howe Sound, British Columbia, Canada

The Sea-to-Sky Highway winds through Howe Sound and stretches just over 100 miles (160 km) from Vancouver to Pemberton, British Columbia.

I n cruise ship commercials and brooding Scandinavian Netflix dramas, Norway's fjords can be depended upon to create an alluring backdrop that elicits sighs of delight and envy from couchbound would-be voyagers. Yet there are other fjords and inlets, just as gorgeous and inspiring, that can be more accessible than shelling out for a flight to Europe or a stateroom on a cruise ship. Consider visiting the fjords near Howe Sound. They're an easy distance from one of Canada's most interesting cities in the province of British Columbia.

The key to these fjords lies in their accessibility. Most of the province's fjords can be reached by car and ferry from nearby **Vancouver**. With its modern steel-and-glass downtown and a relaxed, tolerant vibe (the city is sometimes jokingly referred to as "Vansterdam"), Canada's biggest Pacific coast metropolis makes a pleasant base or embarkation point for the fjords north of it. Howe Sound, with its dramatic landscapes, is an hour's drive on scenic Route 99, known as the Sea-to-Sky Highway, which eventually winds its way up to the Whistler Blackcomb ski resort. A three-hour road trip northwest of Vancouver along the misty Strait of Georgia leads to Egmont on Sechelt Inlet. With its milder, maritime climate, the British Columbia coastline offers an abundance of outdoor activities for explorers at every level. Visitors can hike, bike, rock climb, and scout for wildlife—both on land and in the sea—and always with a stunning natural backdrop. It's a social media feed waiting to happen.

A few sights to see include the **Skookumchuck Narrows** in Skookumchuck Narrows Provincial Park near Egmont. Here watch surfers, extreme kayakers, and divers attempt to master the epic white water. Extreme tides here create both whirlpools and nine-

Climb over moss-covered logs in the lush coniferous Squamish rainforest.

foot-tall (2.7 m) rapids twice a day. Hike the 2.4-mile (3.9 km) **Smuggler Cove** trail at Smuggler Cove Marine Park. There are a number of scene-stealing overlooks, including one rocky outcrop with views of the waters of the Salish Sea, which embraces the Strait of Georgia, Strait of Juan de Fuca, and Puget Sound. The region remains the ancestral home of the people of the Coast Salish First Nations, the first inhabitants of the Canadian Northwest. The cove's name is thought to be inspired by its history with smugglers, some of whom are said to have transported Chinese laborers to the United States (eager to cross the border after building the Canadian Pacific Railway), while others moved whiskey during Prohibition. For an epic view of Howe Sound, board the **Sea to Sky Gondola**. The 10-minute glide up provides visitors with commanding views at 2,900 feet (880 m). Once at the summit you can access scenic trails and walk on a suspension bridge that offers 360-degree views of the steep, forested mountains and waters below.

At the top of Howe Sound is **Squamish**. Once a copper-mining outpost, the destination has transformed itself into a foodie's paradise and outdoor recreation destination. As with many Pacific Northwest towns there are also a number of microbreweries and cider houses, as well as an annual summer beer festival. With a host of hotels it is also a good place to overnight. Accommodations like the **Squamish Adventure Inn** cater to the adventure crowd by offering hostel-style and standard hotel rooms. **Howe Sound Inn & Brewery Company**, a traditional hostelry, is a 20-room hotel built over a brewery. Those visitors wanting an island stay might think about investigating the **Artisan Suites on Bowen** at the mouth of Howe Sound outside Vancouver. You'll need to take a ferry or water taxi to reach it.

The First Nations

In earlier decades, it was easy to overlook the reality that Europeans were not the first people to make their way to the Pacific Northwest. But others called this magnificent scenery home long before explorer-merchants began to chart and settle here. The British Columbia fjords and Vancouver are home to the Coast Salish, the original inhabitants of this area as well as Puget Sound in the United States. These First Nations homelands include the ancestral territories of the Skwxwú7mesh (Squamish), shíshálh, Tla'amin, Klahoose, and Homalco Nations. Much of their histories can be explored in Vancouver at the Museum of Anthropology at the University of British Columbia. Travelers can also contact Indigenous guides. **Talaysay Tours** conducts forest therapy walks and Indigenous excursions in Vancouver's Stanley Park. "There's a magical program called Talking Tree," says cultural explorer Norie Quintos, a regular contributor to National Geographic Travel. "You come away understanding our interconnectedness with nature: that the trees are us, and we are the trees." Other tours introduce visitors to traditional activities on tribal lands. All travelers are advised whenever visiting an Indigenous cultural territory to do so in a respectful and responsible manner. Visit the **Coastal Cultural Alliance** website for activities such as hiking and history walks with a focus on Indigenous cultures as well as lists of museums, heritage sites, and art tours from across the British Columbia coast.

For Hot Springs

Western Colorado, U.S.A.

Instead of Iceland

Stay at Mount Princeton Hot Springs Resort in the winter wonderland of Nathrop, Colorado.

In Pagosa Springs, a resort's natural hot springs line the banks of the San Juan River.

M any travelers to Iceland look forward to at least one splash in the Nordic country's many hot springs. Thanks to the island's geothermal activity there are dozens of them, and the best known hot springs, like the famed Blue Lagoon, are frequently crowded. But Iceland isn't the only destination for a bubbling soak. Other parts of the globe also come paired with gorgeous scenery and steamy waters. Western Colorado's Rocky Mountains, for example, have more than 20 springs perfect for a soak, and water-seeking travelers can craft an epic road trip across the Continental Divide by following the Mile High State's historic hot springs loop.

Colorado finds itself in hot water thanks to the Rockies' relative geological youth, with faults and fissures in the earth bringing magma-heated water to the surface. People have been enjoying a soak in their mineral waters since Native American tribes like the Ute and Arapaho first sought them out for their restorative powers. Later settlers turned many sites into resorts, like the gold miners who struck it rich and built a hotel in 1879 in Nathrop (now called the **Mount Princeton Hot Springs Resort**). Colorado's modern hot springs resorts focus on wellness and relaxation and feature an assortment of vapor caves, terraced pools, and hot pots, and one of the world's largest hot spring pools. Most charge a fee for a soak. A few, like the **Valley View Hot Springs**, are nonprofits. Some are even clothing optional. Others, in various national forests and parks, are free.

Like Iceland's 820-mile (1,320 km) Ring Road, the 800-mile (1,290 km) **Historic Hot Springs Loop** is a good way to get organized. The loop starts in **Denver** and allows visitors to venture through the most scenic parts of the state, with hot springs stops in towns like Buena Vista, Pagosa Springs, and Durango before ending in the laid-back ski-resort town of Steamboat Springs. Here are some of its highlights.

In Chaffee County along the Continental Divide, small mountain towns such as **Buena Vista** and **Salida** offer mineral-rich soaks at sites ranging from large aquatic centers to rustic cabins, such as those at **Antero Hot Springs** in Pike–San Isabel National Forest. Continuing on the recommended loop, visit Pagosa Springs, near **Chimney Rock National Monument**, which preserves 200 ancient homes and structures, including the **Great Kiva**, or ceremonial house, the largest such Native American structure in the region, estimated to have been built in 1084. Surrounded by three million acres (1.2 million ha) of national forest and wilderness areas, **Pagosa Springs** is known for having the deepest hot springs in the world and several comfortable resorts with open-air pools to soak in for a fee. A free roadside spot to try in town is the aptly named **Nathan's Hippy Dip Hot Spring**.

The water has drawn people to **Glenwood Springs** since 1888. The town possesses one of the world's largest mineral hot spring pools, but the region also offers plenty of white water rafting, hiking, and biking as well as winter sports. Lesser known as part of Colorado's geothermal heritage are the naturally occurring underground steam baths at the **Yampah Spa Vapor Caves**, thought to have been historically used by the Ute. Now a commercial venture, the caves are associated with a spa and treatment facility. **Steamboat Springs** is celebrated for its hot water, including **Strawberry Park Hot Springs**, with its series of elaborate natural and human-made pools.

The thermal waters at Strawberry Park Hot Springs are healing and restorative.

Hot Springs Heat Up

With wellness welling up everywhere, hot springs are experiencing a surge in popularity across the globe. Here are a few unexpected destinations with hot waters: Remote and cold, Antarctica's **Deception Island** is an active volcano. Bathers can dig into the black sand beaches to collect hot water and watch icebergs float by while soaking in their steaming homemade bath. At 14,764 feet (4,500 m) high in the Tibetan Himalaya, bathers will find the **Yangpachen Hot Springs**. The springs, which cover 25 square miles (65 km²), produce water so scalding (158°F/70°C) that attendants must cool the temperature for visitors to enter the three bathing pools. Located 56 miles (90 km) from **Lhasa**, the springs' geothermal energy produces much of the electricity for the Tibetan capital. Many travelers know that Iceland is celebrated for its many hot springs, but Greenland also has them. Those on deserted **Uunartoq Island** offer three pools for bathers, who can luxuriate in the 100°F (38°C) water like the Vikings who discovered and frequented these springs 1,000 years ago.

Hikers will be delighted by the native flora and fauna in Tasmania's Walls of Jerusalem National Park.

For Southern Lights

Tasmania, Australia

Instead of Scandinavia's Northern Lights

Greens and purples flicker across Tasmania's sky during a nightly show of the aurora australis.

OPPOSITE: Peer up at colorful art installations at Hobart's Museum of Old and New Art (MONA).

Everyone knows to turn north for a glimpse of the aurora borealis. But here's a notion that's literally poles apart: Head south. The aurora australis, the Southern Hemisphere's version of the famous northern lights, is just as thrilling, and the island of Tasmania, 150 miles (240 km) off the coast of the Australian mainland, is a good place to see them. "Tas," as the island is affectionately nicknamed, is the country's closest point to Antarctica and comes with an added bonus: Travelers are only a kangaroo's hop away from the Australian mainland or New Zealand, where they can commune with koalas and kiwis.

Though the southern lights can appear in any month, prime time for the aurora australis is March through September, in the Southern Hemisphere's fall and winter. They are best viewed in Tasmania's unpopulated areas, where skies are darker, but the lights can be seen throughout the island, even near the city of Hobart. The **South Arm Peninsula**, 25 miles (40 km) south of the Tasmanian capital, is a popular destination, as is **Cockle Creek** on **Recherche Bay**. The bay, a two-hour drive from Hobart, is the southernmost point in Australia reachable by car. Receive information about the lights' schedule and find viewing tips by following the Aurora Australis Tasmania Facebook page.

While a glimpse of the southern lights is the highlight, a visit to Tasmania is far more than just a night sky rave. It's a rugged and beautiful place. The most forested state in Australia, Tasmania boasts diverse ecosystems from temperate rainforests to snowy mountain ranges, and 40 percent of the island's land is protected in parks and preserves. More than 18 national parks protect vistas like **Cradle Mountain** and photogenic **Wineglass Bay**. Other places to visit include **Tasman National Park** for its unique geological formations, including the **Blowhole** and **Tasman Arch**. Hikers will enjoy **Walls of Jerusalem National Park** with its mountainous highland treks. The reserve in **Wellington Park** is worth the 20-minute drive from Hobart. It encompasses 4,170-foot-tall (1,271 m) **Mount Wellington** and spectacular views of Tasmania's capital. Plus, it boasts more than 500 species of native plants and marsupials, like the platypus and bandicoot.

With its mild climate and relaxed manner, **Hobart** is a bright light all by itself. Australia's gateway city to the Antarctic region, it's filled with lively restaurants, Georgian-era cottages, and Victorian homes, giving the city of 220,000 an old-timey feel. Some Hobartian attractions worth investigating are the **Salamanca Market**—with its stalls of fresh produce, baked goods, and local crafts and gifts—and the **Royal Tasmanian Botanical Gardens**, just a short walk from Hobart's Central Business District and considered one of the best urban parks in Australia. Founded in 1818, its 35 acres (14 ha) feature a fernery and the Subantarctic Plant House, an enclosed space full of rare plants from regions just outside the Antarctic Circle, the only one of its kind in the world. The **Museum of Old and New Art (MONA)** features ancient, modern, and contemporary works collected by Australian gambler David Walsh, who calls it a "subversive Disneyland." Native son and swashbuckler Errol Flynn, a rakish 1930s Hollywood superstar, might have agreed. His Tasmanian roots are commemorated at the **Errol Flynn Reserve**, a small seaside park.

The Devil You Know

Credit Warner Bros. and its *Looney Tunes* animators for making the Tasmanian Devil one of the world's best known characters and Tasmania's iconic symbol. The real Tasmanian devil—colored black, not brown, and unable to twirl in a cartoon whirlwind—is a fascinating mammal beyond its Hollywood association. Devils are ferocious and smelly, and they possess one of the strongest bites per body mass of any mammal their size—their jaws open up to 80 degrees, the better to crush the bones of their prey. The island's early European explorers nicknamed the nocturnal hunter "Beelzebub's pup" due to its shrill cries, and eventually the associated name "devil" stuck. With the extinction of the Tasmanian wolf, or thylacine, in 1936, the Tasmanian devil became the world's largest carnivorous marsupial.

Unfortunately, devils are endangered. Opportunistic scavengers, they enjoy snacking on roadkill, a dangerous pastime due to an increased propensity to become victims of automobiles themselves. Even more deadly to the animal is devil facial tumor disease (DFTD), a form of fatal cancer. Efforts to protect regional populations from the disease have included reintroducing devils to the Australian mainland to act as an insurance policy against them vanishing altogether from their native island. Seeing a Tassie devil is hard but not impossible. The nocturnal animals are elusive, but they can easily be found in private wildlife sanctuaries.

GO HERE:

For Majestic Mountains

Sawtooth Mountains, Idaho, U.S.A.

Instead of the Swiss Alps

Team up with friends on a guided paddling tour down the Middle Fork of the Salmon River.

Bike through the flowering meadows of the 18-mile (29 km) Harriman Trail just north of Ketchum.

Consider Idaho's Sawtooth Mountains, not Switzerland, for a vacation surrounded by snowcapped peaks and lively resort towns. With much of the region contained within the national forest system, the Sawtooths offer a wide variety of Alpine sports, ice-blue glacial lakes, and peak-filled scenic drives. And just like dairy-mad Switzerland, there are plenty of cows around. But being the American West, the cattle also come with cowboys.

The central Idaho destination offers a breadth of outdoor adventures that range from easy to demanding. Skiing, hiking, and mountain biking are easily arranged from small towns and regional hubs. While **Twin Falls** and **Boise** can't match Zürich or St. Moritz for urban savoir faire, the two towns possess their own charms. And when it comes to ski trails, cool cash, and social sizzle, the resorts of **Ketchum** and **Sun Valley** can compete with Gstaad and Klosters. They just see fewer royals.

The best way to experience the Sawtooths is by driving right to them. The mountains deliver national park–caliber visuals without the national park crowds—another reason for this western secret to top your list. Federal forestlands extend from the Basin and Range Province of northern Utah to the Idaho Rockies and encompass the headwaters of the Salmon

River. Called the "River of No Return," the Salmon is considered one of America's most magnificent wild waterways, and it was one of the first to receive federal protection. There are plenty of hiking trails in **Sawtooth National Forest**, home to elk, bighorns, mountain goats, black bears, and gray wolves. Salmon, trout, and birdlife thrive here, and, come spring, meadows blaze with wildflowers. A walk on the 10-mile-long (16 km) **Sawtooth Lake Trail** delivers photogenic views of granite crags and summits set against the vivid blues of **Redfish Lake**, the region's largest. It's a good introduction to the Sawtooths' beauty. And while it's allegedly the most popular trail, it's nowhere near crowded. You can also choose more strenuous hikes, including the seven-mile-long (11 km) hike to **Saddleback Lake**, which begins with a boat ride across Redfish Lake. The journey also includes the impressive sight of **Elephant's Perch**, a thrusting rock face that towers over the pines and lakes.

But it's not just the land that beckons. The **Salmon River** is celebrated for its white water. Early American explorers Lewis and Clark thought the river too rough to navigate. But travelers *can* navigate the fast-moving rapids on guided rafting tours that launch from the towns of **Salmon** and **Stanley**, both lying along the 110-mile-long (175 km) Middle Fork of the Salmon. Kayaking and canoeing are also popular, as is fly-fishing. The river is known as one of the best fish nurseries in the country, and visitors can try their hand at casting for rainbow trout. Or simply enjoy a drive along the **Salmon Scenic Byway** for its gorgeous views.

You won't struggle to find a cozy, scenic spot to stay at on a visit here. The Sawtooths are dotted with lodges and dude ranches as well as boutique hotels in more built-up resort towns like Sun Valley. The **Idaho Rocky Mountain Ranch** (open June through September) features a historic lodge with rooms and cabins. The price of your stay includes all meals and activities, from horseback riding to fishing to mountain biking. In Sun Valley try the **Sun Valley Lodge**, a classic inn for all seasons.

McGowan Peak rises above Stanley Lake in Sawtooth National Recreation Area.

Ketchum If You Can

Since it is enveloped by so much wilderness, it is easy to forget the Sawtooths' allure as a social salt lick for the sporty and glamorous from all over the world. Sun Valley and Ketchum are the kinds of places where visitors can savor a sunset at 5,000 feet (1,520 m), then spend the rest of the evening on a dance floor. **Ketchum**, located in the Wood River Valley, was writer Ernest Hemingway's favorite spot on the planet and is his final resting place. He's buried in the local cemetery, and members of his literary fan base frequently leave whiskey bottles on his grave. Celebrities like Tom Hanks have made Ketchum so popular that it's called "New North Hollywood." **Sun Valley** owes its existence to the Union Pacific Railroad. In 1935 its chairman, Averell Harriman, hired Austrian count Felix Schaffgotsch to create a ski resort to attract a well-heeled ridership. It worked. Sun Valley became the first ski resort to install chairlifts (on Dollar Mountain) and is still known for short to nonexistent lift lines. In the summer Sun Valley becomes a base for mountain biking. Come nightfall, visitors enjoy sophisticated dining at establishments like **The Ram**, opened in 1937.

For Bats and Stalagmites

Bracken Cave, Texas, U.S.A.

Instead of Mammoth Cave, Kentucky, U.S.A.

Natural Bridge Caverns, one of the largest cave systems in Texas, is located 180 feet (55 m) belowground.

As its name suggests, Mammoth Cave, near Park City, Kentucky, is elephantine. But the vastness of its chambers pales in comparison to another sprawling underground complex where the superlatives take wing. Literally. If you are spelunking around the internet looking for caverns to visit, consider Bracken Cave in Texas. Here you have the opportunity to witness a jaw-dropping, wing-flapping firestorm as an army of some 15 million Mexican free-tailed bats spiral out from the cave at dusk. Located in Hill County, just outside San Antonio's exurbs, the cave is home to the largest colony of bats on the planet.

The Lone Star State is home to 32 of the 47 species of bats found in the United States. The Mexican free-tailed bat is mostly a migratory species, flying north to Texas from Mexico each February. And Bracken Cave happens to be a key maternity site for the species. By June females give birth to one pup and raise their young in large maternal colonies so crowded there may be as many as 500 pups per square foot (.09 m²). (Male bats batch it elsewhere.) Each night they emerge to feast on insects. The hungry bats eliminate 100 tons (90 t) of pests per night. All their gobbling enriches the mothers' milk, helping their pups grow rapidly and be ready to fly by August. June through September is the best time to watch for bat "emergences," as they're called. In October the bats are ready to return to Mexico for the winter.

Bracken Cave is run by the nonprofit organization Bat Conservation International (BCI), which purchased the private ranchlands surrounding the mouth of the cave in 1991. BCI has since transformed its 1,500 acres (610 ha) of holdings into a nature preserve. Bat-watchers don't actually step foot in the cave. Instead,

Mexican free-tailed bats darken the sky as they leave Bracken Cave to feed.

they sit at a safe distance and observe what many call a "tornado of bats" emerging from the cave's crescent-shaped natural opening.

Bat-watching comes with caveats. The small mammals aren't punctual, and the nightly show can vary due to temperature and weather, so before leaving, check BCI's website for updates. BCI provides seats for observers, who must keep well away from the mouth of the cave. Bright lights, camera flashes, and loud noises are forbidden, as they disturb and confuse the bats. It should also go without saying: Never touch or disturb bats by throwing objects into their swarm.

Visitors must make reservations in advance. Public bat-watches sell out quickly, so book through BCI's website as soon as that summer's dates go live. Joining a bat-watch runs about $30 a person (all funds support the conservation efforts of BCI). Or consider becoming a BCI member ($45–$65 per person), which allows you access to member nights. Members are guaranteed one bat-watch per season and can bring up to five guests. Overnight camping is available, by request and with advance planning, for scouting trips and educational groups.

There are other caves in the area as well. **Natural Bridge Caverns**, discovered by four college students in 1960, features impressive rock formations 180 feet (55 m) belowground. Tours of this family-owned cave can be combined with Bracken. And for those travelers interested in nightlife of the human variety, **San Antonio's Pearl District** makes a vibrant choice. The neighborhood is renowned for its restaurants and clubs as well as the lush steampunk style of the **Hotel Emma**. **Hotel Havana** on the San Antonio River Walk is another atmospheric choice for people who need a roost while in town.

Urban Bats

We associate bats with underground caves deep in the countryside, but these mammals are also citified creatures that can thrive just as well in human environments. Bracken Cave's urban counterpart is the underside of a bridge in the heart of downtown **Austin, Texas. Ann W. Richards Congress Avenue Bridge** shelters the world's largest urban bat colony, estimated at 1.5 million Mexican free-tailed bats and their pups. The bats began roosting in the bridge after its restoration in the 1980s. At the time, few people understood the vital role bats played in controlling insect (specifically mosquito) populations. The bridge's colony devours up to 30,000 pounds (13,610 kg) of them each night. The tiny mammals are also a tourist draw, bringing 140,000 bat lovers to Austin. There are several spots to view the nightly flights, including a bat observation area run by the *Austin American-Statesman*, the city's newspaper. Prime viewing season runs from May through September, and volunteer docents are on hand on weekends to answer questions and convey educational information about the animals. You can also watch the spiraling eruption from the Butler Hike and Bike Trail, atop the bridge itself, and from boats floating on **Lady Bird Lake** below the bridge. Look east as the bats will depart from that direction. In late August Austin throws its annual **Bat Fest,** which features musical acts, local food and drink, craft vendors, and a bat costume contest.

For a Meaningful Hike
Alishan National Scenic Area, Taiwan

Instead of Muir Woods, California, U.S.A.

A grove of ancient trees prompts travelers to contemplate both epochs of time and their own insignificance when measured against the sight of such ancient and mighty giants. The towering redwoods in Muir Woods National Monument, north of San Francisco, or farther north, the goliaths of Sequoia National Park in Tulare County, California, have been an inspirational draw for nature lovers since the days of John Muir. But in Asia there's another sylvan setting with misty cedars and cypress high in the mountains of Alishan on the island of Taiwan. The rugged and scenic landscape offers an intriguing Eastern twist on a walk in the woods.

Located in the rugged center of Taiwan, Alishan National Scenic Area is a protected 160-square-mile (415 km²) region of steep mountains, waterfalls, and high-altitude tea plantations threaded with hiking trails. With the cool of the mountains meeting lowland, Alishan generates thick layers of clouds that swaddle the valleys, while wisps of mist creep through the groves of trees. The fog and mist transform Alishan's collections of Formosan red cedar and yellow and red cypress trees into a watercolor-like scene that draws visitors to its beauty. And like the coniferous California behemoths, Alishan's trees are also impossibly ancient. Protected within the park's boundaries are trees more than 2,000 years old, with several individual ones designated as sacred because of their extreme age, size, or both. "For comparison's sake, the largest still standing tree at Alishan is the 2,300-year-old Xianglin Old Tree," says Nick Kembel, a Taiwanese travel expert, "while fallen Sacred Tree is thought to be over 3,000 years old." General Sherman, the largest tree in the world, which grows in Sequoia National Park, is estimated to be only about 2,200 years old.

Walk through Alishan National Scenic Area on a wooden boardwalk and bridge.

The Alishan Forest Railway offers a scenic tour of the region's lush landscape.

Many Alishan visitors brave the chill and come at dawn to catch the sunrise over the peaks, a popular pastime. Kembel recommends getting into the woods by utilizing Alishan's many hiking trails. "It's a good way to experience giant trees without crowds," he says. He recommends the **Giant Tree Plank Trail** to experience its collection of lofty trees, including what's believed to be the world's tallest camphor tree, a species of evergreen found in Asia. The trail is an uncrowded loop that's accessible from Shenmu's rail station. The **Shuishan Trail** is even more remote but ends in front of a memorable sight, an immense 2,700-year-old red cypress that's 98 feet tall (30 m) and 59 feet (18 m) in circumference.

Many of these spots are reached by a trip through a narrow-gauge on the **Alishan Forest Railway**. The train's antique wooden cars were crafted from local cypress and originally built for loggers in the early 20th century when Taiwan was a colony of Japan, which exploited the island's timber resources. The ride's a good option for older or special-needs visitors interested in taking in the scenery at higher elevations without too much demanding physical exertion. But keep in mind the railway is likely to be packed. Reservations are advised. A bus is another option to visit the park; the drive features plenty of switchbacks.

Many visitors will opt to stay overnight, while others prefer to do a day trip. **Alishan** has a lot to explore beyond the national scenic area. There are bamboo forests to hike through, or visitors can poke around small historic towns like **Shizhuo**, where many of Alishan's tea farms are located. **Fenqihu**, a staging area from which to reach the park's higher peaks, is a good place to find a bento box lunch.

A High Tea

Taiwanese love tea, and Alishan is just their cup with its highly coveted home-grown variety of tea called **Alishan high mountain oolong**, which smells like orchids and has sweet tasting notes of jasmine and fruit. Taiwanese travel expert Nick Kembel describes it as the "champagne of teas" because of its fame and deep connection with Alishan's high-altitude terroir. Many of the tea plantations offer simple rooms or homestays for travelers who want more time to hike the forest trails that meander through the fields and villages and adjoining national scenic areas. Owners will usually serve a basic breakfast, but visitors should be prepared to bring their own food for other meals, as restaurants are rarely within walking distance. Kembel recommends **Cuiti B&B** for its working tea farm, incredible sunset views, and vistas of misty peaks in the distance. Also look into **Long Yun Leisure Farm**, another homestay with rooms boasting scenic overlooks. "It has the feeling of a very remote rural escape," Kembel says. "The kind of place you go to find solitude, sip tea all day, meditate, write a book, and forget that cities exist."

For Plentiful Ocean Life

Ningaloo, Australia

Instead of the Great Barrier Reef, Australia

Western Australia's Ningaloo reef is teeming with more than 500 animal species, including the flashy convict tang.

The Great Barrier Reef beckons us even as disaster looms. Divers and snorkelers arrive in Australia eager to explore its underwater marvels while the climate grows ever warmer, threatening the natural world beneath its waters. For fin-flapping visitors worried about making things worse, there's another reef down under that makes a tempting alternative. Located on the edge of the Indian Ocean three time zones west of the Great Barrier Reef, Ningaloo's reef in Western Australia is one of the largest fringing and near-shore reefs on the planet. Stacked with coral and sponge gardens and swarmed by fish, Ningaloo offers visitors a magnificent, still viable ocean reef bordering a mostly deserted stretch of coastline some 685 miles (1,100 km) north of Perth.

Ningaloo (the word means "promontory" in the Australian Aboriginal Wajarri language) is a UNESCO World Heritage area. It stretches 300 miles (480 km) along Western Australia's coast and is populated with more than 500 animal species, including the rare dugong (a species of manatee), leopard sharks, sea turtles, and manta rays. It also features acres of vibrant coral beds. Though it's one of Australia's most accessible reefs, Ningaloo's onshore landscape features mostly solitary beaches and a desertlike topography. If you want to splash away from the crowds, this is the place.

The base from which to explore the reef is the **Ningaloo Coast World Heritage Area**, which encompasses both the underwater **Ningaloo Marine**

The clear waters of Ningaloo look especially blue against the desertlike landscape of Western Australia.

OPPOSITE: Divers can swim with massive whale sharks at Ningaloo.

Park and Australia's Cape Range National Park, 117,760 acres (47,655 ha) located directly off the reef on the North West Cape. Cape Range features 190 miles (305 km) of pristine coastline and white sand beaches.

Beneath the ocean surface the marine park shelters a multitude of fish and corals. Ningaloo is also noted for its marine megafauna—orcas, whales, and whale sharks. The shallow lagoons offer excellent snorkeling opportunities that visitors can easily access right from the beach, including sites at **Lakeside**, **Turquoise Bay**, and **Oyster Stacks**. The **Exmouth Gulf** (a nursery for many Ningaloo reef species) should be considered as well.

Back on terra firma, **Cape Range National Park**, with its dramatic limestone hills and arid landscape, offers up wild beauty for nature lovers. The park features a diverse array of mammals including kangaroos, wallabies, and echidnas, as well as birds such as emus. Most traditional Aboriginal cultural sites in the park remain off-limits as archaeological sites are still being discovered. Of particular note are **Shothole** and **Charles Knife Canyons**, both of which are four-wheel drive accessible, and **Yardie Creek**, which forms a gorge that can be explored by trail and boat (be alert for sightings of rare black-footed rock wallabies). Eleven campgrounds dot the park, making for an affordable and memorable stay. Take precautions for arid conditions (bring water and sunscreen, for example) and rent a vehicle capable of traversing both paved and unpaved roads.

For a taste of civilization, not to mention breakfast, the small town of **Exmouth** (population 2,500, plus a daily group of tourists) provides dining options and activities of all kinds. Try the **Ningaloo Aquarium and Discovery Centre** and the **Jurabi Turtle Centre** to see turtles nesting and hatching. Lodging options include an all-inclusive glamping experience at the eco-luxury resort **Sal Salis**, which offers guided walks, kayaking, stargazing, and whale and whale shark swims, and **Bullara Station Stay**, a working cattle ranch partway between Coral Bay and Exmouth.

Whale Sharks

Enormous, slow-swimming pacifists of the seas, whale sharks are the largest nonmammalian vertebrates in the world. One of the largest—and, according to the Western Australia government, one of the best managed—whale shark schools in the world is the population of 300 to 500 of the massive beasts that make their way to Ningaloo each year. Growing up to 60 feet (18 m) in length and with a life span of up to 130 years, whale sharks navigate the planet's tropical oceans, vacuuming up plankton, their food source, into their five-foot-wide (1.5 m) mouths. Peaceful and serene, these massive creatures are no threat to humans. At Ningaloo, some 85 percent of the sharks are juvenile males. Schools of whale sharks arrive off Western Australia in late March and linger through late July, timed to the mass coral spawning and the accompanying increase in marine nutrients that are found here. Under strict guidelines and at a distance, visitors can enter the water with these marine tweens for a once-in-a-lifetime experience. All-day tours, operating from Exmouth and Coral Bay, are regulated by the government and designed to minimize human impact on the whale sharks' behavior. The restrictions include the number of swimmers and their proximity to sharks to prevent crowding these placid plankton-eating youngsters. Divers eager for an encounter should be reassured by the fact that a portion of tour proceeds goes toward funding research on one of the world's most impressive species.

For Prairie Landscapes and Bison
Zuid-Kennemerland National Park, Netherlands

Instead of Custer State Park, South Dakota, U.S.A.

Zuid-Kennemerland National Park's visitors center offers information on the park's flora and fauna and a café.

The foreign tourists cavorting in Amsterdam's Red Light District drinking Heinekens and eating french fries aren't the only wildlife to be seen in the Netherlands. Only 45 minutes from the Rijks-museum, a herd of wild buffalo grazes peacefully near the North Sea coast in the country's Zuid-Kennemerland National Park. It might seem incongruous, but if you want to see some wild bison, don't strike out for Yellowstone or South Dakota's Custer State Park. Instead, pack your bags and head to the Netherlands for an unexpected encounter with one of the world's most captivating mammals.

Bison are such quintessential American beasts it often comes as a surprise to learn they have a European cousin. European bison, or wisent, are rarer than the bison in North America. Their numbers are fewer than those of the wild black rhino in Africa. Considered a keystone species of their environment, European bison were hunted to extinction in the wild throughout Europe before a captive breeding program in Poland saved them in the nick of time. Now, Europe's largest wild herbivore is gradually returning to some of its original range.

The Dutch bison herd forms the basis for a conservation effort that began in 2007 at Zuid-Kennemerland National Park. The **Wisentproject Kraansvlak**, or Kraansvlak bison project, measures the impact of the large grazing mammals on the dunes along the Dutch North Sea coastline. The herd helps maintain the sand dunes, keeping the grass in check and the ecosystem resilient—all desired outcomes as the Netherlands confronts the effects of climate change.

Almost two million people visit Zuid-Kennemerland National Park each year for hiking and wildlife-viewing.

Catching a glimpse of the wisent requires a little luck. These are elusive creatures. Bison in the Dutch herd, consisting of more than 20 total, wander a large southern section of the 15-square-mile (39 km²) park and aren't always visible. Travelers can take the path closest to the visitors center and follow a marked trail that leads past tidy houses into grassy meadows and wetlands populated by herons, ducks, and swans and through an oak forest to an observation area. Farther west is an additional 1.8-mile-long (2.9 km) trail that directly traverses the wisents' range. It's an electrifying sight when visitors spy the animals grazing or nibbling on bushes. European bison are taller at the shoulder than American bison, with longer horns and tails but less body mass. Their streamlined appearance resembles the animals depicted in cave paintings thousands of years ago. Visitors should show respect and allow them to graze undisturbed by keeping a distance of 150 feet (45 m) between themselves and the animals.

Zuid-Kennemerland is accessible by car, or by rail via the always efficient Dutch transit system. Catch the train from Amsterdam to Haarlem; the pretty city center makes a good spot for a meal before or after your safari. From there a bus (#81) drops people at the park's visitors center or at the start of the yellow path, or bison trail. The center contains several exhibits about the wisent, as well a café selling coffee and proper Dutch cakes. During certain times of year volunteer guides lead walks through the bison's habitat. Private bison-watching tours are also available (times are posted on the park website). A search for one of Europe's most fascinating survivors in a landscape worthy of Rembrandt makes for a fine day away from Amsterdam.

Back From the Brink

All European bison living today are descended from a group of captive animals reintroduced to the wild in Poland's Białowieża Forest in 1929. In the 1930s, additional breeding programs started in Germany (one Nazi leader even became obsessed with reviving extinct Teutonic forest species). After World War II the bison resumed their slow expansion. Today rewilding teams are busy reestablishing the endangered herbivore across the continent, with a goal of increasing genetic diversity. A 2019 census counted 8,400 bison. **Rewilding Europe** and the **WWF (World Wildlife Fund)** have overseen bison releases in Romania's Tarcu Mountains at the edge of the Southern Carpathians since 2014. Another group of European bison thrives in the country's northwest. There are now herds in the Netherlands, the Baltic countries, Germany, Romania, Italy, Sweden, Bulgaria, and even the United Kingdom, where a calf was born in the wild for the first time in 1,000 years in 2022.

For Mountainous Rainforests

Nantahala National Forest, North Carolina, U.S.A.

Instead of Costa Rica

A rushing creek in the Fires Creek Recreation Area is one of many water systems that nourish Nantahala National Forest's trees.

Everyone knows what tropical rainforests should look like: verdant green with spouting waterfalls and filled with birds. Americans would probably think of Costa Rica's cloud forests or Puerto Rico's El Yunque National Forest as the rainforests nearest to them. But they'd be wrong. In fact, there's one that's as wild as anything near the Equator on U.S. soil. The temperate rainforests of western North Carolina are as lush as any found in the tropics, but just a few hours' drive from Hartsfield-Jackson Atlanta International Airport.

Centered around Pisgah and Nantahala National Forests, which sprawl across the southern Blue Ridge Mountains and the escarpment marching across North Carolina into South Carolina and Georgia, the region is known for its abundant rainfall and wild forests. With annual rainfall between 60 and 80 inches (150–200 cm), these temperate forests can be rainier than Seattle and are filled with 130 types of trees including spruce, fir, and oak, with robust rhododendrons and delicate dogwoods below. The local roads, most notably **U.S. Highway 64** and the **Blue Ridge Parkway**, are mostly winding two-lane highways that can drop jaws with their views. In the space of two miles (3.2 km), the land jounces down between 1,500 and 2,500 feet (460–760 m)—one of the steepest descents east of the Rockies. The dramatic inclines feature granite cliff

For arresting views, take a sunrise drive along the Blue Ridge Parkway.

OPPOSITE: Shop in posh boutiques or dine at local pubs on Main Street in Highlands, North Carolina, a resort town tucked against the Blue Ridge Mountains.

domes, 50 waterfalls, and one of the world's largest assortments of salamander species.

There's plenty to do in the woods: hike mountain trails, search for wildflowers like trilliums and lady slippers, and visit the many waterfalls. A favorite cascade of Hollywood location scouts includes Nantahala's **Dry Falls**, which co-starred with Daniel Day Lewis in *The Last of the Mohicans*. In **Dupont State Recreational Forest**, head out on a one- to two-hour looped hike to eyeball the impossibly photogenic **High Falls** and **Triple Falls**. The latter was a literal scenery-chewer competing with Jennifer Lawrence in *The Hunger Games*. (Arrive early. Thanks to the waterfalls' star turns, the visitors center parking lot can fill up by 10 a.m.) Stay on the marked trails. Waterfalls are seductive in their beauty, but every year people injure or kill themselves slipping on wet rocks.

It's not only the forests that are lush along the Blue Wall, a large parcel of protected land in the Blue Ridge Mountains. Western North Carolina is home to a series of old-school resort towns, Brevard, Cashiers, and Highlands among them. Mostly protected from overdevelopment by the surrounding national forests, the towns serve as cool retreats from summer heat for the wealthy. In June the perspiring upper crust of Georgia, the Carolinas, and Florida ascend here to escape the humidity of places such as Buckhead, Myers Park, and Sanibel Island. While Cashiers possesses no real downtown, **Highlands' Main Street** is a bustling spot with restaurants and shops. Overnights might include the rambling **Old Edwards Inn and Spa**, where the outdoor wine garden is great for people-watching. The woodsy mid-century modern **Skyline Lodge** feels like Bigfoot and the Rat Pack cooked up the ultimate stylish retreat. Revamped in 2020, the property is as chill as one of Dino's vodka martinis. But the Blue Ridge's allure remains the scenery, not the money, as the sunset atop **Satulah Mountain** will remind you.

A Real Hogwarts

Towns like Highlands, North Carolina, aren't the only surprising mountain communities in the Southern Appalachians. High on Tennessee's Cumberland Plateau sits the town of **Sewanee**. "The Domain," as it is called by those who know it best, is a college community exuding a magical sense of place similar to Harry Potter's Hogwarts. The reason is Sewanee's college, the **University of the South**. Founded in 1857 as an Episcopal school, the university grew gradually into a stately assortment of Gothic Revival buildings scattered across its campus. And like certain young wizards, many of the school's 1,700 undergrads are apt to stroll to class wearing their black gowns, a tradition connected to their academic achievements.

Wander over to the **Quad** and **All Saints' Chapel**, a Gothic glory finished in 1959 (go inside and search for the stained glass window featuring a Volkswagen Beetle). Or explore any of the 50 miles (80 km) of hiking trails ringing the slopes, making sure to catch the sunset from the overlook at the **Memorial Cross**. The views of farmlands and meadows in the Tennessee Valley far below are at once stunning and contemplative. After checking out both the campus and the surrounding nature, try a meal at the **Sewanee Inn**, an oak-beamed hotel known as the college's "living room," or the **Lumière**, a nearby bistro filled with parents, alums, and faculty. Both are refreshingly social without the "media."

For Down Under Landscapes
Wilpena Pound, Australia

Instead of Uluru, Australia

At Ikara-Flinders Ranges National Park, visitors can hike one of the many eucalyptus-lined trails or sign up for a cultural tour led by an Aboriginal guide.

The solitary sandstone monolith Uluru, formerly known as Ayers Rock, is a quintessentially Australian icon and symbol of both the country's vastness and its spirit. Yet there is another, even larger, rocky formation down under that's just as compelling despite being obscured by Uluru's superstar status. The lesser known, immense natural amphitheater named Wilpena Pound, located in the outback of South Australia, is eight times Uluru's size, measuring 11 by 7 miles (18 x 11 km), and surrounded by 800-million-year-old mountains. Like its more famous rock cousin, Wilpena Pound possesses a similar capacity to inspire awe. This is a place few outsiders know about, but it's one they most certainly should.

Wilpena Pound is a geological wonder. The site is located within **Ikara-Flinders Ranges National Park**, a 360-square-mile (930 km²) natural preserve named for the Flinders Ranges, a 235-mile-long (380 km) mountain chain stretching south to the coast. Wilpena's signature interior valley—or pound, an old English term for a stone livestock enclosure, brought to the region by sheep farmers who emigrated from Britain in the 19th century—was formed when the original mountains eroded, leaving behind the remaining quartzite cliffs. This wall includes the Flinders Ranges' highest mountain, 3,840-foot-high (1,170 m) St. Mary Peak. Enclosed and surrounded by this curtain of mountaintops, the pound's valley floor measures five miles (8 km) long and two miles (3.2 km) wide and gives visitors a protected feeling, as if cupped in the palm of a giant hand. That enthralling association may have inspired the Aboriginal name of Wilpena, or "bent fingers." The local Adnyamathanha people call the place Ikara, and their legends say the mountains are actually a sand wake created by two giant inter-

An aerial view of Wilpena Pound showcases its unique bowl shape and many layers of sandstone and quartzite.

Adelaide, Capital of South Australia

In a rush to explore Sydney or Melbourne, many travelers ignore Adelaide. Big mistake. The capital of South Australia is a lively city with a foodie bent. It's also surrounded by five wine regions, including the **Barossa Valley** and **McLaren Vale**, that nurture some of Australia's oldest vines. A stop at Adelaide's **Central Market** to wander its 70 stalls makes a great introduction to the region's fresh produce and foodstuffs, while the **Art Gallery of South Australia** contains the world's largest collection of Aboriginal artifacts and artworks. More contemporary Indigenous work can be found at the **Tandanya National Aboriginal Cultural Institute.** The region's plants are on display in the 130-acre (53 ha) **Adelaide Botanic Garden** and its ornately Victorian all-glass Palm House. The nearby coast has numerous beaches, notably those at **Semaphore** and **Port Noarlunga**. Alert drivers may even spot kangaroos and emus while exploring scenic roads. Lastly, drive to the top of **Mount Lofty** and **Cleland National Park** to catch a view of the Adelaide skyline.

twined serpents slithering their way south. Mystical and isolated, Wilpena Pound, like Uluru, will fascinate travelers drawn to it for its timeless, rock-ribbed majesty and creation legend.

It's also fun to explore. The 270-mile (435 km) drive from Adelaide Airport to Wilpena Pound takes about five hours, but there is no shortage of ways to recover from a long car ride upon arrival. This is a place made to stretch your legs and get your heart pumping. Rock climbing and hiking, or bushwalking as it's known in Australia, are popular pastimes at Wilpena, with trails for all difficulty levels, including short walks for beginners. More experienced hikers can try climbing St. Mary Peak, though the mountain's summit is considered sacred to the traditional inhabitants so the respectful will bear that in mind. There are also cultural tours led by Aboriginal guides who teach about Wilpena's spiritual significance to the local people. Maybe one of the best ways to appreciate Wilpena's dramatic landscape and vast size is via a half-hour soaring air tour of the area.

Night holds a different fascination at Wilpena Pound. As dusk gathers, the valley begins to stir with nocturnal noises as the park's animals begin their forage. Like other parks across the globe, Wilpena keeps a list of must-see wildlife. The big three here are eagles, emus, and yellow-footed rock wallabies. The endangered rock wallaby is considered a conservation success story. Reduced in 1992 to a population of only 40, the rare marsupials number more than 1,000 today.

The park has three types of accommodations. The 60-room **Wilpena Pound Resort** offers traditional hotel rooms, while its **Ikara Safari Tents** offer a glamping experience with air-conditioning. There's regular camping, too. At night, gathered by the fire and with starry views above, Wilpena Pound is a dreamy story worth telling.

GO HERE:

For a "Big Five" Safari

Denali National Park, Alaska, U.S.A.

Instead of Kruger National Park, South Africa

Mist settles beneath the Alaska Range and over Denali National Park and Preserve's colorful tundra landscape.

Spring is an excellent time for viewing mother grizzly bears and their cubs (from a distance).

OPPOSITE: If you take the *McKinley Explorer* from Denali to Anchorage, make sure to sit in the upper level for 360-degree views.

Few travelers would spurn a trip to Africa and its many parks to catch a glimpse of rhinos, elephants, leopards, lions, and African buffalo—known familiarly as the "big five." But the African continent is not the only place to see a collection of mammals bearing that same sobriquet. North America has its own version of the big five, which includes moose, caribou, Dall sheep, wolves, and grizzly bears. To spot this impressive group, consider heading to Denali National Park and Preserve for a memorable encounter with Alaska's big five.

Larger than the state of New Hampshire, Denali encompasses more than six million acres (2.4 million ha), part of a 600-mile-long (965 km) mountain range that includes the eponymous peak, which means the "High One" in the language of Alaska's Athabaskan people. Denali contains three distinct landscapes: forest, tundra, and, at its highest elevations, an alpine zone—a mix of rocks, snow, and glaciers of which **Kahiltna** is the largest. Altogether, 39 species of mammals inhabit Denali, including black bears, foxes, and marmots, but the big five are the main draw.

The big five range across Denali, but individual species cluster in particular sections. Moose inhabit the north side of the park's **Alaska Range**, preferring deep woods close to lakes and other bodies of water. The park's caribou herds roam more or less near the park's northern boundaries and east of the **Foraker River**. Dall sheep thrive in the high peaks on the park's eastern and western sides. Grizzlies roam throughout the park, either alone or in family units of mothers and cubs searching for food like alpine berries or moose calves. Last on the list are the wolves, and Denali is one of the best places in the world to catch a rare glimpse of them. They're often spotted loping along the side of 92-mile (148 km) **Denali Park Road**, the park's only thoroughfare. Along with the big five, Denali harbors numerous birds, including golden eagles, mew gulls, gray jays, and ptarmigans—all worthwhile reasons to look to the sky.

Wildlife-watchers headed to Denali should remember to pack binoculars and consider taking one of Denali's bus tours. A guided tour makes wildlife-watching easier, as it affords visitors a higher vantage point and time to get the best shot without worrying about the steering wheel. For the most commanding vantage point, consider booking a seat on a "flight-seeing" tour. Denali's website provides a list of operators.

There are numerous other activities in Denali as well. Cycling trails allow bikers an opportunity to explore the park on two wheels, though they should watch for bears. Visitors can also meet sled dogs and watch a mushing demonstration. Because of its wilderness there are few marked trails in the national park; those available are short, less than two miles (3.2 km) in length, and found close to Denali's visitors center. The two-mile (3.2 km) **Savage River Loop Trail** has windswept views and offers the opportunity to explore **Savage Canyon** between Mount Margaret and Healy Ridge. Travelers interested in a longer off-trail hike should talk to a ranger first for insights and tips. Hikers should always be careful of wildlife encounters.

For overnight stays, Denali sports six campgrounds within the park itself. But for those who want a cozier stay, there are numerous hotels, such as the **Denali Grizzly Bear Resort**, rustic cabins at **EarthSong Lodge**, and in the park, the **Denali Backcountry Lodge**.

Salmon Fishing in Anchorage

The wildlife in Alaska doesn't always listen to the call of the wild. Alaska's city dwellers are accustomed to seeing the occasional moose or bear roaming their streets. Therefore, it shouldn't be a surprise to discover some of the state's best salmon fishing happens in downtown Anchorage. The fish is an important part of contemporary Alaskan identity. Its importance transcends its role as a tasty source of protein and symbolizes both heritage and economy. In Alaska, salmon fishing generates an estimated $1.5 billion annually, supporting livelihoods and local economies. The state accounts for 95 percent of the total U.S. commercial wild salmon catch. And part of that haul comes from the urban precincts of Anchorage. From late May through early September, runs of king and silver salmon head up Ship Creek, a 25-mile-long (40 km) waterway running through Anchorage (population 291,000), and anglers in Alaska's biggest city can legally fish for them. But visitors mustn't overlook bureaucracy: Out-of-state fishers must purchase a state fishing license before casting their lures. A pair of waders is recommended, as the riverbanks can get muddy. Happily, nearby bait shops will rent you what you need and offer advice on the best fishing spots and the best times to reel in a catch. Properly outfitted and positioned, lucky visitors will be rewarded with a 20- to 30-pound (9–14 kg) salmon caught in sight of Anchorage's skyline.

The Riga Cathedral, built in the early 13th century, and Dome Square are two of the Latvian capital's most recognizable landmarks (page 112).

CHAPTER 3

ROMANTIC RECALIBRATIONS

Gorgeous scenery and glittering cities will make for a memorable romantic getaway. But there's often trouble in paradise when everyone sets their sights on the same place. Rethink an expected dream destination and opt for a surprising replacement, from an American stand-in for the French Riviera to an English manor with a twist.

For a Lavish Coastal Escape
Santa Barbara, California, U.S.A.

France's Mediterranean coast is celebrated for its physical beauty, sublime weather, and relaxed—some might say indulgent—lifestyle nourished by its delectable local wine and produce. Perhaps it's no surprise that a California locale equally blessed by geography, climate, and fortune could mirror the glittering French playground. There are a lot of compelling reasons why Santa Barbara is called the "American Riviera," but it's mostly due to its Mediterranean climate and its residents' love of the good life.

Set sail from Santa Barbara Harbor for a cruise down the California coast.

Just 90 minutes from Los Angeles up U.S. Route 101, Santa Barbara's ingredients of sky, sea, and the dramatic Santa Ynez Mountains make up a fairly identical recipe to the one that visitors find in Cannes or Saint-Tropez. Like in those French towns, the glow in Santa Barbara radiates not only from the sunshine but also from bank accounts. This California seaside town is a "one percent" kind of place. In neighborhoods like Hope Ranch—and even a community christened "the Riviera"—live some of the world's wealthiest people. Proud of their hometown, they've helped sustain institutions like the **Santa Barbara Museum of Art** and the **Santa Barbara Museum of Natural History**.

Santa Barbara's earlier history, however, was rougher. Though the Jesuits established the **Old Mission Santa Barbara** in 1786, the town remained a dusty, Western-style hamlet before wealthy Easterners made it famous as a health resort in the late 19th century. Briefly, in the 1910s, Santa Barbara became an epicenter of silent film production before the movie industry settled permanently in L.A. That legacy helped shape the **Los Angeles International Film Festival**, which is housed in theaters such as the **Granada**, a spectacularly decorated 1920s film palace

Shoreline Park's position atop a mesa creates a lookout for migrating whales.

dotted with movie artifacts and memorabilia, including an uncomfortable-looking couch from the set of *Gone With the Wind*.

The more a visitor searches, the more similarities they can find between Santa Barbara and its Mediterranean counterparts—from the red-tile roofs and azure waters bobbing with yachts and sailboats to street markets selling lavender sachets. And there's wine, too. Santa Barbara knows its grapes. The county boasts 283 wineries and seven AVAs, or wine regions. Grenache and rosé are available in most of its cafés and bistros.

And like the Rainiers of Monaco, Santa Barbara can now boast its own royal house of sorts: Prince Harry and Meghan Markle, formerly of the United Kingdom, live in adjoining Montecito and often pop up unexpectedly all over town. The prince is supposed to be a generous Lyft rider, sometimes adding a $50 tip to his fare.

That's not to say the place doesn't have distinctly American features. Santa Barbara redeveloped its industrial areas along U.S. Route 101 and turned the old warehouses and industrial buildings into the **Funk Zone**, a trendy collection of cafés, shops, and restaurants. Such attractions draw visitors, and the city's hotels have been redone to accommodate them. Come sunset, take a walk to **Butterfly Beach** on the **Cabrillo Bike Path** —which runs past many of the area's oceanfront attractions. If you arrive before sunset, the beach is a great spot to surf or kayak. Or head up to the **Douglas Family Preserve**, named for the movie star Michael Douglas, who donated the money to purchase the land. Enjoy a cliffside walk during golden hour with ocean views in the Golden State's most golden of towns.

Central Planning

Though Santa Barbara is called the "American Riviera," its buildings are decidedly more Spanish than French. With its red-tile clay roofs, white stucco, and wrought iron, Santa Barbara resembles a version of Old Spain, without the years. The city is actually an example of 20th-century urban planning, which was instituted after a 1925 earthquake. The powerful temblor reduced the city to rubble, and Santa Barbara decided to rebuild itself in the Spanish Revival style that was popular at the time, resulting in landmarks like the Moorish **Santa Barbara County Courthouse** and the **Lobero Theatre**. Montecito's **Casa del Herrero** museum is a good example of how eastern industrialists, in this case the heirs to a machinery fortune, created a fantasy world on the Pacific coast. Redone and reimagined, the **Mar Monte Hotel** evokes 1930s glamour, while the 121-room **Hotel Californian**, opened in 2019, offers a rooftop pool and spectacular views. Travelers enjoy discovering the whimsy of native Santa Barbara architect Jeff Shelton at **Ablitt Tower**. More than 60 of Shelton's designs keep Santa Barbara's tradition of lively vernacular architecture thriving.

For Mediterranean Indulgence

Montenegro

Instead of Croatia's Dalmatian Coast

Trek up to the mountains for aerial views of the old coastal town of Kotor, Montenegro.

At more than a mile (1.6 km) high, Njegoš Mausoleum in Lovćen National Park is the highest mausoleum in the world.

OPPOSITE: Kotor's St. Tryphon Cathedral displays valuable artifacts and art.

B eginning in June, the world makes a dash to the sea. In Europe, nowhere do the beelines buzz louder than along Croatia's Dalmatian coast. This stretch of shoreline along the Adriatic Sea spent the long Cold War on ice and then, in the 1990s, on fire during Croatia's war for independence. In the 21st century Croatia's coast has become world famous. Cruise ships now disgorge thousands of tourists who crowd ancient towns like Split and Dubrovnik. Lines form everywhere, and there are few uncrowded views. Yet, farther south, another Adriatic destination remains largely unknown while sharing a similarly dramatic coastline, historic architecture, and an ancient culture. Small and beautiful, Montenegro has become a favorite hidden gem for Europeans.

Montenegro's history is complex. Once ruled by the Venetian Republic and then the Ottoman Empire, this former Balkan kingdom was known, with Serbia, as the Federal Republic of Yugoslavia from 1992 to 2003. Only in 2006 did Montenegro become a fully independent entity. Such a rich, variegated history has resulted in a 183-mile-long (295 km) attraction-filled coastline and a slew of picturesque ports of call. Center your visit around the charming old towns that hug Montenegro's Adriatic coast and fjord-like Bay of Kotor, or Boka Kotorska. Numerous resorts and beaches lie within easy reach, and the historic towns, with their orange-tiled roofs and twisting streets full of outdoor cafés, are perfect embarkation points for activities such as boat tours and hikes into the surrounding hills.

Surrounded by steep mountains and graced by an ancient walled city, the **Bay of Kotor** looks less like a candidate for the European Union and more like it belongs in J. R. R. Tolkien's Middle Earth. Originally Venetian, Kotor's old town is now a UNESCO World Heritage site filled with venerable buildings and churches. Its seagoing heritage can be explored at the **Maritime Museum**. Or consider a hike along the upper walls for spectacular views of town and the bay beyond.

The seacoast town of **Budva** traces its existence back 2,500 years. Today it's considered one of Montenegro's liveliest places and the center of the **Budva Riviera**, a collection of beach towns extending in either direction. Of note are the fortified medieval town of **Starigrad**, also a World Heritage site, and pebbly, curving **Jaz Beach**, which is a magnet for sun lovers. Just 15 minutes south, **Sveti Stefan**, a fortified town from the Middle Ages, sits like a jewel box open to the sea. Now a private resort, the surrounding beaches remain open to the public. Stay in Budva at the **Avanti Hotel & Spa**. The influence of the Ottomans, who ruled Montenegro for 500 years, is on display in the far southern coastal town of **Stari Bar**. The ruins of its old town lie some two miles (3.2 km) from the coast.

Should the beach become too hot, hit Montenegro's interior and the former royal capital of **Cetinje**. Nearby **Lake Skadar National Park** is renowned for its green mountains, tiny towns, and nesting pelicans. Or strike out to **Durmitor National Park**, in the wild Dinaric Alps, for a rafting or kayaking excursion on the white water of the **Tara River**, the site of Europe's deepest gorge (4,265 feet/1,300 meters). The dramatic alpine landscapes of **Prokletije**, another Montenegrin national park, are also worth attention.

Albania, the Med's Last Frontier?

Albania is the next, and maybe the last, frontier along the Adriatic coast. One of the most remote nations in Europe, the country features a mix of sandy beaches along a dramatic and rugged coastline stretching from Montenegro in the north to the Ionian Sea and the Greek border in the south. Originally known as a backpacker's idyll, Albania's shoreline has gradually been developed, but coastal areas like **Divjakë-Karavasta** and **Llogara National Parks** are still havens for nature, including birdlife such as flamingos and endangered Dalmatian pelicans. Reminders of Albania's long history include the ruins of **Apollonia**, a former Greek city just a short drive from the city of Fier; an ancient Roman amphitheater in **Durrës**; and **Butrint**, a UNESCO World Heritage site protecting both classical ruins and the surrounding marshes. But it's Albania's gorgeous beaches that lure international travelers most, especially the coastline stretching in both directions from the town of **Sarandë**, the center of the "Albanian Riviera." Sarandë is bordered by pristine beaches, and its city center is nestled between beautiful hills of olive groves and the Ionian Sea. A few beaches to consider include **Ksamil** and its three small islands across the water from Corfu, Greece, or the beaches at **Borsh** and **Dhërmi**, farther north but with the same turquoise-color water and relaxed pace. Albania's beaches are cheaper and less crowded than their Italian or Croatian counterparts, but don't wait: The secret is out.

For British Aristocratic History

Knepp Estate, West Sussex, England, U.K.

Instead of Blenheim Palace or Highclere Castle, England, U.K.

Tours of aristocratic English estates and stately manor homes such as Blenheim Palace or Highclere Castle—the location of the TV series *Downton Abbey*—are considered the quintessential "must-dos" for visiting Anglophiles who roam across the British countryside each summer. But there's another grand estate redefining what an English country home should be or could become. Knepp Estate in West Sussex turns the idea of an English manor on its head, and it's worth it to see why.

At **Knepp Estate**, located south of the town of Horsham (about an hour via train from London's Victoria Station), there are no clipped and manicured lawns nor tidy wheat fields. Instead, its owners have allowed their 3,500 acres (1,415 ha) to return to nature in all its shaggy glory. The results make for a vivid display. Walking onto Knepp's grounds from the main road, the English landscape sounds junglelike in its decibel level: Birdsong fills the air, as does the buzzing of insects, with butterflies fluttering and dragonflies swooping and dancing. Alongside the drive, scrubs and saplings sprout from what were once managed agricultural fields. Far above the regenerating woodlands, a circling stack of white storks rides the thermals. It's all going according to plan, or rather, the lack of a human one. Instead of imposing a top-down strategy, Knepp's owners—Sir Charles Burrell, the 10th Baronet, and wife Isabella Tree—allowed nature to take its course when their efforts at more traditional farming, with attendant investments in pesticides and machinery, no longer made economic sense.

Hear live music at Knepp Estate, where flora and fauna have overtaken the English manor.

Thanks to extensive conservation efforts, native white storks once again can call the Knepp Estate home.

Following their back-to-nature successes, the couple have become advocates and authors and invite people to participate in the experience of rewilding, aka returning spaces to nature. Visitors can stay in a variety of seasonal properties including glamping tents, yurts, and tree houses. A former dairy barn transformed into a rustic cabin is available year-round. There are hiking paths around the estate, and Knepp's walking safaris, led by trained guides, allow visitors to explore the grounds and search for free-ranging Exmoor ponies or Tamworth pigs, an heirloom species. Fallow deer and a herd of longhorn cattle also roam the estate, while birds like goldfinches, kingfishers, and kestrels populate the sky above. Other safaris are devoted to beavers, nightingales, and even butterflies.

In fact, Knepp has played a key role in reintroducing the white stork to England. Two pairs of white storks arrived at Knepp in 2016 and built the species' trademark stick nests and hatched chicks in 2020—the first ones in the United Kingdom since 1416. The growing population is monitored by the White Stork Project, a partnership with several conservation groups including the Durrell Wildlife Conservation Trust and the Warsaw Zoo. The project's goal is to reestablish permanent populations of white storks in southeast England.

Perhaps even more fascinating than the safaris are the walks focused on the ecological impacts of rewilding and how animals, from scrabbling beetles to rooting hogs and grazing cattle, play a key role in re-creating new habitats and expanding the biodiversity of this small but increasingly influential plot of England. Knepp Estate will continue to be a center for the rewilding movement as it grows in influence.

Salamanders and Time Machines

Located in the apple orchards of rural Somerset near Bath, **The Newt** is another memorable English estate. Its cheeky name, inspired by the discovery of endangered salamanders on the grounds, belies the elegance of its hotel and jaw-dropping gardens. But it's the reimagination of a third-century Roman villa that turns the luxe hotel into a time machine. Owners and hoteliers Karen Roos and Koos Bekker spared no expense to conjure their villa in authentic detail beside the ruins of an ancient one discovered on the property. The reimagined version has Roman furniture, art, and even baths heated with a traditional wood-burning hypocaust system. The couple even flew in a team of Florentine fresco restorers to create the colorful murals and designs on the walls. Unlike a traditional museum, visitors are offered a hands-on experience of daily Roman life. Finger the curtains, rattle the pots and pans, and root through the shoe closet. The docents on staff provide interpretation and explanation. There's also an on-site museum that provides historical and archaeological perspective.

For Waterside Pastorals
Lake Atitlán, Guatemala

Instead of Lake Como, Italy

There's stunning, and then there's Lake Como. The North Italian *lago* is rightly celebrated for its magnificent scenery: steep verdant hills dotted with resorts, cream-colored villas, and even creamier movie stars—and all of it topped with a large dollop of la dolce vita. But there's a comparable lakeside pastoral in a place far from the flight paths of *Succession*-style billionaires. For anyone after gorgeous views without a Hollywood or Wall Street travel budget, Lake Atitlán, in Guatemala, rivals those watery vistas in Italy or elsewhere.

Lake Atitlán offers clear views of three massive volcanoes: San Pedro, Tolimán, and the still active Atitlán.

Like Como, Atitlán is all about a dramatic setting. Nestled in the Guatemalan highlands, the lake lies in an enormous volcanic caldera formed 84,000 years ago following what must have been a spectacular eruption. Atitlán, in the country's southwest, is fringed by small Maya-speaking towns and dominated by the escarpments of three volcanoes (San Pedro, Tolimán, and Atitlán) in the Sierra Madre mountains. While the first two volcanoes are now considered dormant, Atitlán is still geologically active—its last recorded eruption was in 1853. Other acts of nature include tropical storms, hurricanes, and a 1976 earthquake that killed more than 20,000 people and caused water levels in the lake to drop six feet (1.8 m).

Seismology and weather events aside, Atitlán manages to be at once both serene and sublime. The English writer Aldous Huxley compared the view to the more famous Italian lake by saying, "Lake Como, it seems to me, touches on the limit of permissibly picturesque, but Atitlán is Como with additional embellishments of several immense volcanoes. It really is too much of a good thing." The German explorer and scientist Alexander von Humboldt was more direct, calling it the "most beautiful lake in the world."

Colorful buildings and hanging umbrellas line the quaint town of San Juan la Laguna, Guatemala.

Guatemala declared the area surrounding Atitlán a national park in 1955, and this century has seen a rise in adventure-seeking travelers who are eager to climb the trails that lead to the volcanic peaks, kayak across the lake, or both. (There's cliff diving, too, for the very brave.) Many more visitors just want to slow down and meld into the view, taking in the lake's supreme sunrises and sunsets or immersing themselves in the Spanish language. Spanish is spoken in the waterside communities, though most of the residents default to their native Maya tongue.

With such a relaxed tempo, visits frequently extend to longer stays. While you can spend just a weekend here, many travelers opt to linger a week or longer to investigate Atitlán's surrounding 11 villages and towns. Most can be reached by water taxi (for about two dollars) or by renting your own boat for the day. Each town exudes its own character and style. **Panajachel** is the largest, and a tourist gateway, with all that this implies, from expat-focused services, medical clinics, and Spanish language classes to bars to shopping. **San Marcos** became famous as a hippie destination. Today there are yoga studios and probiotic eateries that give it the feel of a Northern California–style retreat. **Santa Catarina Palopó** is renowned for its striking murals, a project started by a journalist in 2017 to help beautify the village with colors and patterns based on the designs of traditional *huipil* blouses, which are still woven by the local women. In fact, Atitlán's local artisans make an array of beautiful crafts. Look for pottery, weavings, ceramics, and textiles. **Casa Palopó**, a 15-room luxury hotel in Santa Catarina, is a villa for those who want pampering. Otherwise, check out Airbnb listings for budgets of every sort. Wherever you stay, Lake Atitlán's captivating beauty makes the trip to Central America well worth the effort.

The Mistake in the Lake

Most people agree that the exquisite scenery surrounding Lake Atitlán needs to be carefully protected from overtourism, but what about the lake itself? A story involving Atitlán, a hungry fish, and an American airline illustrates the dangers of unintended consequences. It began in 1958 when executives of Pan American Airways decided to expand Atitlán's tourist potential (and Pan Am's passenger loads) by transforming the lake into a fisherman's paradise. Having pioneered air travel to Central America in the 1930s, Pan Am executives convinced Guatemala to seed the lake with largemouth bass fingerlings. The plan was to attract sportfishers from the United States and elsewhere eager to fly down to Central America for an opportunity to hook an aquatic trophy in an exotic locale.

But there was a problem. Voracious predators, bass devour anything they can eat. An invasive species introduced into a body of water with no natural predators, the bass were soon feasting upon much of the lake's indigenous fish and crabs, which were also the food of the rare giant Atitlán grebe, or poc, a bird found nowhere else in the world. With the bass too big for the birds to eat, the pocs, as documented by American wildlife conservationist Anne LaBastille, soon disappeared from the lake. By 1990 they were extinct. Pan Am followed the poc into oblivion. It went bankrupt a year later.

For Innovative Arts and Crafts

Asheville, North Carolina, U.S.A.

Instead of Santa Fe, New Mexico, U.S.A.

Nestled in the Blue Ridge Mountains, Asheville is known for its arts scene, craft breweries, and outdoor activities.

The mural-filled River Arts District is the center of Asheville's creative scene.

Those attracted to Santa Fe's culture of craft should turn their gaze to Asheville in the Blue Ridge Mountains. The booming North Carolina city's reputation for artisanal beer, outdoor recreation, and New Age vibes (there's a weekly drum circle in downtown's Pritchard Park on Fridays) sometimes obscures the city's deep and vibrant Arts and Crafts tradition. Add a burgeoning music scene and the outdoor allure of nearby national forests, and Asheville is a worthy rival to the New Mexico town for those who hunger for art in an inspirational setting.

Asheville's craft roots stretch back to the Indigenous Cherokee and earliest European settlers who fashioned furniture from rhododendron bushes and pots from local clay deposits. But its modern reputation got started in 1895 when New Yorker George Washington Vanderbilt II moved there and built the **Biltmore Estate**, a stupendous Gilded Age palace with 250 rooms. His "little summer escape" remains the largest private home in America. Tours of the French-style château and gardens are a major draw. Vanderbilt's wife, Edith, founded Biltmore Industries to train local young-sters in woodworking, weaving, and needlework. Her altruism coincided with a new interest in progressive design and decor, known as the Arts and Crafts Movement. Proponents, including the Roycroft community and

Gustav Stickley, two furniture manufacturers based in upstate New York, emphasized native materials, honest construction, and handcraftsmanship—the perfect complement to a town with a growing tourist industry, says Bruce Johnson, an Asheville historian.

The movement found one of its fullest expressions in 1913 with the opening of the **Grove Park Inn**, now owned by Omni. Constructed with granite hewn from the nearby mountains, the 140-room resort grew to contain the largest collection of Arts and Crafts furniture anywhere in the world—more than 1,000 pieces, according to Johnson, who organizes the annual **National Arts & Crafts Conference** held at the hotel since 1988. Other hotels to consider are **The Foundry**, part of an old factory complex in the heart of the city's historic African American community, and the **Abbington Green Bed & Breakfast Inn and Spa**, whose attention to detail and breakfasts of strawberries with balsamic vinegar make it a favorite. All offer a staging ground to investigate Asheville's burgeoning craft scene.

"Craft was here way before many things, certainly before the outdoor industry," says Stephanie Moore, executive director of the Center for Craft in Asheville. "You have a city perfectly situated for small business; you've got little shops and an entrepreneurial spirit. Those two things have married—and married well. It's produced a fertile environment for makers of all kinds."

Asheville's downtown is speckled with galleries and print shops, glass-blowing studios and breweries. Institutions such as the **Center for Craft** and the **Asheville Art Museum** host changing exhibits. The **River Arts District (RAD)** is an entire neighborhood filled with art studios and plastered with creative graffiti that resembles the tattoos sported by its shopkeepers. There's a skateboard park and an 8.9-mile (14.3 km) bike path along the **French Broad River Greenway**, numerous coffeehouses, and a well-loved barbecue joint called **12 Bones Smokehouse** known for its pulled pork sandwiches.

There is no escaping the artisanal in Asheville. "Craft," says Moore, "is in our DNA."

Explore Asheville's natural side atop a paddleboard in the nearby French Broad River.

Musical Notes

Music is an art form that thrives in Asheville and the Southern Appalachian Highlands. Folk, or roots music, and bluegrass have always been popular here. Since 1928 the city has hosted the **Mountain Dance and Folk Festival**, the oldest continuous folk festival in the United States, and Asheville's reputation as a mecca for modern bohemians has drawn performers like the Avett Brothers and Gladys Knight to make their homes nearby. Visitors can catch live performances in clubs like the **Orange Peel** and the **Grey Eagle**, local breweries, and even on the street, where buskers frequently play impromptu concerts. And music is growing as an Asheville industry. The city counts six recording studios and a vinyl record factory. **Citizen Vinyl** is located downtown in the streamlined former headquarters of the local *Asheville Citizen Times* newspaper. Its pressing plant, busy turning mounds of black plastic goop into platters, is visible to diners in the lobby restaurant. Many of the records contain music captured upstairs in the store's recording studio.

The Nam Khan meets the Mekong River in Luang Prabang, the former royal capital of Laos and now a UNESCO World Heritage site.

For a Spiritual Experience

Luang Prabang, Laos

Instead of Sedona, Arizona, U.S.A.

Comparing the red rocks of Sedona, Arizona, with the emerald green jungles of Laos isn't obvious. Yet for travelers in search of a place both soul-nourishing and peaceful, both towns offer a feeling of serenity and an escape from the rush of daily living. But the former Laotian imperial capital of Luang Prabang offers a far more complex history than the Arizona town known for crystals and New Age vortexes. The small, misty Southeast Asian city of Buddhist temples and palaces is a unique place indeed.

What gives Luang Prabang such a dreamlike atmosphere? Its setting, for one. Built on a peninsula formed by the confluence of the Nam Khan and Mekong Rivers, the city seems more watercolor than real, evoking a time when boats filled with cargoes of rubies, tiger skins, and teak floated down from the mountains. There's also its spiritualism. Long a center for Buddhism, the city is filled with temples and monasteries nurturing rituals dating back centuries, such as morning alms, when orange-robed monks wander the streets while locals and visitors fill their bowls with small gifts of food. Lastly there's Luang Prabang's unique history. Between the 14th and 16th centuries, the city served as the capital of Lan Xang, or "kingdom of a million elephants." In 1893 Laos fell under French rule, becoming a protectorate, and Luang Prabang became a royal capital again.

Climb Mount Phousi's more than 300 steps to see the famous reclining golden Buddha.

OPPOSITE: Try Laotian grilled meats from open-air restaurants.

French administrative buildings fill the historic core, giving the city a unique Parisian flair. The combination of Buddhist and colonial architecture creates a unique heritage that's now protected as a UNESCO World Heritage site.

There's a rich itinerary for visitors, from touring Luang Prabang's many temples (including its biggest, the 16th-century **Wat Xieng Thong**) to renting one of the trademark slender riverboats for an afternoon cruise on the caramel-colored **Mekong River**. Climb **Mount Phousi**, the city's sacred hill, for a view of the surrounding town. Or visit **Haw Kham**—the royal palace—a beaux arts confection built in 1904 that possesses a throne room decorated with warriors and elephants in mirrored glass. Don't miss the 1958 white Ford Edsel, a gift from the U.S. government, that's parked in the garage.

When dusk approaches and the air cools, follow vendors toting bundles to the night market on **Sisavangvong Road**. It's filled with colorful, easy-to-pack souvenirs like cotton and silk scarves, silver bangles, and embroidered textiles. Luang Prabang is chock-full of roadside family restaurants offering tempting dishes. Two hotels close to all the action are the romantic, French-influenced **Satri House** and the more contemporary **Avani+ Luang Prabang Hotel** across the street from the market. Perhaps Luang Prabang's real power is how it fosters serenity through ordinary experiences: enjoying a rice-and-eggplant stew in an open-air restaurant during a tropical downpour or wandering its old streets while a temple's gong reverberates in the distance. Like the plumeria blossoms locals reverently set atop fence posts and doorstops as offerings, such moments are a reminder of the power of life's underappreciated details that can rejuvenate a traveler's spirit.

Laotian Cuisine

Sometimes a gateway to a country is a soup bowl. The Southeast Asian cuisine most people in Europe and North America know is either Vietnamese or Thai, but Laotian dishes are well worth exploring, too. Lao cuisine makes the most of fresh produce like green onions, mushrooms, and cabbage and proteins like pork, chicken, and fish. These are usually served in traditional family-style dishes that are often accompanied by sticky rice. Lao soups are both sublime and earthy, like *tom kha kai*, a coconut chicken soup with aromas of lemongrass and lime. Citrusy lemongrass is served extensively in Lao cooking, and aromatic makrut limes also accompany spicy stews (*or lam* is a popular one) and soups. There are marinated fish or mincemeat dishes called *larb* served with spices, herbs, and signature greens. Green papaya salad, first popularized in Thai restaurants, is also a Laotian dish. It is often mixed with *padaek*, a popular sauce made from fermented fish, rice bran, and salt. Where to sample them in Luang Prabang? The city is full of restaurants of every variety, so travelers should follow the locals. Look for small, family-run restaurants like those along the old city's historic Sakkaline Road, a thoroughfare lined with temples and French colonial homes. Discover noodle shops where iron pots are heated by wood fires and low-to-the-ground tables are clustered with customers stirring a dollop of *jeow bong* sauce, a sweet and spicy paste, into their soups. The experience is as flavorful as the food itself.

Evening lights illuminate
the Piazza del Duomo's Lecce
Cathedral, located in the center
of town.

For an Instagrammable City

Lecce, Italy

Instead of Florence, Italy

An ancient Roman theater was buried under Lecce for centuries until construction workers discovered it in the early 1900s.

Florence may be the shiniest eyelet on the Italian boot, but down in the heel is a fleck of gold called Lecce. Located in Puglia, on the Salento peninsula, and often referred to as "little Firenze" because of the magnificent churches and civic buildings in its old town, this city of 95,000 is worth visiting for its soft, Southern California–like climate, less frenetic tourism industry, and gorgeous architecture.

Lecce's allure is immediate. At night the narrow streets fill with families enjoying its charms. The city prides itself on its Italian, and the Leccese, who have a reputation for ornate and indirect speech, like similarly expressive buildings, says Awdie Coppola, a local tour guide and Lecce authority. "During the 16th century, Lecce was the most eastern part of the Spanish Empire. They conceived it as a showpiece town where the [architectural] influences came from the top: the clergy, merchants, and princes." Such patronage gave rise to the detailed baroque architecture that populates its narrow streets. The buildings are at once exuberant and sly, with emphasis on decoration—pediments and reliefs full of flowers, fruit like pomegranates, and *putti*, the flirtatious cupids that gesture and grin from the Corinthian columns.

Such creative chiseling seems to have reached its climax with the **Basilica di Santa Croce**, a baroque church built in 1695 with a facade slathered with sculptures, garlands, and statues. Designed to knock the socks off anyone lucky enough to glimpse it, Santa Croce defines over-abundance and is, perhaps, the most spectacular of the town's many churches. Lecce also possesses a fine cathedral in its main square, the **Piazza del Duomo**. The grand Naples Gate—**Porta Napoli**—a triumphal entrance to Lecce, was built in 1548 and is one of three surviving entries into the densely packed old town. The **Museo Ebraico**, or Jewish Museum, recounts the history of Lecce's Jewish community and is located in the historic medieval Jewish neighborhood called the **Giudecca**.

Travelers will want to stay in the heart of the old city. Splurge at the **Palazzo Maresgallo Suites & Spa**, a gorgeously restored residence with 12 highly individual and spacious rooms, each one integrating art and design, and gardens from courtyard to rooftop in easy reach. There are numerous short-stay accommodations as well; one of the more spectacular is a one-bedroom with kitchen and sleeping loft overlooking Lecce's partially excavated Roman amphitheater, built during the emperor Hadrian's reign in the second century.

But perhaps the greatest pastime in Lecce lies in what the Italians call *dulce far niente*—the sweetness of doing nothing. Stop for a scoop or two of *fior di latte* from a nearby gelateria and promenade like the locals do through the tapered flagstone streets as the setting sun turns the buildings' limestone blocks, made from "Lecce stone," the color of Thracian gold. Tourism will surely grow in Lecce as Americans and others discover its warm weather, nearby coastline, and bucolic countryside dotted with olive groves and *masserie*, the traditional fortified farmhouses found on estates across the peninsula. For the moment, though, there's a chance to discover Lecce's timeless beauty before your neighbors do.

Dine on delectable Italian eats in the streets of Lecce.

Masserie Love Company

Tuscany has elegant villas of the sort made famous by the film *A Room With a View*, but Puglia is known for retreats without any views at all. Such buildings are called *masserie*, or *masseria* in the singular. Found across southern Italy, but especially in Puglia, masserie are fortified farm compounds featuring high walls with few windows, grouped around a central courtyard surrounded by the owner's farmhouse and various outbuildings for animals, crops, and the peasants who tended to both. In Puglia, the masseria boom occurred in the 16th and 17th centuries when Spain ruled southern Italy and built a series of watchtowers dotting the coast as a warning system against seafaring invaders. Today many of the old farmsteads have been restored as guest accommodations or private homes that give travelers the chance to experience the rural life of southern Italy. Among the favorites are Masseria San Domenico for its seaside location and Masseria Muntibianchi AgriResort, which offers massages in a cave.

For a Maker Culture
St. Ives, England, U.K.

Instead of North Adams, Massachusetts, U.S.A.

Artists flock to St. Ives for its charming cottages and narrow roadways.

North Adams, Massachusetts, is a small place with a big art scene. As the home to the Massachusetts Museum of Contemporary Art (MASS MoCA), the largest contemporary art museum in the United States, the former mill town is now known for its artistry, not its manufacturing. Travelers looking for another small town with equally creative ambitions might want to visit St. Ives on Britain's Cornish coast. With its own branch of London's Tate Museum, St. Ives offers a mix of modern art and low-key allure that's turned the picturesque English fishing village into a flourishing creative community an ocean away from the maples and pines of New England's Berkshire Mountains.

St. Ives (population 15,558) is in the far west side of Cornwall, north of Penzance and facing the Celtic Sea, a part of the Atlantic Ocean with a setting that gets rave reviews from visitors and residents alike. Since the Middle Ages it has operated as a busy fishing town. St. Ives's picturesque, narrow streets lined with small houses and cottages—affectionately called the "Warren"—have lured artists for 200 years, beginning with the 19th-century marine and landscape painters J. M. W. Turner and Henry Moore (the latter not to be confused with the 20th-century sculptor of the same name). The writer Virginia Woolf spent much of her childhood in St. Ives. After World War II, contemporary artists had found their way here, including modernist sculptor Barbara Hepworth. Her former studio is now the **Barbara Hepworth Museum and Sculpture Garden**. Such a tradition means St. Ives has numerous art galleries, especially along **Fore Street**. It's the kind of town where the art is everywhere and on offer. Visitors can purchase items ranging from paintings to pottery.

Works from the late Barbara Hepworth are on display at her eponymous museum and sculpture garden, located at her former studio.

The biggest cultural draw is the **Tate St. Ives**. The innovative and architecturally significant museum opened in 1993 on the site of an old gasworks overlooking the town and beach. Featuring the work of many St. Ives artists such as Alfred Wallis and Partou Zia, the hub of the London-based Tate doubled in size following a 2017 expansion. Today the Tate St. Ives is one of the most popular attractions in the United Kingdom. It schedules numerous exhibits and talks, and its rooftop café is a favorite place to take in views of the town and the sea.

Art may be the biggest draw, but St. Ives offers other things to do as well. **Porthmeor Beach** is popular with surfers. There are even surfing schools available for beginners tempted to try to catch a wave. It also attracts swimmers and diners. The latter can grab a meal at one of the beachside cafés and restaurants. The low-ceilinged **Sloop Inn** dates from the 1300s and is one of the oldest inns in Cornwall, if not the United Kingdom. Visitors interested in seal-watching along a group of small islands known as the **Carracks** can take excursion boats that leave from the harbor, while hikers can walk the coastal cliffs or head out along the **Cornwall Coast Path**. The 17-mile (27 km) trail south of St. Just is known as one of Britain's most beautiful hikes, with gorgeous views beloved by British writer D. H. Lawrence, who lived at Higher Tregerthen with his wife. Also good for a stroll is **Steeple Woodland Nature Reserve**, a 40-acre (16 ha) forest of beech and oak that holds **Knill's Monument**, a would-be mausoleum to an 18th-century customs official, John Knill (1733–1811), who stipulated a party be held there every five years. The annual ritual is still observed, and it is exactly right for this creative, eccentric community. "It's the greatest outdoor theater in the world," says St. Ives storyteller Shanty Baba.

Captain Sir Richard Francis Burton

It seems fitting that one of history's most extraordinary travelers should have his own fan tribute in St. Ives, a town accustomed to unconventional lives. The **Captain Sir Richard Francis Burton Museum** is a private museum open by appointment and run by St. Ives storyteller and tour guide Shanty Baba. (Bookings for the museum can be arranged by phone or email; entrance is £8, approximately $10.50.) Inside are 28 exhibits celebrating the legendary Burton (1821–1890), a soldier, diplomat, and explorer who challenged the racial and sexual prejudices of his day. Burton smuggled himself into Mecca, a journey at the time punishable by death for non-Muslims, and published a book on his exploits.

In 1856 he embarked on an expedition to find the source of the Nile and became one of the first Europeans to glimpse Lake Tanganyika. A multilinguist, Burton was said to have spoken 29 languages, and at one time he kept a tribe of tame monkeys to see if he could learn their vocalizations. He shocked the Victorians by translating the *Kama Sutra of Vatsyayana* and an unexpurgated version of *The Arabian Nights* into English.

Burton and his wife, Lady Isabel, are buried in London in the graveyard of St. Mary Magdalene, a Catholic church in Richmond upon Thames. Their mausoleum is made of sandstone that is carved in the shape of the tent that the couple used on their travels, incorporating both Christian and Islamic symbols in its design.

For La Dolce Vita
California's Central Coast, U.S.A.

Instead of Tuscany, Italy

Golden sunlight floods the Central Coast's rolling hills and prized vineyards.

Hearst Castle, newspaper baron William Randolph Hearst's former estate, offers tours of its extravagant rooms and grounds.

Tuscany is a place where glamour has overpowered the simpler pleasures of the countryside. Travelers searching for a bucolic destination with vineyards, olive groves, centuries-old churches, and inspiring scenery might head in another direction: California's Central Coast. The stretch of coast between Los Angeles and San Francisco centered in and around the county of San Luis Obispo (often called SLO) serves up similar rural delights to those found in Tuscany. No one is speaking Italian, but the Central Coast of California may just be an American Tuscany.

The Central Coast's mild climate gives it a year-round growing season, so it's no surprise that it's packed with farms and orchards harvesting fruits, vegetables, and legumes, ranging from strawberries to walnuts. A farm trail knits together many of the local producers and offers experiences from kelp harvesting in the Pacific to soapmaking. In the city of San Luis Obispo there's a farmers market held every day of the week. The biggest one, covering more than five city blocks, is the Downtown SLO Farmer's Market, held every Thursday evening. While no one could mistake San Luis Obispo (population 47,545) for anything but a small California town, its relaxed feel—Oprah Winfrey once called it the happiest city in America—and array of restaurants make for low-key exploring and dining.

The region is also a rising wine star. San Luis Obispo County alone supports at least 300 wineries and two wine regions. The vineyards closest to the Pacific make up the **SLO Coast Wine Region** and are known for lighter reds and whites, like pinot noir and albariño. Farther inland and at a higher elevation, the **Paso Robles Wine Region** is known for heavier reds. Both regions feature wine trails and wineries that exude an Italian feel, such as **Niner Wine Estates** and **DAOU Vineyards** in Paso Robles.

The California equivalent to the frescoed churches scattered throughout the Tuscan countryside are Spanish missions. Established by Jesuits, the missions march up the coast about every 30 miles (48 km). **La Purísima Mission State Historic Park** boasts almost a dozen restored buildings where visitors can watch reenactments of 1820s mission life including weaving, pottery, leatherworking, and blacksmithing. **Mission San Miguel** dates from 1818 and contains interior frescoes designed by Esteban Munras. It has preserved many of the original buildings and adobes, including a stagecoach inn. Located in the middle of a modern downtown, **Mission San Luis Obispo de Tolosa** has a museum with Native Californian, mission-era, and American settlement artifacts. Protected from the 21st century by an 86-acre (35 ha) sanctuary, **Mission San Antonio de Padua** in Monterey County seems to evoke an older California, maybe even that of the year of its founding, 1771.

Villas are an essential part of a Tuscan holiday, but the Central Coast possesses the biggest, grandest villa of them all. **Hearst Castle** is no turreted, medieval fortress, but it is a celebration of Mediterranean style and filled with art treasures from across Italy, France, and Spain. Located in San Simeon, the sprawling estate was conceived by media tycoon William Randolph Hearst. Built between 1919 and 1947, the castle is now a museum, and its 82,000 acres (33,185 ha) form a state park and conservation trust. For villa-style stays, accommodations like **CaliPaso** and **Allegretto Vineyard Resort** give guests a chance to sleep among the vineyards.

A blacksmith works on a nail during a reenactment at La Purísima Mission State Historic Park in Lompoc.

An Italian-Style Renaissance

You can't become a serious alternative to Italy without olive trees. When it comes to olive groves, California's Sonoma County has been a surprising pioneer in their cultivation. As climate change roils the state, Sonoma is nurturing both sustainable agriculture and tourism, supporting farmers and growers who diversify their offerings with quality olive oils. For travelers, it can mean a tasty adventure as they roam the county sampling the best varieties, especially extra-virgin olive oils (EVOOs). Sonoma's olive oil renaissance began in 1990 when the **B.R. Cohn Winery** near Glen Ellen pressed California's first estate olive oil using fruit from a grove of more than 450 trees that date back to the mid-1800s. The county's first olive press was introduced at the **Jacuzzi Family Vineyards**. Some 16 acres (6.5 ha) of the **Jordan Vineyard & Winery** in Healdsburg are devoted to growing four types of olives that are sold at the estate and used in its kitchen. Also in Healdsburg, **DaVero Farms & Winery** offers tours of its olive groves, gardens, and vineyards that include pairings with olives, wine, and charcuterie.

For Art Nouveau Architecture

Riga, Latvia

Instead of Prague, Czechia

Riga's stunning cityscape includes the Freedom Monument, honoring lives lost during the Latvian War of Independence, and St. Peter's Church, the tallest church in the city.

E ven if they can't identify the style by name, few travelers can resist the allure of a neighborhood of art nouveau buildings. The curvy, ornamental art movement that blossomed from around 1890 until World War I was inspired by the organic shapes of nature. The style is characterized by wavy and sinuous lines in a manner that broke with earlier classical traditions. Popping up in architecture, interior design, jewelry, and posters, art nouveau became a favorite in Brussels, Paris, and Vienna. Prague, in particular, is noted for it. However, few people realize that the largest assemblage of art nouveau buildings found anywhere on the planet is actually located in Riga, the capital of the small Baltic country of Latvia.

How did Riga end up with so many art nouveau buildings in its historic center (which is listed as a UNESCO World Heritage site)? It was due to timing. In the early 1900s, when the style was at its height, Latvia underwent an economic boom. Eager for jobs in new industries, Latvians moved from rural farms to Riga, which meant buildings needed to be built to house them. The city also liberalized its zoning rules, allowing newly prosperous families to commission homes in the art nouveau style outside the medieval city. The results left Riga with at least 50 noteworthy art nouveau buildings in the historic city center and another 300 or so within the city limits.

Dine alfresco on Riga's narrow, cobbled Jauniela Street.

OPPOSITE: Latvia's capital is famous for its art nouveau architecture, such as this building on Elizabetes Street designed by Mikhail Eisenstein.

Founded in 1201, Riga grew to become one of the Baltic region's most prosperous cities in eastern Europe's trading bloc, known as the Hanseatic League, which peaked in the 13th to 15th centuries. Riga's medieval center is on the right bank of the Daugava River and dominated by church steeples, like those of the **Riga Cathedral** and **St. Peter's Church**. The Old Town is filled with landmarks such as the **House of the Blackheads**, a resurrected, ornate merchants guild house from the 17th century.

A tour of Riga's art nouveau buildings takes travelers through neighborhoods where ordinary Latvians live and work, allowing the opportunity to get a real feel for the city. The place to begin is Riga's **Art Nouveau Centre**, a museum devoted to the style and located in an ornate 1905 apartment building on the corner of Alberta and Strēlnieku Streets, in a neighborhood filled with many other buildings of the period. You can sign up with guides who specialize in Riga's architectural history, or rely on online maps to lead you past some of the best highlights.

More areas to explore include **Vilandes Street**, which features many fine examples of the style and which the museum calls "a jewel." Other strolls take you past **Valdemāra** and **Brīvības Streets**, and, just a few miles from downtown, the more suburban **Mežaparks** neighborhood, where wealthy residents left the older city to build villas and mansions. Don't miss the building at **Kalēju 23**. The facade is decorated with daisies and a golden rising sun. At **Elizabetes 10b** the robin's egg blue facade, with its heroic heads, is also a riot of design and feeling. Finally, to supplement your architectural experience, stay at the boutique **Hotel Neiburgs**, another art nouveau landmark in the Old Town. The 55-room property makes a good base camp for your explorations.

Barcelona

Like Latvia, Spain also experienced a flowering of art nouveau architecture, known as *modernisme* in Spanish. At the turn of the 20th century, Barcelona was an epicenter of the style. It was where creative architects such as Lluís Domènech i Montaner, Josep Puig i Cadafalch, and, above all, Antoni Gaudí designed and built arresting and beautiful landmarks. It is well worth a walk through the busy capital of Catalonia to see them. Stops should include **Casa Batlló**, Gaudí's curvaceous town house built in 1904, and the **Palau de la Música Catalana**, a concert hall celebrating Catalonian culture with dazzling mosaics on its supporting columns and a spectacular skylight featuring 18 stained glass muses. Next door is another landmark, **Casa Museu Amatller**, a Willy Wonka–ish building once owned by the Amatllers, a family of wealthy confectioners and candymakers, in the early years of the 20th century. The restored house, now a museum, displays the original bespoke furniture. A few blocks away is another Gaudí original, the **Casa Milà** apartment building. **Casa Fuster**, designed by Domènech i Montaner as an apartment building, has been reborn as a five-star hotel. Perhaps the most memorable example of Barcelona's delirious modernisme is Gaudí's **La Sagrada Família**. Under construction for 136 years, the massive edifice remains unfinished; it is scheduled to be completed in 2030. That's the plan, anyway. But even unfinished, Gaudí's masterpiece is one of Barcelona's most popular tourist attractions.

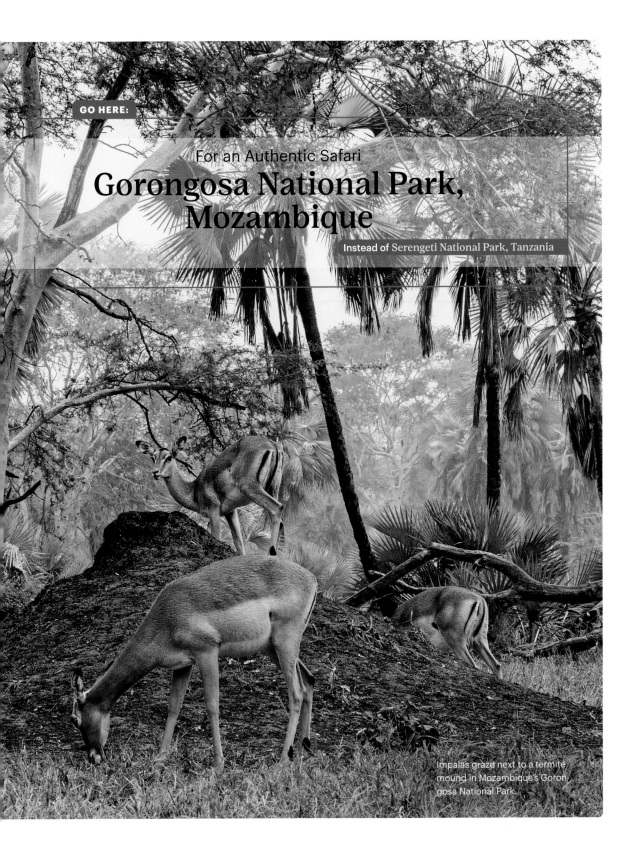

GO HERE:

For an Authentic Safari

Gorongosa National Park, Mozambique

Instead of Serengeti National Park, Tanzania

Impalas graze next to a termite mound in Mozambique's Gorongosa National Park.

Marvel at lions—one of the big five—on a guided safari.

If there is still an African safari that resembles those before they became as easy to assemble as a five-day Caribbean cruise, its spirit might be geolocated to Mozambique's Gorongosa National Park at the southern end of the Great Rift Valley. Known as the "Serengeti of the South" for its varied landscapes of savannas and forests filled with bushbucks, lions, and elephants, Gorongosa is an alluring and authentic experience in a little-traveled region of Africa. This is a safari that's far removed from most of the more crowded parks found in Kenya or South Africa, and one that rewards visitors with wildlife made even more compelling by their triumph over human cruelty.

Gorongosa is, quite rightly, one of Africa's natural wonders. Yet not too long ago, in the 1990s, the park was a tarnished crown following a bloody civil war that resulted in the extermination of some 90 percent of Gorongosa's large animals. Now a sustained conservation effort has restored the park's luster. Established as a game reserve in 1920 during the years Mozambique was a Portuguese colony, Gorongosa became a national park in 1960. Until the mid-1970s it was known for its large population of game animals. But after independence, the ensuing civil war proved disastrous for Mozambique and Gorongosa when opposing armies used the park as a battlefield. Soldiers on both sides slaughtered Gorongosa's elephants for ivory, machine-gunned lions for sport, and shot herds of zebras and wildebeests for food. When the war ended in 1992, Gorongosa was a silent, ravaged place empty of animal life. The devastation slowly began to reverse itself as Mozambique recovered and conservation efforts began anew. By 2018 an aerial survey estimated that more than 100,000 large herbivores were again roaming the park. Meanwhile, the park expanded to 1,500 square miles (3,885 km²), encompassing **Mount Gorongosa**, the only refuge of the Mount Gorongosa pygmy chameleon.

It's the park's large mammals that bring visitors here, first and foremost by safari. The best months to come are in the dry season from April to October (the park is closed from mid-December to the end of March during the rainy season). Organized camping and daily safaris are available through **Wild Camp Gorongosa**, which features an array of creature comforts. Trained guides can be hired for a half or full day to do an open game drive and explore the floodplains and palm forests to find wildlife including buffalo, elephants, antelopes, and primates. There are also bushwalks on foot and several excursions by boat on **Lake Urema**, located in the very heart of Gorongosa, where you can encounter floats of crocodiles, hippo pods, and flocks of birds.

For anyone interested in local culture, bicycle tours introduce visitors to the local communities and offer a chance to see current park conservation projects. Such community and conservation efforts helped make Gorongosa a model across the world for integrating biodiversity conservation with human development. Nothing worthwhile is easy, however.

The park's magnificent animals rely on the several rivers that flow into Lake Urema.

Travelers wishing to visit the park usually need to connect from Johannesburg, South Africa, and fly to northern Mozambique, then ready themselves for a three-hour drive to the park. With an abundance of wildlife and a compelling story of renewal and revival, Gorongosa is very much worth the effort.

How Gorongosa Was Recovered and Restored

How to restore a broken world? That was the challenge facing Gorongosa National Park's employees in the 1990s after armed conflict wiped out entire species of animals. Their efforts got a big boost in 2004 when American telecom entrepreneur Gregory C. Carr pledged more than $100 million to return and protect the park's biodiversity by reintroducing species from other places. So far Gorongosa has reintroduced seven keystone species, including 180 blue wildebeests, 35 elands, and 14 African wild dogs. In addition, the park planted three million trees on Mount Gorongosa in an effort to restore the mountain's landscape. Hippos, wildebeests, and zebras have yet to approach their preconflict populations, but antelope, hartebeest, and waterbuck numbers have soared. The elephant population has recovered from fewer than 200 individuals to more than 800. To help ensure the park's long-term viability, conservation teams reach out to the bordering villages to educate people on the benefits the park brings while also encouraging youngsters to seek employment opportunities as safari guides or staff.

Red mangroves, which create essential habitat for young fish and crustaceans, grow in shallow waters in Florida's Biscayne National Park (page 154).

CHAPTER 4

UNCONVENTIONAL PARKS

Famous forests, iconic seashores, and beloved national parks attract herds of SUVs. However, if you're looking to avoid crowded landscapes and long wait times, you may want to consider exploring breathtaking spots on Lake Michigan dunes, jaw-dropping Arizona mountains, and a green space in Oklahoma that rivals New York's Central Park.

For a Taste of Appalachia

Cumberland Gap National Historical Park, Kentucky, U.S.A.

Instead of Great Smoky Mountains National Park, Tennessee, U.S.A.

Fog pours over deciduous trees in early fall at the Pinnacle Overlook in Cumberland Gap National Historical Park.

Snow covers an old barn in Cumberland Gap National Historical Park's Hensley Settlement.

Great Smoky Mountains National Park is the most visited national park in the United States. For a similar mountain adventure without the crowds, traffic jams, and other frustrations, give another Appalachian national park—located only 90 miles (145 km) from its more famous cousin—a try. While the Smokies drew 14.1 million visitors in 2020, Cumberland Gap National Historical Park counted only 814,000. Cumberland offers an opportunity to revel in uncongested mountain vistas marked by beauty, geology, and the history of American pioneers who sought a westward passage to Kentucky and the lands beyond.

Authorized by Congress in 1940, the 24,000-acre (9,710 ha) Cumberland Gap National Historical Park straddles three states (Tennessee, Kentucky, and Virginia) and contains one of the three natural breaks in the Appalachian mountain wall that marches down the eastern seaboard. It was once the portal between the English colonies and the Ohio River Valley for both animals and Indigenous tribes, like the Shawnee and Cherokee, who followed the game trails. Late in the 18th century, settlers took up the same route, intent on expanding from the 13 original states to the Ohio River Valley through the "first doorway to the West." Their path became Wilderness Road, through which white settlers came into

Kentucky. One of those travelers was Daniel Boone, who recommended pioneers bring along "a good gun, a good horse, and a good wife." Historians estimate 300,000 people navigated the rough, narrow road through the mountain pass.

The trek is much easier today. The **Cumberland Gap Parkway** (Route 25E) takes drivers through some of the park's best scenery. And the park's more than 85 miles (135 km) of hiking trails include some 14,000 acres (5,670 ha) of protected wilderness. The trails range from easy quarter-mile (0.4 km) strolls to days-long backcountry adventures. There are also **ranger-led walking tours** that detail the Cumberland Gap's rich history and aspects of its natural beauty. On the **Tri-State Peak Trail**, hikers can even straddle three states; a marker designates where Virginia, Tennessee, and Kentucky come together.

There are more than 30 caves in the park. While most are restricted to the public, there is one spectacular exception: **Gap Cave**. Here, park rangers conduct two-hour tours of 3.5-million-year-old subterranean chambers filled with stalagmites and minerals. The park's collection of aboveground geological formations is equally impressive. On its eastern border rise 500-foot-tall (150 m) cliffs called **White Rocks**. Towering above the forest, they give hikers a 360-degree panorama. Another drop-dead view is the one from the **Pinnacle Overlook**, a short, if winding, drive from the park's visitors center. The summit's elevation of 2,440 feet (744 m) affords a three-state view as well as one of the Cumberland Gap itself.

For a glimpse of what mountain life was like in the early 20th century, reserve a tour of the **Hensley Settlement**. Established in 1903, the village is a collection of buildings, including log cabins, a one-room schoolhouse, and a blacksmith shop, on top of Brush Mountain. Overnight accommodations can be found within the park at the 154-site **Wilderness Road Campground** (reserve far in advance) or **The Olde Mill Inn Bed & Breakfast**, which has eight guest rooms, including a log cabin from the 1700s.

White-tailed deer can be easily spotted at dusk and dawn in the park.

Knoxville's Musical History

While the world knows Nashville as the capital of country music, Knoxville, Tennessee, is where the industry first began. The closest city for musicians from Southern Appalachia, Knoxville and its radio stations nurtured the careers of many musicians from the region including Roy Acuff, Chet Atkins, and Kenny Chesney. Other country singers passing through included the Everly Brothers, Lester Flatt and Earl Scruggs, and Kitty Wells.

Knoxville's musical history can be discovered on a self-guided walking tour found on the city's visitor website. It concentrates on downtown including **Gay Street**, where a seven-year-old Dolly Parton first sang on the radio, and **Market Square**, where a record store manager pressed a copy of an unknown Elvis Presley's "That's All Right" into the hands of an RCA record scout. Nashville would eventually win out, thanks to its geographic position and more powerful radio stations, but Knoxville was the city to first rock country's cradle. Today the downtown bustles with restaurants, brewpubs, and, naturally, music venues.

For an Urban Green Space
Gathering Place, Tulsa, Oklahoma, U.S.A.

Instead of Central Park, New York, New York, U.S.A.

Oklahoma's second largest city is one where traditional values are central. "Sir" and "ma'am" follow "thank you," and there's a reverence for religion—Tulsa's blessed with large and ornate churches: Baptist, Greek Orthodox, Catholic, and Methodist (one church is topped by a stylized art deco sculpture representing praying hands). The city also celebrates U.S. restlessness—Route 66, the fabled "Mother Road," plunges through it. But faith and highway signs aren't the only attractions. Tulsa is also home to one of the world's most unique city parks. Travelers who think New York's Central Park is the last word in urban greenery should head to the heartland to explore Tulsa's Gathering Place, an innovative space in the best sense of the word and hardly traditional at all.

The brainchild of the local nonprofit George Kaiser Family Foundation, Gathering Place opened in 2018 and features 100 acres (40 ha) of playgrounds, outdoor concert lawns, tree-shaded walking paths, and fountains on the east bank of the Arkansas River just south of downtown. Built with some $445 million in funding, Gathering Place reserves a large part of its operating endowment for programming, which features everything from Native American storytellers to circus troupes. There are also 18 full-time horticulturalists who lavish attention on Gathering Place's flowers as well as 6,300 trees, 16 acres (6.5 ha) of butterfly-nurturing prairie grasses, and 400 species of other plants, many native to Oklahoma.

Sprinkled throughout are creative public art installations and imaginative slides and playground equipment, like those in the **Skywalk Forest**, a colorful, Seussian collection of bridges and climbing structures

Children will delight in the bird-themed structures at Gathering Place's Chapman Adventure Playground.

A restored canoe filled with plants is one of Gathering Place's public art installations.

designed by German and Danish artists. There's a bustling flea market of bric-a-brac in the **Cabinet of Wonder**, an installation by artist Mark Dion containing collectibles such as model skyscrapers that guests are invited to rummage through. Even the rentable paddleboats, kayaks, and canoes are made to be unique, with decorations and embellishments by Tulsa artists.

Gathering Place helped transform Tulsa into a pop music shrine with the creation of **Guthrie Green**, a new park in the downtown Tulsa Arts District. The urban square is named for Oklahoma-born Woody Guthrie, the Depression-era folk singer and songwriter of "This Land Is Your Land." It fronts the **Woody Guthrie Center**, which contains a museum devoted to his work. Thanks to the museum's popularity, its operating foundation acquired the papers of legendary 1960s balladeer Bob Dylan and opened the **Bob Dylan Center** in 2022 as a repository for his works. Rounding out Tulsa's musical hits is **The Church Studio**, a shrine to 1970s rocker Leon Russell, the purveyor of the Tulsa Sound, once embraced by musicians like Eric Clapton and others.

Tulsa's downtown is worth walking to explore its notable assortment of **art deco skyscrapers**, constructed in the 1920s when the young city sloshed with cash from an oil boom. **Tours of Tulsa** offers wanders throughout the historical Deco District, including through the many tunnels that connect the buildings below street level. There's also a stop at the **Tulsa Club Hotel**, a Hilton property housed in a landmark building. Tulsans, it should be noted, have big appetites. Boutique ice-cream parlors, bakeries, and donut shops (a local passion) abound, and the **Mother Road Market** is the site for sampling a variety of unique foods and craft cocktails under one roof. The bustling food hall is located just off 11th Street, better known as Route 66.

The Tulsa Massacre

In 1921, Tulsa was riven by a racially motivated massacre as white residents torched more than 40 blocks of Greenwood, a Black neighborhood and thriving commercial sector known as the "Black Wall Street." More than 39 African American residents were killed and another 800 injured. The horror of the event is recounted in a searing exhibit at **Greenwood Rising**, a digital museum that takes visitors on a sobering journey from the inception of Tulsa by Native Americans, European Americans, and African Americans to the rise of Greenwood's soaring entrepreneurial ambitions.

The museum also remembers the neighborhood's sense of community. One of Greenwood Rising's highlights is a period barbershop where three holographically projected barbers invite viewers to sit for a haircut and listen while they talk and share their dreams. Their optimism is obliterated in the next gallery, in which a multimedia presentation plunges visitors into the ensuing violence made more visceral and immediate through imagery and sound. The final exhibit showcases Greenwood's recovery and highlights the community from the 20th century to present day. Nearby **John Hope Franklin Reconciliation Park**, with a 27-foot-tall (8 m) bronze-and-granite sculpture by Ed Dwight. Called the **Tower of Reconciliation**, the 26-foot-tall (8 m) monument depicts the African American experience in the United States and honors prominent African American figures in Tulsa's history.

For Hoodoos and Uncrowded Trails
Chiricahua National Monument, Arizona, U.S.A.

Instead of Bryce Canyon National Park, Utah, U.S.A.

Hike past towering hoodoos on the Ed Riggs Trail.

When it comes to extraordinary western landscapes, Utah's Bryce Canyon is a perennial favorite, celebrated for its sandstone rock formations called hoodoos (pinnacles of weathered rock eroded by time, rain, and wind). No wonder 2.5 million visitors flock here annually. But there's a lesser known alternative that comes equipped with a cluster of similar rock formations, arrayed in a long canyon in a 19-square-mile (49 km²) park in a remote part of southwestern Arizona.

Despite its modest size, Chiricahua National Monument captivates travelers with the bewitching voodoo that hoodoos do well (to riff on Frank Sinatra). How fitting that this small protected landscape has been called a "wonderland of rocks."

Rising southeast of Willcox, Arizona, the Chiricahua Mountains shelter an area known for its biological diversity and its forestlands. Here, animals like the collared peccary and coati live alongside plentiful species of birds. The mountain range also represents the southernmost reach of the West's quaking aspen, named for their leaves' tendency to tremble or flutter in the slightest breeze. But it's the rocks and pinnacles that are the park's real draw. This was Apache territory, and they described the area as the "Land of Standing-Up Rocks." So it may come as a surprise, then, that Chiricahua National Monument sees so few visitors—only about 61,377 in 2022. But that is also its blessing; it's spared the crush that invades Bryce. In Chiricahua, there are no long lines and fewer parking issues. Instead, visitors feel like they have this geological petting zoo all to themselves.

Chiricahua owes its unique formations to volcanic activity. When the immense Turkey Creek Caldera erupted

Take in the hoodoos from a bird's-eye view at Inspiration Point.

27 million years ago, it spewed out nearly 2,000 feet (610 m) of volcanic ash and pumice. Once cooled, the hot mess hardened into rhyolitic tuff. This relatively soft, porous stone eroded over millennia, becoming the hoodoos and balancing boulders that distinguish this part of southern Arizona's "sky island" geography.

Ease into your explorations with a 0.8-mile (1.3 km) hike that takes you to the **Echo Canyon Grottoes** for an introduction to the park's trademark hoodoos. Because of the trail's relative ease, it's a favorite with children. The more ambitious can head to a series of trails that join up with the **Ed Riggs Trail** for a three-mile (4.8 km) walk through ever more riveting scenery. If you have more in you, continue to the **Big Balanced Rock Trail**, which, as the name implies, leads you to a gravity-defying rock formation—an enormous boulder barely balanced on a rock beneath it. Continue on to the **Heart of Rocks Loop**, where more balancing boulders and hoodoos turn the landscape into a not unreasonable facsimile of a Flintstone family outing. Return to the visitors center by taking the **Sarah Deming Trail** to the **Rhyolite Canyon Trail**. It's a seven-mile (11 km) hike through some of the best geology in America.

The monument and surrounding area are also a birder's paradise. More than 200 species of birds frequent the Chiricahua Mountains. The American Bird Conservancy lists Chiricahua as home to many threatened and endangered species, including the Gould's turkey, the largest and rarest subspecies of gobbler, now successfully reintroduced into its former range. With Mexico so close, the monument regularly shelters birds from that country. Many of the 13 types of hummingbirds found here are Mexican species rarely seen elsewhere in the United States.

Night Skies and Telescopes

Besides birding and hiking, Chiricahua National Monument also offers travelers excellent opportunities to stargaze. In 2021 the park became an International Dark Sky Park, marking it as a place where it is possible to experience the night sky the way the ancients did, devoid of light pollution. The International Dark-Sky Association calls the quality of Chiricahua's night sky "nearly pristine," with only limited light pollution from faraway cities. That and the pure air quality, atmospheric conditions, low precipitation, and higher altitude mean the skies are frequently afire with stars, affording visitors the chance to see the Milky Way in its grandeur year-round. The **Chiricahua Astronomy Complex (CAC)**, located 15 miles (24 km) west of the national monument and run by the Tucson Amateur Astronomy Association, sometimes allows the general public to utilize its sky-viewing platforms. Twice a year, CAC hosts an Evening Under the Stars, when you can look through telescopes and learn from on-site volunteers.

For Desert Explorations

Anza-Borrego Desert State Park, California, U.S.A.

Instead of Death Valley National Park, California, U.S.A.

Dune evening primroses, among other wildflowers, add a splash of color to Anza-Borrego's desert landscape.

A 90-minute drive from San Diego, California's Anza-Borrego Desert State Park is a vast, wild, and inspiring locale that rivals Death Valley's arid beauty—without the long schlep from the city. In Anza-Borrego, Southern California visitors can spend their day hiking a dramatic desert and its hills before returning to their hotel to sip wine and watch the sun sink into the Pacific—Southern California traffic permitting, of course.

Anza-Borrego encompasses 12 wilderness areas across 650,000 acres (263,045 ha) of San Diego County, making it the country's largest state park. It sprawls across the Colorado Desert, a section of the Sonoran Desert, and between the Mexican border in the south and the playgrounds of Greater Palm Springs in the north. Save for the park's southern entrance, where giant white windmills generate renewable energy to feed the Golden State's insatiable electrical appetite, the park seems gloriously void of civilization and its malcontents.

Indeed, there's an End of Days feel to Anza-Borrego's dry washes, slot canyons, and towering boulder-strewn escarpments of the Santa Rosas and San Ysidro mountain ranges, the quiet broken only by the scuttling of ghostly zebra-tail lizards. Desert winds tease the ocotillos, cacti, and California fan palms (the state's only native palm tree). In years when the winter rains come, carpets of wildflowers bloom in February or March. Deer, mountain lions, and the park's namesake bighorn sheep wander in the hills. ("Borrego" is a Spanish word for sheep, and "Anza" honors 18th-century Spanish explorer Juan Bautista de Anza.) More than 200 species of birds nest here,

Desert bighorn sheep skillfully climb Anza-Borrego's rock faces.

depending on the time of year, including buntings, thrashers, and hummingbirds. Park planners are attempting to protect such populations with habitat corridors contiguous with nearby **Cuyamaca Rancho State Park**; their goal is to provide wildlife safe passage from Anza-Borrego to the Mexican border.

For humans, hiking and biking opportunities are numerous, though anyone entering this harsh environment should follow park safety rules. Information on local conditions is available at the park's visitors center in **Borrego Springs**. Two popular trails include **The Slot**, a 2.3-mile (3.7 km) trip to a slot canyon, and the **Cactus Loop Trail**, a 0.7-mile (1.1 km) trail past a variety of cacti. The park has 500 miles (800 km) of dirt roads, and anyone who wants to explore needs a vehicle equipped with four-wheel drive. Guided tours are a safe option. They take you to some of the more spectacular vistas including **Fonts Point**, which looks out across an enormous valley of eroded canyons—a cross between Mars and the Forbidden Zone in *Planet of the Apes*. Anza-Borrego is also an International Dark Sky Park. Protected by its mountains from the glow of Southern California's cities, the night sky dazzles with stars.

Though visitors can make the (long) day trip and return to San Diego or L.A. for dinner, there are **12 designated park campgrounds** ranging from RV-ready to primitive sites (reservations in the busy months are recommended). There are also a number of upmarket resorts in or near Borrego Springs, the park's nearest town. These include **La Casa del Zorro Desert Resort & Spa**, which hosts a mix of private adobe-style casitas on landscaped grounds and sit-down dinners. Two others include the *Mad Men*–mod **Palms at Indian Head**, or the **Hacienda del Sol** in town.

Bighorn Sheep

A glimpse of Anza-Borrego's namesake bighorn sheep herd is considered a memorable highlight. The park is one of the last California redoubts for an animal that once ranged across the West. The male, or ram, sports curling horns weighing up to 30 pounds (14 kg). Rams engage in intense headbutting during mating season to establish dominance and access to mates. These contests can grow so fierce that the sound of the collisions can be heard from a great distance. Bighorns are elusive, using their split-toed hooves to inhabit hard-to-reach mountain slopes where predators like mountain lions have a tougher time tackling them. They are adapted to extreme temperatures, with the ability to endure both freezing winters and scorching summers. Their capacity to conserve water allows them to survive in arid regions, and they rely on their efficient digestive system to extract moisture from the sparse vegetation they consume. One good place to find bighorns is hiking along the **Palm Canyon Trail** near Borrego Springs. During the fall mating season, the headbutting of rival males sometimes echoes through the hills. If you're absolutely determined to see a bighorn, try joining the park's annual summertime **bighorn sheep count**, one of the country's longest-running volunteer wildlife censuses. Enthusiasts have braved the scorching summer temps for more than 50 years to tally the health of Anza-Borrego's bighorn population, currently estimated to be no more than 300 animals.

For Glaciers and Wildlife

Adamello-Brenta Nature Park, Trentino, Italy

Instead of Glacier National Park, Montana, U.S.A.

The Cornisello lakes, as seen from atop the Brenta Dolomites

visit to Italy doesn't necessarily mean city destinations divided into equal parts Florence, fashions, and alfresco dining. The nation also possesses wild regions that travelers frequently overlook to indulge in Gucci and gastronomy. In fact, the Italian boot boasts 20 national and 130 regional parks, each as compelling as any found elsewhere in the world—and no more so than in Italy's northeast, where the Alps meet the Dolomites in a dramatic, mountainous mash-up that presents visitors with vistas of sheer cliffs, waterfalls, and mighty crags overlooking Alpine meadows and icy lakes. For anyone wanting a landscape and peaks that match the scale of Montana's Glacier National Park, consider Italy's Adamello-Brenta Nature Park, a UNESCO-designated global geopark. It's got the glaciers. It's got the 10,000-foot (3,050 m) peaks. And it even has the bears.

Located in Trentino, Adamello-Brenta is an hour's drive from the provincial capital of Trento and comprises some 153,000 acres (61,920 ha) covering 230 square miles (595 km²). The park's namesake, the **Adamello**, is one of the largest glaciers in Europe, though it's now seemingly in permanent retreat as climate change warms the planet. The park's arresting,

Mountain bike the Vallesinella trail for waterfall views.

though threatened, scenery helped it win its UNESCO designation in 2008. A third of Adamello-Brenta is covered by forest, which includes maples, beeches, and stands of conifers such as larch and pine in the higher altitudes. Rhododendrons and edelweiss are also abundant. The park is also an ark for an extraordinary number of wild species including birds (partridges, grouse, and kestrels) and mammals (badgers, ermines, roe deer, mouflons, ibexes, and chamois). Like Glacier's grizzly, the brown bear—the European apex predator—is iconic, and its image is used in the park's logo.

The best way to see Adamello-Brenta's glories is by striking out on one of the many hiking trails that thread the park. Some of the most stunning are those that take hikers into the Alpine valleys between the surrounding peaks. Two worth considering are **Vallesinella**, celebrated for its roaring waterfalls, and **Brenta**, a trail through valley meadows and pastures called the "pearl" for its glorious views of the cliffs, peaks, and glaciers that ring the trail like an amphitheater. One of the park's most challenging hikes is the vertiginous **Bocchette**. The *via ferrata*, or iron trail, features iron grips and footholds embedded in the mountain face, affording adventurous hikers the opportunity to ascend like mountain goats for a prize of stunning overlooks. Other trails reward hikers with waterfalls. More than two dozen can be seen during the late spring and summer, when the snowmelt sends flumes of water cascading downward. Highlights include **Nardis Waterfalls** and its 311-foot (95 m) drop (it's also a popular ice-climbing spot in winter) and **Grasei Waterfall**, fueled by runoff from the Amola glacier above.

Where to stay? If you're hiking across the park you can book a *rifugio*. There are more than 20 of these hostel-style huts in the park that are available to hikers and mountain climbers. They are primarily open during the summer. If you're not for roughing it, there are hotels located in and around the park. For one with a view of the Dolomites try the **Alpen Suite**, a boutique hotel located in Madonna di Campiglio.

The Tuckett Refuge is one of many places to spend the night in the Brenta Dolomites.

The Bears of Italy

In the spring of 2020 a video of a 12-year-old Italian hiker's close encounter with a brown bear in Adamello-Brenta Nature Park went viral. Neither boy nor bear were harmed, but the footage surprised many international YouTubers who never imagined bears living in Italy. But bears have always been here, mostly inhabiting the country's mountains. Hunted for centuries, the bears dwindled in number in the 20th century to the point of extinction.

Now a conservation program has given Italy new hope for its bears. The environmental group **Rewilding Apennines,** a partner of Rewilding Europe, is working to secure the future of the approximately 60 Marsican brown bears, a critically endangered subspecies of Europe's more widespread brown bear. They might take heart from the experience of Adamello-Brenta's bear population, which had declined to an estimated four individuals before conservationists relocated 10 Slovenian bears to the park between 1999 and 2002. By 2022 the park's bear population was estimated to be 90 individuals.

The Llaima volcano towers over araucaria trees in Chile's Conguillío National Park

For Watery Sojourns
Lake District, Chile

There are few more lyrical destinations than England's Lake District, a dreamy, windswept, and frequently wet corner close to the Scottish border that inspired poets like William Wordsworth and Samuel Taylor Coleridge. But might you consider Chile's Lake District instead? Girdling the narrow South American country's midriff, Chile's version also possesses landscapes ravishing enough to compose odes to its beauty. Los Lagos, as it's called by the Chileans, may not be as well known as its British counterpart, but there's plenty worth discovering there, including a long list of outdoor activities and six inspiring national parks.

The Lake District region has an interesting cultural history as the traditional home of Chile's Indigenous Mapuche people, who fought the conquistadores and, later, the Chilean government to a standstill. It also attracted German immigrants in the late 19th century. The European settlers gave the place a Teutonic feel, establishing numerous dairy farms and small Alpine-looking towns where *kuchen*, a uniquely German mash-up of cake and pie, is still sold in bakeries in the region's many resort towns.

Termas Quimey-Co, a spa in the Araucanía region, offers massages and access to natural hot springs.

OPPOSITE: Windsurf across Todos los Santos Lake in Vicente Pérez Rosales National Park.

About 600 miles (965 km) south of the capital of Santiago, Chile's Lake District extends for some 215 miles (345 km) along this spine-shaped country until reaching the Patagonia region. Its climate—humid and wet—is similar to the Pacific Northwest of the United States. Chile's lakes region is blessed with a varied mix of seductive landscapes: rivers and lakes, misty woods, snow-crowned volcanic peaks, and glaciers—all seemingly hand-crafted for a social media feed. Its forests shelter an array of rare plants and trees including the sequoia-size alerce (a giant that can live more than 3,000 years), and the araucaria, a species of evergreen also known as the monkey puzzle tree that grows in Chile and Argentina at altitudes above 3,000 feet (915 m). The Lake District is also one of the world's best spots to white water raft, with rafters seeking out the **Río Futaleufú** (the name means "grand waters" in the Mapuche tongue). Some 40 miles (64 km) of the rapids are powered by the ice of glaciers melted by the underground heat of the area's volcanoes.

Six Chilean parks are the jewels of Los Lagos and include **Conguillío National Park**, which is known for its lush flora, birding around Captrén lagoon, and views of the Princesa Waterfall. There's also **Villarrica National Park**, designated to protect the mountain the Mapuche call Villarrica, or "great spirit house." This is the site of one of South America's most active volcanoes, and at its base are fern-filled valleys abubble with hot springs. **Vicente Pérez Rosales National Park**, along the border of national park-lands in Argentina, is Chile's oldest national park. Together with Argentina, this international consortium protects 5,792 square miles (15,001 km²) of mountains, temperate rainforests, and lakes, such as the irresistibly photo-genic **Lago Todos los Santos**, which is surrounded by snowcapped Andean peaks.

As a magnet for outdoor enthusiasts, the Lake District features an array of imaginative accommodations. Some, like the hobbit-like, moss-covered **Montaña Mágica Lodge**, are idiosyncratic, while others, like **Hotel Antumalal** in Villarrica, offer a modern, clean-lined look.

Threads of Conservation

Few people are lucky enough to have a national park named for them. North Dakota's Theodore Roosevelt National Park is named for the legendary conservationist and U.S. president. Outdoor fashion tycoon Doug Tompkins is another. Chile's **Pumalín Douglas Tompkins National Park** honors the founder of the American clothing firms North Face and Esprit. Tompkins—an environmentalist, mountain climber, and adventurer—made millions from his companies' fleece and outdoor wear. He then used his fortune to buy and protect endangered landscapes threatened by logging and other extractive endeavors in Argentina and Chile, including parts of the Lake District. Over time Tompkins purchased 2.2 million acres (890,310 ha) stretching from the Andes mountains to Chile's Pacific coast, including 715,000 acres (289,350 ha) of temperate rainforest known as **Pumalín Park**, named for the pumas that once roamed its forests. Tompkins's large landholdings and opposition to dams and salmon farms generated resentment in some quarters, but following the 72-year-old American's death in 2015, Chile renamed Pumalín in his honor. Preservation efforts continue in his name. **Tompkins Conservation** has helped create or expand 15 national parks and two marine reserves and has established more than 20 conservation and monitoring projects—a permanent legacy for a clothing manufacturer who became an environmental pioneer.

For Wooded Wonders

Adirondack Park Forest Preserve, New York, U.S.A.

Instead of Olympic National Park, Washington State, U.S.A.

It's rare to find primeval wilderness close to a major urban center. Olympic National Park, a three-hour drive from Seattle, comes to mind, but it is far rarer to discover wildlands on the United States' crowded East Coast. Look no further than Adirondack Park Forest Preserve, an uncrowded destination with miles of pristine wilderness and more old-growth forest than anywhere else east of the Mississippi. And it's just 200 miles (320 km) from the Empire State Building.

On the way up Algonquin Peak, hike past a waterfall in the High Peaks Wilderness Area.

The Adirondack region is a big one. The official park, created in 1892 by the state legislature and comprising both private and public lands, is nearly three times the size of Yellowstone National Park. Adirondack Park covers six million acres (2.4 million ha) and one-fifth of New York State. In fact, it is the largest park in the lower 48 states. There's no entrance fee for the Adirondacks since some 130,000 people live inside the "blue line," as the park boundary is called. The area is dotted with 105 towns and villages sustained by park tourism.

Outdoor recreation abounds in the Adirondacks. Hunting, fishing, camping, skiing, and even snowmobiling are in easy reach. But it's the park's wilderness that stirs the soul. And there's a lot of that. More than 2.6 million acres (1 million ha) of the Adirondacks are designated as forest preserve. Its mountains contain the headwaters of five major watersheds with 30,000 miles (48,280 km) of rivers and streams as well as 3,000 lakes. Hikers will find 2,000 miles (3,200 km) of trails to enjoy. Some of the most spectacular spread across the 46 mountains that stand over 4,000 feet (1,219 m) tall, known collectively as the "High Peaks."

Hikers who reach the top of Cascade Mountain are rewarded with striking views of the High Peaks.

The **Cascade Trail** leads to the 4,098-foot (1,249 m) **Cascade Mountain**, where a climb to the summit offers 360-degree views. Meanwhile, the **Moose River Plains Wild Forest** near the towns of Inlet and Indian Lake is good for wildlife-watching. Its hills, low mountains, and river valleys support deer, bears, and moose. The **Wildway Overlook Trail**, near the town of Essex, is an easy 1.5-mile (2.4 km) hike up the shoulder of **South Boquet Mountain** that's suitable for families. The trail ends at an outcropping with lovely views of **Lake Champlain Valley**. A picnic on **Prospect Mountain**, 2,030 feet (620 m) above **Lake George**, is a good alternative to the strenuous hiking of the area. You can reach it by driving the 5.5-mile (9 km) **Whiteface Veterans Memorial Highway** and then taking a short shuttle to the summit for views of Vermont's Green Mountains, New Hampshire's White Mountains, and the High Peaks.

Shopping, dining, and hotels are found in towns like Saranac Lake and Lake Placid. A two-time Winter Olympics host, in 1932 and 1980, **Lake Placid** sits alongside Mirror Lake. During the winter months, the town fills with visitors interested in skiing and snowboarding at nearby **Whiteface Mountain**, a ski resort boasting the East Coast's steepest vertical drop. There's even a toboggan run with of a 30-foot-tall (9 m) chute that sends sledders clattering onto iced-over **Mirror Lake**. Just outside town is abolitionist **John Brown's farm**, a New York State historic site. Accommodations in Lake Placid include the 100-year-old **Mirror Lake Inn Resort & Spa**, a 131-room resort that's as cozy as a pair of fleece-lined moccasins. For those who like to rough it there are 44 campgrounds in Adirondack Park and a number of lean-to shelters and primitive tent sites in the wilderness areas.

Adirondack Furniture

It wasn't long after the creation of Adirondack Park Forest Preserve that wealthy New York City and Boston families began building large summer homes, which they called "camps," in the area. The mansions, characterized by their rough log and natural stone exteriors, are fashioned in the "Adirondack style." Their interiors mirror the style, with furniture and decor fashioned from sticks, twigs, and planks gathered from the Great North Woods. The perennially popular Adirondack chair is the most famous example. Today visitors can tour some of the surviving estates including **Camp Pine Knot** on Raquette Lake and Saranac's **Great Camp Sagamore**. Some, like **The Point** on Saranac Lake and the **Waldheim** on Big Moose Lake, have found new life as luxury hotels. Those interested in Adirondack furniture can find authentic pieces on display at the **Adirondack Experience** in Blue Mountain Lake. The **New York State Museum** in Albany also has examples of the style on display.

For Lighthouses and Fishing Villages

Grand Manan Island, New Brunswick, Canada

Instead of Mount Desert Island, Maine, U.S.A.

The ocean off Grand Manan Island's rugged shoreline is home to whales, porpoises, and seals.

Grand Manan Island has a rich fishing history, with many old fish houses and smokehouses still standing.

OPPOSITE: Pack some binoculars to see Atlantic puffins up close.

A highlight of any trip to Maine is a visit to Mount Desert Island. Home to Acadia National Park, granite-bordered shores, and some of the most delightful blue-sky August days along the eastern seaboard, the island and its postcard-pretty views help make Acadia the second most visited national park in the country. It is not unusual for 650,000 people to swarm Mount Desert in August alone, resulting in long lines and lost patience. But there's another island where the views are equally sublime, the towns as quaint, and the seafood as delicious. You've got to drive farther east to Canada to reach Grand Manan Island, but it offers the same lighthouses, lobster rolls, and rocky-ribbed shores as Maine. Just with fewer folks.

Grand Manan Island lies in the Bay of Fundy in the province of New Brunswick, almost a five-hour drive from Mount Desert, including a 90-minute ferry ride from the port of Blacks Harbour. The 16-mile-long (26 km), seven-mile-wide (11 km) retreat is quieter than Mount Desert, and that's the entire point. Serene and secure Grand Manan always stood apart. An influx of British loyalists fleeing the American Revolution in the 1790s made the island home; Grand Manan was also visited by Passamaquoddy people and French traders in the 1800s. Today with few shops and restaurants and no bank, Grand Manan is a respite from the madding crowds, though that's not to say it isn't popular. Summer visitors are advised to make ferry reservations well ahead of their travel, but the numbers come nowhere near Acadia's.

Island activities include beachcombing, picnicking, hiking the coast, kayaking, and scouting for a multitude of marine animals. The whale-watching is excellent. The area is a haven for finback, humpback, minke, and the rare North Atlantic right whale. You'll also spot harbor porpoises, white-sided and white-beaked dolphins, and harbor and gray seals off the shores. Grand Manan's birdlife has been celebrated ever since American naturalist John J. Audubon dropped by in 1833. Today visitors can look for puffins, shearwaters, loons, and albatrosses, to name just a few species. At **Anchorage Provincial Park** visitors can search for some of the 30 documented warbler species known to visit the island. All in, some 360 species flock here.

Biking (rentals available) and hiking are popular along 44 miles (71 km) of shoreline, cliffside, and beach trails. There are also ATV trails.

Islanders often urge visitors to try the local dulse, a dried seaweed snack that's a New Brunswick signature, if an acquired taste. Its best batches, allegedly, hail from Grand Manan's **Dark Harbour**.

Accommodations on Grand Manan range from short-stay rentals to inns. One to investigate is **Whale Cove Cottages**, which includes a two-bedroom that once belonged to author Willa Cather and overlooks the cove. The Nebraskan summered on the island for 20 years with her partner, Edith Lewis. The **Grand Manan Museum** has more information about her time there. The museum's collection numbers more than 4,000 local objects found in attics and barns or recovered from the sea.

Fundy Funday

Some of the world's most beautiful scenery can be found along the **Bay of Fundy**. Shaped like a mackerel's tail, the bay surrounds Grand Manan and borders both Nova Scotia and New Brunswick. Its coast is filled with fishing villages and busy ports, such as St. John, New Brunswick, as well as a collection of parks including **Fundy National Park**, where beachcombers can explore mudflats full of marine life and kayakers can explore the shorelines. Thanks to its narrowness and the Atlantic's movement, Fundy creates twice daily tides of unimaginable power: 100 billion tons (90 billion t) of water flow in and out of the bay every 12 hours, double the flow of all the world's rivers combined. Whereas most tides measure little more than three feet (0.9 m) in height, Fundy's regularly reach 52 feet (16 m). Also worth investigating is **Kouchibouguac National Park**'s estuaries, golden-colored sand dunes, and the starry skies of its dark-sky preserve. **Campobello Island**, the summer home of U.S. president Franklin Roosevelt, is also worth a visit. In Nova Scotia, the rural municipalities of **Clare** and **Argyle** are great places to immerse yourself in Acadian culture. Tour **Grand-Pré National Historic Site**, commemorating the Acadian diaspora depicted in Henry Wadsworth Longfellow's classic 1847 poem "Evangeline." The poem tells the tale of an Acadian exile, Evangeline Bellefontaine, and her lifelong search for her lover Gabriel during the time of the expulsions (when the British forcefully removed inhabitants from Acadia, from 1755 to 1764).

For One-of-a-Kind Shores

Sleeping Bear Dunes National Lakeshore, Michigan, U.S.A.

Instead of Cape Cod, Massachusetts, U.S.A.

While no longer in use, the South Manitou Island Lighthouse directed boats from 1871 to 1958.

Curling into the Atlantic like a WWE wrestler's muscled arm, Massachusetts' Cape Cod National Seashore bulges with crowds during the summer—more than 3.9 million visitors in 2022, making it the busiest national seashore in the country. If you're looking for a more solitary but still lovely coastline, cast your eyes westward along the northeastern shore of Lake Michigan to Sleeping Bear Dunes National Lakeshore. Though the signature towering sand dunes can pack them in, Sleeping Bear counts less than half of Cape Cod's visitors. The park also possesses 65 miles (105 km) of mostly empty shoreline featuring gold sand beaches speckled with driftwood and pebbles worn smooth by breaking waves. At night, with few large cities nearby, the skies glow with stars. Sleeping Bear's unique landscape awaits those with the imagination to pick a lake, not an ocean, for a shoreside holiday.

The national lakeshore lies on Michigan's Leelanau Peninsula, running along the northwest "pinkie" of that mitten-shaped state. Its lyrical name derives from a Native American Anishinaabe (Ojibwa) legend. Fleeing a terrible Wisconsin forest fire, a bear and her two cubs swam across the lake to Michigan. Mother bear clambered ashore first to await the cubs. But the two little bears, exhausted from their paddling, drowned. Their grieving mother stayed where she was, waiting and gradually being covered by sand. Taking pity on the family, the Great Spirit transformed the cubs into two islands, **North** and **South Manitou**, and their mother became the immense **Sleeping Bear Dunes**—guarding her children until time's end. The dunes' geological rationale is less romantic. Lake Michigan's constant east-

A steep dune at Sleeping Bear Dunes National Lakeshore descends into Lake Michigan.

erly winds mounded the sands, left here from Ice Age glaciers, to their massive height of 450 feet (140 m).

Today visitors clambering atop mother bear from the 7.4-mile-long (11.9 km) **Pierce Stocking Scenic Drive** can gaze down at the azure blue and turquoise water below. Many will descend the steep dune, or "vertical beach," that spills into Lake Michigan. Warning: The climb up is significantly harder. The view is certainly the national lakeshore's signature one, but just to its south and north are accessible and mostly empty beaches. Offshore, the two wild and primitive Manitou Islands are serviced by a seasonal ferry from Leland.

On the mainland Sleeping Bear is divided into three large parcels, with the dunes at the center. The prettiest beaches lie in the park's north section along **Good Harbor Bay** stretching west to **Pyramid Point** and accessible by dirt roads paralleling the shoreline. The third section, south of the **Philip A. Hart Visitor Center** in the town of Empire, contains additional beaches perfect for shoreline wanders. They're reachable from Esch Road and Platte River Point via the Lake Michigan Road. There's an unexpected bonus to Sleeping Bear, a collection of **farmsteads**. More than 369 historic buildings preserve the region's agricultural heritage. The open fields are no longer tilled, but they bloom with wildflowers in warmer months. The old frame houses, neat and tidy, evoke a simpler time and place.

The park supports two campgrounds: **Platte River Campground** boasts hot showers and electricity. **D.H. Day Campground** is more rustic with pit toilets and no hot water. Both book up months in advance, so interested parties are advised to check the park's website to reserve the next available date. Much of the park can be biked or hiked on the **Sleeping Bear Heritage Trail**, a portion of the park's 100 miles (160 km) of trails that allows visitors an opportunity to roam without a car.

Cherry Town, U.S.A.

Traverse City (population 15,902) is Sleeping Bear's welcoming resort community. The pretty Craftsman bungalows and Victorian cottages are decked with rainbow flags and Black Lives Matter signs as frequently as they sport the red, white, and blue. The town sits at the bottom of West Bay, a 32-mile-long (51 km) inlet between the Leelanau and Old Mission Peninsulas dotted with cherry orchards (sour not sweet) and vineyards (the area's known for its Riesling). **Downtown Traverse City** possesses a more artisanal, urban feel. Its restaurants, distilleries, and more than 20 breweries are on top of national food trends. Every July the city plays host to an annual film festival founded by political gadfly Michael Moore. The former site of a state psychiatric hospital, **Grand Traverse Commons** is a tree-shaded campus with stately 19th-century Italianate buildings now full of shops, restaurants, businesses, and apartments. It's recognized as one of the largest historic preservation sites in the country. The working lighthouse atop the **Park Place Hotel**, a 10-story hostelry opened in 1930, can't flick off without the U.S. Coast Guard's permission.

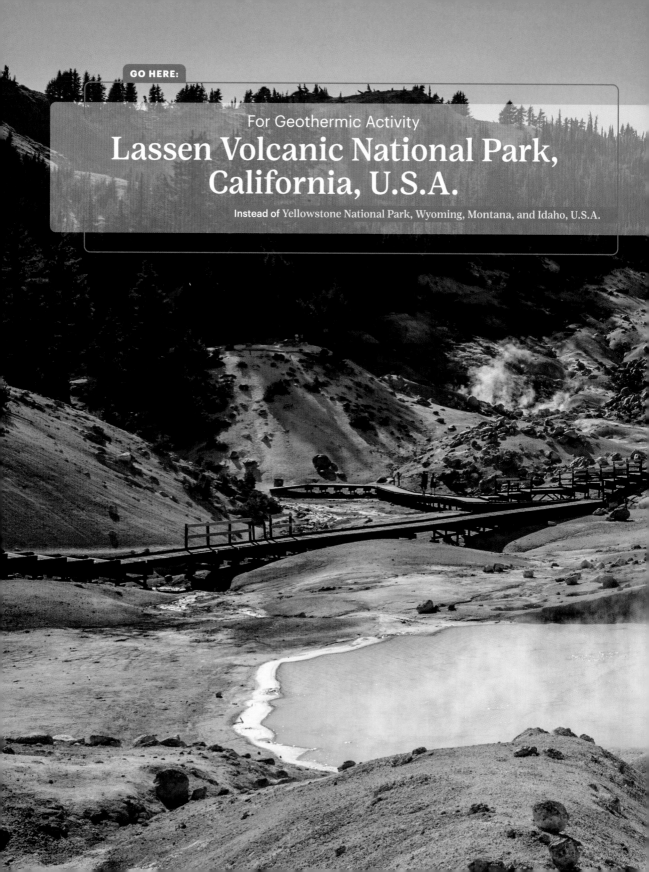

For Geothermic Activity

Lassen Volcanic National Park, California, U.S.A.

Instead of Yellowstone National Park, Wyoming, Montana, and Idaho, U.S.A.

Hot springs and mud pots bubble up at Bumpass Hell, Lassen's most heavily trafficked hydrothermal area.

Look down to Painted Dunes, Fantastic Lava Beds, and Snag Lake atop the Cinder Cone volcano.

OPPOSITE: A mountain lion stalks through the snow.

Plopping mud pots, boiling hot springs, and other burbling geothermal activities have long drawn visitors to Yellowstone National Park, one of the most geologically active places on Earth. But such geology makes Yellowstone one of America's most popular destinations, and during the summer thousands flock to Wyoming, Montana, and Idaho to see its many attractions. For anyone intrigued by geothermal activity without the crowds, Lassen Volcanic National Park is a good alternative. The park's 106,542 acres (43,116 ha) are a volcanologist's dream. The spooky, smoking landscapes resemble Hades far more than 21st-century California.

Lassen is just under a four-hour drive from San Francisco. Despite a pandemic bump, just 446,291 visitors made the trip in 2022, according to the National Park Service. For comparison: 4.8 million people arrived in Yellowstone the same year. Established in 1916, Lassen is one of America's oldest national parks and contains all four types of volcanoes: plug dome, shield, cinder cone, and stratovolcano. It is home to the largest plug dome volcano in the world, the park's namesake **Lassen Peak**. The area is dotted with active boiling mud pots, fumaroles (vents in the earth that release volcanic gases and vapors), lava beds, and hot springs.

The park's western landscape has an assortment of lakes and streams, sulfur vents, craters, and lava pinnacles, formations created by cooling lava flows. The southern reaches contain a number of hot springs, like Boiling Springs Lake and **Devils Kitchen**. To the east, there is an enormous lava plateau with many geological landmarks including **Cinder Cone** and its **Fantastic Lava Beds**. Though the latter sounds like a 1960s psychedelic rock band, it's a cinder cone volcano and a popular draw. The volcano erupted at some point in the mid-1600s and formed the 750-foot-tall (230 m) peak. The surrounding lava beds, formed when basalt lava flowed from the cone's base during the eruption, eventually covered 30 square miles (78 km²).

Other geological sites to experience in Lassen include the hydrothermal areas dotted with mud pots and steam vents, which are accessible via short hikes. (Visitors must stay on designated trails and follow park guidelines to avoid injury from scalding water.) Check out **Bumpass Hell Trail**, which brings you to the park's largest and most popular region of hydrothermal activity, **Boiling Springs Lake**. The lake's bubbling water heats to 125°F (52°C). Also visit **Terminal Geyser**, a steam vent that puts on a geyser-like show. Or linger by **Manzanita Lake**, with its postcard views of Mount Lassen.

Though the park's animals are not as visible as Yellowstone's, they include cougars, bears, and mule deer. A wolf pack, one of the few in California, has recently taken up residence.

Warner Valley, though impacted by the 2021 Dixie forest fire, is home to **Drakesbad Guest Ranch**, a rustic lodge with bungalows that make for a good place to stay. Numerous campsites are scattered throughout the park, though some may be closed due to fire impacts.

Rwanda's Volcanoes National Park

On the opposite side of the world is another assortment of volcanic parks that shelters some very special inhabitants: bands of mountain gorillas, one of the world's most endangered primates. Rwanda's **Volcanoes National Park**, the adjoining **Virunga National Park** in the Democratic Republic of the Congo, and Uganda's **Mgahinga Gorilla National Park** all lie in the Virunga Mountains, a tangle of deep forests and eight dormant volcanoes set along the border of the three countries. Rwanda's mountain gorillas are nest builders, using vegetation on the ground or in trees as material. They live in large groups—some have been documented with as many as 68 members—led by a dominant silverback. Humans can observe the usually gentle giants from a safe, but relatively close, distance during gorilla treks.

In 2022 the Rwandan government expanded its park to 89 square miles (230 km²). Though the gorillas are the stars, they are not the region's only animals. The park shelters some 178 bird species, bushbucks, spotted hyenas, and rare golden monkeys. But it is the gorillas that attract international travelers. Visits with the animals are short, not always guaranteed, and expensive. Uganda gorilla-trekking permits are, at the time of writing, $1,500 per person. The expensive access fees aid conservation efforts and provide financial incentives for local residents to preserve park habitats and work in the mostly upmarket lodges that have opened for gorilla-seeking sightseers.

For Canyon Views

Letchworth State Park, New York, U.S.A.

Instead of Grand Canyon National Park, Arizona, U.S.A.

The autumn foliage is stunning along the Genesee River Gorge in Letchworth State Park.

The grandeur of the red-and-orange-colored Grand Canyon has inspired poets, painters, photographers, and Hollywood filmmakers. Thelma and Louise drove their car over its edge, and it became the title of a 1991 movie by director Lawrence Kasdan. But if you've already visited the national park, are far from Arizona, or are looking for a less crowded canyon, there's an East Coast alternative with similar awe-inspiring views. While there are more canyons spread across the American West, consider instead a green and dramatic 17-mile-long (27 km) canyon, or gorge, located in an underpublicized part of western New York. Both verdant and beautiful, Letchworth State Park prompts superlatives from those who know about it. And for those who don't, perhaps they should plan on making a visit.

Indeed, Letchworth is often described as the "Grand Canyon of the East" for its dramatic cliffs rising as high as 550 feet (170 m) from the both banks of the 160-mile-long (260 km) Genesee River as it flows north, out of Pennsylvania and through upstate New York on its way to Lake Ontario. The 14,350-acre (5,810 ha) park is located near the small college town of Geneseo, southeast of the Finger Lakes, and is scarcely 1.5 miles (2.4 km) wide at any point. The park also encompasses the most dramatic sections of the gorge: There are 50 waterfalls including four major ones, the highest of which, **Middle Falls**, roars down into the chasm from a striking drop of 107 feet (33 m). Geologically the gorge's exposed walls are estimated to be three million to five million years old and consist of shale, sandstone, and other rocks.

Float above Letchworth State Park on a hot-air balloon tour.

The park's genesis began with a local fortune fashioned from horse whips, harnesses, and buggy bridles manufactured by a 19th-century Buffalo businessman. William Pryor Letchworth went for a visit and fell madly in love with the region and the view from Middle Falls. In 1859 he purchased the surrounding acreage and developed it into the **Glen Iris** estate, named after the ancient Greek goddess of rainbows. The far-thinking Letchworth eventually acquired 1,000 acres (405 ha) and in 1906 donated them to the people of New York. His generous gift formed the beginnings of the park. His mansion is now a 100-year-old, 16-room hotel. Glen Iris also has several lodges that can accommodate larger groups, and the park itself offers 257 campsites and 81 cabins scattered throughout.

It's easy to see why the park regularly makes media "best lists." Letchworth is full of things to do, like exploring its beauty and geological wonders on 66 miles (106 km) of hiking trails. The most popular, the seven-mile-long (11 km) **Gorge Trail**, starts at the **Genesee Arch Bridge** and runs along the park's three main waterfalls. The 24-mile (39 km) **Finger Lakes Trail** follows the continuous length of the slender park from the towns of Portageville to Mount Morris.

Letchworth also contains two constructed swimming pools and provides other activities such as horseback riding, fishing, kayaking, and, in the winter, snowmobiling. Two of the more adventurous undertakings are white water rafting on the **Genesee** or floating in a hot-air balloon over the gorge itself. Rides are available from May through October, when the leaves are transformed from green to gold, orange, and red. For a few autumn weeks, anyway, Letchworth takes on the same fiery hues as its mighty western icon.

The Big Canyon in the Northwest

Spread across Washington State are canyons like those found in Letchworth State Park. However, these aren't the result of millions of years of slow, steady erosion. All were created in a catastrophic event some 18,000 to 15,000 years ago when a warming climate melted Ice Age glaciers holding back the waters of vast prehistoric lakes. When the ice dams broke, a series of titanic deluges, known as the Glacial Lake Missoula floods, coursed across Washington with incomprehensible speed and force. Scientists estimate one two-day deluge drained the equivalent of Lakes Ontario and Erie in a wall of water hundreds of feet high that carried 10 times more volume than all the rivers on Earth. Today visitors can see the results by following the **Ice Age Floods National Geologic Trail** through several Washington State parks. These include **Steamboat Rock**, the waterfall and canyons of **Palouse Falls**, **Sun Lakes–Dry Falls**, and **Wallula Gap National Natural Landmark**. The canyons and landscapes are an impressive testimonial to nature's power and the impact of a warming climate.

More than 500 species of fish, including French and white grunts, live in Biscayne National Park's reefs.

For a Marine Life Adventure

Biscayne National Park, Florida, U.S.A.

Instead of Everglades National Park, Florida, U.S.A.

Boca Chita Key's historic lighthouse is a great spot to catch the sunset.

OPPOSITE: Paddle through the mangroves for firsthand wildlife-viewing on Biscayne Bay.

The Everglades is called a "river of grass," and seeing it, plus an alligator or two, is considered a rite of passage for many visitors to Florida. But few realize there's another fascinating national park close to Miami. Following a leisurely South Beach breakfast, spend the afternoon snorkeling in one of the top three coral reefs on the planet. Biscayne National Park is 173,000 acres (70,010 ha) of parakeet green and turquoise water dotted by red mangrove forests, intact shipwrecks, and deserted keys. With 95 percent of the park lying beneath the waves, this natural kingdom's array of undersea wonders would make even Ariel envious.

Biscayne didn't start off as a mermaid's delight. Located south of Miami and north of Key Largo, the bay and its archipelago of barrier islands, or keys, were long a haven for Native Americans, Spanish pirates, loggerhead turtles, and, in the 20th century, bootleggers. Overlooked by the first frenzy of Florida's development, Biscayne was a place for hardy pioneers and rich men. On **Adam's Key** automobile entrepreneur Carl G. Fisher's Cocolobo Cay Club entertained tycoons and U.S. presidents including Lyndon B. Johnson, whose administration designated much of Biscayne Bay as a national monument in 1968. (The designation ended developers' dreams of oil refineries and resorts.) Biscayne became a national park in

1980. Paradoxically, Biscayne Bay's one industrial site, the **Turkey Point** nuclear power plant on the park's mainland, is now a haven for manatees and the endangered American saltwater crocodile—both are attracted to the plant's warm-water canals.

The focus of the park is its water-based activities. With the vast majority of the park underwater, visitors need to get wet to see it. Twice a day, morning and afternoon, there's a flurry of activity at the docks of the **Dante Fascell Visitor Center** as departing boats run by the nonprofit Biscayne National Park Institute motor out with their passengers. Each vessel heads to a specific destination and activity, including sailing, paddleboarding, kayaking, snorkeling, scuba diving, and history excursions. Other institute-led tours depart from the **Coconut Grove** neighborhood in Miami. All tickets should be booked in advance. Rentable snorkeling gear and wet suits are available at the visitors center.

The biggest draw is the opportunity to explore the park's coral reefs by snorkel or scuba. Stretching from the Marquesas, 20 miles (32 km) west of Key West, to Key Biscayne, is the Florida Reef. Fringing the coast like a crenellated wall, the reef is 171 miles long (275 km), making it the third largest reef system in the world—and the only one in North America. The reefs form and protect an underwater city populated by huge numbers of marine life, including parrotfish, angelfish, and barracuda, totaling more than 600 species in all. Biscayne reefs also contain numerous shipwrecks. The park's **Maritime Heritage Trail** offers visitors the chance to explore some of this sunken history. It has mapped six wrecks, placing buoys above them as boat moorings. Three of the ships can easily be accessed by snorkeling parties. They include the Scottish steamer **Arratoon Apcar** (sunk in 1878) and the **Mandalay**, a jazz age schooner that sank in 1966.

The Fruits of Labor

One of the unsung heroes of America's national park system is an African American farmer named Israel Jones (1858–1932). From Raleigh, North Carolina, Jones migrated to southern Florida in the 1890s to find work as a farm laborer. Eager to build his own business, he bought several Biscayne Bay islands (Porgy, Totten, and Old Rhodes Keys). His family cleared the land in a backbreaking effort to grow pineapples and key limes, eventually becoming the region's largest supplier of both fruits.

Jones was instrumental in the founding of Florida's Negro Industrial School (later called the Florida Baptist Academy, and today Florida Memorial University), and enrolled his two sons, King Arthur Lafayette Jones and Sir Lancelot Garfield Jones, for an educational opportunity he never had.

Mexican competition had shuttered the family fruit business by the time Jones died in 1932. By the 1960s developers tried to pressure his family to sell their property, but Lancelot (Arthur had died in 1966) refused. To protect his islands, Lancelot sold them to the National Park Service for $1.2 million with the stipulation he could live out his years there. Though the Park Service agreed, it wasn't meant to be. In 1992 Hurricane Andrew decimated Lancelot's home, forcing him to the mainland. Lancelot died in 1997 at age 99. His islands, now part of Biscayne National Park, are a monument to the vision of a remarkable American family.

CHAPTER 5

WEEKEND ALTERNATIVES

You don't need to spend a fortune on Broadway tickets for excellent theater. Nor is all the glamour in Miami and San Francisco. America's heartland cities are undergoing a renaissance and providing experiences from Oktoberfests to mountain biking comparable to those found in far-off destinations, as well as unique offerings entirely their own.

The Milwaukee River meanders past Milwaukee's Historic Third Ward and into Lake Michigan (page 172).

An art deco–style foyer decorates downtown Detroit's Guardian Building, originally named the Union Trust Building when it was built in the late 1920s.

For Art Deco Style
Detroit, Michigan, U.S.A.

Instead of Miami, Florida, U.S.A.

RETAIL
PROMENADE

Miami Beach's colorful art deco hotels roost along Ocean Boulevard like a pandemonium of parrots. But anyone wanting to explore another city with equally splendid examples of that streamlined architectural style should make Detroit their destination. The Motor City, the only UNESCO City of Design in the United States, features spectacular jazz age skyscrapers, factories, watering holes, and private homes. And just like Miami, Detroit sports a couple beaches where you can work on your tan between sightseeing (but only in the summer).

How did Detroit come to possess so many art deco buildings? The modern style, marked by geometric shapes, streamed lines, and sculptural forms celebrating speed and movement, flourished in the 1920s and 1930s when the city boomed along with its auto industry. Detroit grew rapidly, and art deco proved the perfect complement to the city's 0-to-60 economy.

In 1933 Mexican painter Diego Rivera immortalized the spirit of the age; his 27 epic frescoes depicting an automobile assembly line are permanently displayed at the **Detroit Institute of Arts**. Today Detroit's downtown is full of skyscrapers from that era, including the **Metropolitan Building** (now the Element hotel), the *Detroit Free Press* **headquarters**, and the **Penobscot Building**. But the two spectacular must-sees are the Guardian Building and the Fisher Building. Both offer guided tours of their dazzling interiors. The

Visitors admire an automobile industry fresco by acclaimed Mexican painter Diego Rivera at the Detroit Institute of Arts.

36-story **Guardian Building**, called the "Cathedral of Finance," boasts stunning Aztec-influenced design and Technicolor terra-cotta tiles (locally produced by the Pewabic Pottery company) as well as industrial glass and brick. The 30-story **Fisher Building**, in the New Center neighborhood near the **Motown Museum**, is celebrated for its mosaics and frescoes, and the use of more than 40 types of marble in construction. After the building's 1928 opening, the Architectural League of New York proclaimed Fisher the "most beautiful commercial structure in the United States." Another 1920s deco building is the **Fox Theatre**, which also opened in 1928. "Experts don't consider it primarily art deco," says author Rebecca Binno Savage of the Detroit Art Deco Society. "It's Byzantine-Siamese." Whatever you call it, take a tour of the Fox, scheduled weekly. The glittering decor and the history behind how it was built make an entertaining few hours.

Other local art deco landmarks include Albert Khan's 1927 **Maccabees Building** on Woodward Avenue, known for its dazzling ceilings. The **National Shrine of the Little Flower Basilica** in Royal Oak is an imposing 1931 Catholic church with a zigzag facade; it was founded by Father Charles Coughlin, the controversial "radio priest" known for his conservative views. Bloomfield Hills' **Cranbrook Art Museum** and **Saarinen House** are also both worth a visit. The two were designed by Eliel Saarinen, a pioneer of modernist architecture.

Then there are Detroit's bars and nightclubs. Some, like the gloriously swanky downtown jazz club **Cliff Bell's**, are authentic to the time. Others, like the Metropolitan Building's **Monarch Club**, an open rooftop bar with superb views of downtown, are new but evoke the glamour of that bygone era. The local hotels lean into 20th-century design as well. The **Siren Hotel** cultivates an Old Hollywood look, and its piano bar, **Sid Gold's Request Room**, seems a film noir set. The **Shinola Hotel**, a branch of the Detroit design firm, features rooms with the clean lines of a 1935 Packard coupe. That's appropriate, as Detroit's art deco buildings and their interiors are sumptuous, romantic, and filled with vroom.

One of many gilded figures on the highly decorated Fisher Building

Belle Isle

Detroit possesses the country's only art deco lighthouse, according to the Detroit Area Art Deco Society. The white marble **Livingstone Memorial Lighthouse** sits on Belle Isle, moored in the middle of the Detroit River just north of downtown. Both a nature reserve and well-used city treasure, Belle Isle is easily accessed by car via the MacArthur Bridge, or, even better, by bike after a pedal along the ever expanding **Detroit International RiverWalk**. The 14-mile (22.5 km) promenade was voted the best in the country by *USA Today* readers in 2021. Belle Isle, designed by Frederick Law Olmsted (famed designer of Central Park) in the 1880s, contains some of Detroit's greatest landmarks, including its **aquarium**, the glass-domed **Anna Scripps Whitcomb Conservatory**, the new **Oudolf Garden Detroit** by Manhattan's High Line landscaper Piet Oudolf, and the splashing, spouting **James Scott Memorial Fountain**. Decorated with marble lions, the fountain predates Detroit's famously feline professional football team. Meanwhile, if the freighters that plow past Belle Isle's shoreline spark curiosity, the **Dossin Great Lakes Museum** tells their story, including that of the wreck of the famous *Edmund Fitzgerald*.

For Live Theater
Cleveland, Ohio, U.S.A.

Playhouse Square runs through the Euclid Avenue theater district's 10 theaters and one outdoor performance space.

It's always showtime on Broadway. New York City's Theater District is one of the world's biggest tourist draws. In a good year the plays and musicals in Midtown Manhattan attract more than 13 million people to its legendary venues. But with average ticket prices at $150—and higher—a show on the Great White Way, plus hotel and airfare, is a hit to the wallet. For entertaining stagecraft without financial drama consider visiting Cleveland, Ohio, for a theatrical weekend.

The city on Lake Erie supports a surprising and vibrant theater scene centered around **Playhouse Square** in its muscular downtown. Stretching along Euclid Avenue are 10 theaters and one outdoor performance space. The cluster makes it the largest performing arts district in the United States west of the Hudson, and the offerings are diverse. "If you came for a weekend, you would have three or four choices to see, from classics to comedy to touring Broadway musicals," says Gina Vernaci, former president of Playhouse Square, the nonprofit tasked with running the historic theaters. Furthermore, she adds, a subscription to several shows can cost less than a single Broadway ticket.

How did Cleveland come to have the nation's second largest performing arts center? The beginnings go back a century to an earlier pandemic. The end of the 1918 influenza outbreak sparked renewed interest in building entertainment venues. In 1920 several Cleveland real estate developers saw the need for more theaters, including motion picture and vaudeville houses. They built a group of ornate theaters on Euclid Street that all opened within 19 months of each other. Decline started in the 1960s. By the 1970s the neighborhood was a ghost town, the theaters mostly shuttered, and the ornate lobbies filled with dead pigeons and fossil-

Every summer, U.S. Bank Plaza hosts weekly public dance lessons called "Dancing Under the Stars."

ized Jujubes. Then, in the late 1970s an impassioned band of preservationists and theater lovers developed and executed a plan to save the five grandest ones.

Today the restored theaters, with their dazzling lobbies and brightly colored murals, are complemented by the world's largest outdoor chandelier, hung with 4,200 crystals and suspended over the intersection of Euclid Avenue and East 14th Street. On select Saturdays visitors can learn more about the theaters with **free backstage tours**. Playhouse Square offers seasonal outdoor walks in the neighborhood. Showgoers can stay in the neighborhood: The **Crowne Plaza Cleveland** at Playhouse Square is located right on Euclid. For something different, the **Glidden House**, a boutique hotel on the Case-Western Reserve University campus, feels like a cozy faculty club.

There are a lot of other things to see and do in Cleveland before showtime. Zip over to the **Rock & Roll Hall of Fame** along the shores of Lake Erie. Explore **Cuyahoga Valley National Park**, a crazy quilt of forests, farms, and fields just south of the city that somehow avoided urban development. Try exploring the park on bike. Rentals are available for a whiz down the **Ohio & Erie Canal Towpath Trail**. The five-mile (8 km) round-trip along the Cuyahoga River to the **Boston Mill Park Visitor Center** is easy and pedalers will learn how this 1827 piece of nation-building infrastructure ignited Ohio's industrial revolution. Back in town, the **Cleveland Botanical Garden** offers an array of dazzling plantings, though the horticulture might get some competition from the all–stainless steel 1966 Lincoln Continental located down the street at the **Western Reserve Historical Society**. Lastly, make a point to visit the **Cleveland Museum of Art**, one of the nation's most important for the breadth and quality of its more than 45,000-piece collection.

Onion Domes and Onion Rings

Cleveland's century-old eastern European heritage is easy to find. Travelers will almost certainly encounter the spires and onion domes of an Eastern Orthodox church as they meander through the city. They're also likely to find a restaurant selling pierogies or *pączki*, or the local "Polish boy"—a kielbasa hot dog topped with barbecue sauce and coleslaw. Slavic immigrants were first attracted by Cleveland's booming factories and steel mills in the 19th and early 20th centuries. By 1920 the city counted more than 150,000 eastern European immigrants including Poles, Slovenes, and Romanians, with Ukrainians still one of the most visible communities. Today the suburban town of Parma, Ohio, supports a thriving **Ukrainian Village** with several churches, including St. Vladimir Ukrainian Orthodox Cathedral, and stores selling Ukrainian goods, arts, and crafts. Cleveland also has the **Ukrainian Museum–Archives**, which houses a large collection of historical photos, costumes, and brightly colored Easter eggs, a tradition throughout Ukraine. Another place to explore Cleveland's eastern European heritage is **Rockefeller Park**, which holds numerous "national cultural gardens" that celebrate the city's many ethnic groups. Ukraine's is surrounded by cherry trees and bronze busts of Ukrainian historical leaders including Vladimir I, a 10th-to-11th-century Ukrainian leader and grand prince of Kyiv, who was integral in bringing Christianity to the region.

For Vibrant Neighborhoods
Indianapolis, Indiana, U.S.A.

Instead of Amsterdam, Netherlands

Choose Indianapolis not Amsterdam for a three-day, two-wheeling adventure through vibrant urban neighborhoods. Like the Dutch city, Indianapolis has miles of traffic-free urban bike paths that reach into every part of town. There's also a thriving food scene and a host of regional museums befitting Indiana's capital. And, like Amsterdam, Indy even has canals, affording you the chance to pedal along, or stroll through, the city's busy downtown without crossing a street.

For biking it helps that Indianapolis is as flat as an iPad screen. Millennia ago, glaciers sanded down any hills and smoothed out the area's terrain. Since its founding in 1821, Indianapolis has been known for its all-American practicality; it's a place where accents are as "un-ornamental as a monkey wrench," mused native son and author Kurt Vonnegut. Indianapolis is no longer the plain-and-proper town of the past that unfairly earned the city the nickname "India-no-place." Today you'll find the **Children's Museum of Indianapolis**, the largest of its kind in the world; craft breweries like **Deviate** and **Sun King**; and artisanal bakeries (**Amelia's** and **Leviathan Bakehouse**). You can explore lively neighborhoods like **Broad Ripple** and **Fountain Square**, which isn't square at all but does boast a **classic bowling alley**. And all of these places are reachable without renting a car. Instead, utilize Indy's network of urban bike lanes, old railway lines, and canal towpaths to crisscross the city.

The **Indianapolis Cultural Trail** is an eight-mile-long (13 km), two-lane bike trail set with paver stones and separated from traffic by medians planted with daylilies and greenery. Wide and well marked, it bisects the city's downtown making it easy to spend a full day stopping at various attractions like the **Eiteljorg Museum of American Indians and Western Art**. The **Indianapolis**

The Children's Museum of Indianapolis is the largest museum of its kind in the world.

Dusk falls over downtown Indianapolis.

Zoo is a worthwhile stop off the trail, too. The city is packed with monuments, with more war memorials than any other U.S. city save Washington, D.C. Two impressive ones are the soaring **Soldiers & Sailors Monument**, located in the very heart of downtown, and the **Indiana World War Memorial**. The **state capitol**, constructed from Indiana limestone, naturally, sits in a park that contains several trees planted by Indiana governors. The coolest one is the Bicentennial Moon Tree, a sycamore planted on April 9, 1976, that sprouted from one of the seeds the Apollo 14 astronauts carried to the moon and back.

Don't miss the **Murat Shrine**: This Shriners International facility, decorated with crescent moons and spires, evokes the Arabian Nights. The entertainment venue lies just north of **Massachusetts Avenue**, a percolating mix of outdoor restaurants and diverse pubs that leads to the city's newest neighborhood, the **Bottleworks District**, which is centered around a 1931 Coca-Cola bottling plant that has been transformed into the **Bottleworks Hotel**, adjacent to the Cultural Trail. **The Alexander**, a 209-room downtown property, provides free bikes for its guests and prides itself on its modern art collection.

Bikers can use the Cultural Trail to reach longer, more traditional bike routes that take you to Indy's farthest reaches. The **Monon Trail**, developed on a defunct railroad track, runs more than 20 miles (32 km) from downtown to northern suburbs, with Broad Ripple a favorite destination for weekend brunch. The 5.2-mile (8.4 km) **Central Canal Towpath** cuts through northwest Indianapolis and delivers you to Newfields, site of the **Indianapolis Museum of Art**. "India-no-place" is, these days, very much *some* place indeed.

Madam C. J. Walker

In 1910 Black entrepreneur Madam C. J. Walker (1867–1919) picked Indianapolis as a distribution center for her line of African American beauty products because of its thriving Black business community and central geographic location. The shrewd decision was typical for Walker, who is regarded as the first self-made female millionaire in the United States. Born to formerly enslaved Louisianans, Walker, née Sarah Breedlove, worked as a washerwoman before finding fortune and fame. Breedlove adopted the surname of her third husband, transforming herself into Madam C. J. Walker. It was under that name that she gained fame for a hair-care regimen—and accompanying line of schools, salons, and products. Walker died before completing her Indianapolis headquarters. The building opened in 1927 with its own theater aimed at African Americans, who in the era of segregation could not easily enjoy a state-of-the-art entertainment facility. Embellished with African motifs, the restored **Madam Walker Legacy Center** welcomes visitors today as a touchstone and inspiration for a new generation of Black entrepreneurs.

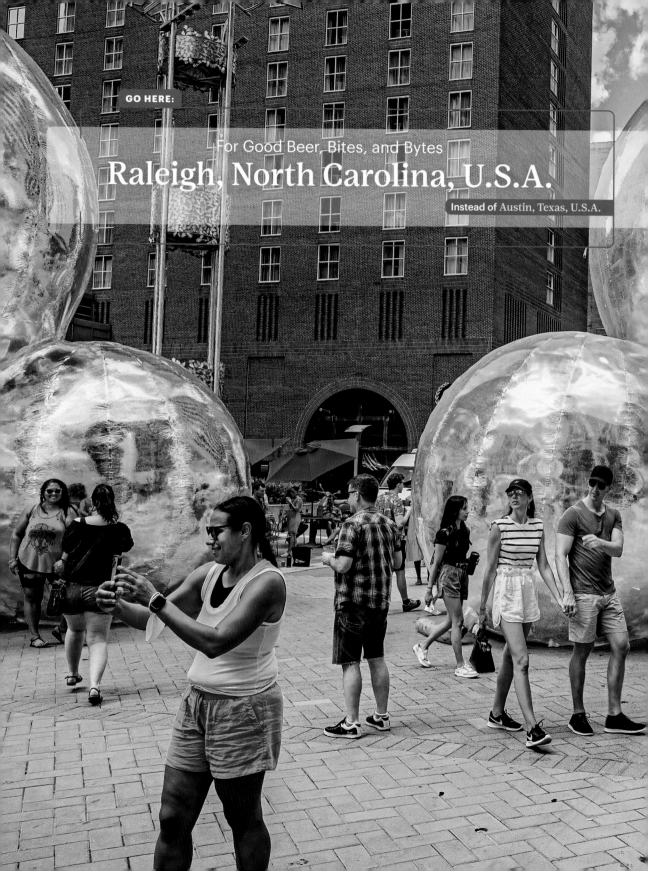

GO HERE:

For Good Beer, Bites, and Bytes

Raleigh, North Carolina, U.S.A.

Instead of Austin, Texas, U.S.A.

Raleigh's two-day Artsplosure festival showcases the works of artists from across the United States.

Take your pick of Raleigh's locally owned rooftop restaurants.

OPPOSITE: The ever popular North Carolina Museum of Natural Sciences displays a massive whale skeleton.

Raleigh, North Carolina, is all in on tech. The vibrant city (population 469,000) possesses a large and growing number of start-up companies as well as established names including Apple, Google, and Red Hat, all drawn to a town where 66 percent of the residents have an undergraduate degree. Despite its growth, Raleigh remains small enough to retain the local charm that has evaporated in bigger tech hubs like Austin, Texas, where prices for everything from housing to margaritas are more expensive than ever. Raleigh also offers visitors a large number of outdoor recreational activities including parks, greenways, and water sports in a relatively mild climate.

Besides technology, or maybe because of it and its battalions of well-compensated young geeks, the parallel with Austin is stronger than ever with Raleigh's lively nightlife and restaurant scene. Within two miles (3.2 km) of downtown are more than 165 restaurants, 87 percent of them locally owned and operated, and half run by women or minorities. The food is equally diverse, with chefs offering dishes from traditional North Carolina barbecue to Laotian pork belly soup. Some 22 Raleigh chefs have been nominated for James Beard Awards. The **Morgan Street Food Hall** and the **Transfer Co. Food Hall**, inside an old bus depot, are both good places to sample the tasty local fare. For thirsty visitors there are 80 bars and clubs, and 18 craft breweries—with some 35 in total across Wake County. In milder weather the **Glenwood South** neighborhood along Glenwood Avenue is jammed until late in the evening with weekend revelers crowding its many bars, clubs, and restaurants.

Also like Austin, Raleigh is a state capital, with a large number of North Carolina government employees and political organizations, as well as universities, drawing a mix of people from diverse backgrounds. No surprise the city is filled with cultural destinations, including 72 art galleries, museums, entertainment venues, performing arts spaces, and other outposts. Because many of them are state supported, free admission has been a long tradition with Raleigh's institutions. Many are located in the downtown **Capital District** neighborhood, home to a number of state museums including the **North Carolina Museum of History** and the **North Carolina Museum of Natural Sciences**, the home of the **SECU DinoLab**, opened in 2024, which allows visitors direct contact with the scientific team's examining dinosaur fossils. Also nearby is the new **North Carolina Freedom Park** honoring the African American struggle for freedom in the state. Designed by Phil Freelon, architect of the Smithsonian's National Museum of African American History and Culture in Washington, D.C., the park features moving quotations by Black North Carolinians. Farther afield, the **North Carolina Museum of Art** transformed its galleries in 2023, when it reimagined its **People's Collection** to create a more dynamic and inclusive visitor experience.

There are a number of new hotels in the city, but two reach back into Raleigh's past. The **Heights House** is a nine-room boutique hotel in an 1860 mansion in the historic Boylan Heights district. Its opposite is the **Longleaf Lodge**, a revamped 1960s motor lodge done in a fizzy style mixing fire pits and Danish modernism.

The Greenway

Raleigh's pride is its Greenway, an emerald necklace of trails and parks more than 100 miles (160 km) long. It is used by cyclists, commuters, runners, rollerbladers, and walkers eager to escape traffic and reconnect with nature. The Greenway took shape in the 1970s, when Raleigh began acquiring land along the Neuse River and other nature corridors. The first major section, the **Neuse River Greenway Trail**, opened in 1979. Stretching 27.5 miles (44 km) from Falls Lake Dam to the Johnston County line, the paved trail follows the winding Neuse River through the city and offers a variety of experiences for hikers, bikers, and runners. The diverse range of landscapes, including wetlands, forests, and meadows, is peppered with interpretive signage about the ecosystem and Raleigh's history including the landmark **Milburnie Dam**, built in the early 1900s as part of a hydroelectric power plant that supplied electricity to the city. Connected to the Neuse River Trail is the 15-mile-long (24 km) **Walnut Creek Greenway Trail**, another linear park offering scenery and recreation for pedestrians, cyclists, and other non-motorized users. The **Falls Lake trailhead** provides access to the **Falls Lake State Recreation Area**, a state park covering approximately 12,000 acres (4,860 ha) situated around a human-made reservoir. The **Crabtree Creek Greenway Trail** connects to the Neuse River Greenway Trail at **Anderson Point Park**, a great spot for wildlife-viewing, walking trails, and canoeing.

For a Great Lakes City

Milwaukee, Wisconsin, U.S.A.

Instead of Chicago, Illinois, U.S.A.

F ancy apartments with views of Lake Michigan and shoreline parks graced with museums and sandy beaches. A squeaky-wheeled train rumbles across a river rail trestle, delighting a pod of kayakers below. Sniping gulls curlicue far above brick, broad-shouldered warehouses reborn as condos. It sounds like Chicago, but the Windy City is a 90-minute drive south. This is Milwaukee, Wisconsin, a smaller, less expensive, but no less rewarding Great Lakes city you pass up at your peril.

Milwaukee is a find—one of the few remaining American cities to possess an idiosyncratic urban culture that's both sophisticated and working class. Think San Francisco before it pulled on yoga pants and stuffed itself with tech start-ups. Milwaukee's a broad-beamed town filled with individuality and quick to flash a smile as wide as Laverne DeFazio's, one of the comic characters of the 1970s Milwaukee-based TV show *Laverne & Shirley*. There's a belly-up-to-the-bar sensibility here that's epitomized by good beer, loud billboards, and even louder music. No surprise the **Harley-Davidson Museum** feels right at home. This isn't a town for putting on airs.

Like Chicago, Milwaukee centers itself on Lake Michigan. Lakeside parks are graced by Santiago Calatrava's soaring **Milwaukee Art Museum**, sandy beaches, and festival grounds. But instead of one river, Milwaukee has three—the Menomonee, the Kinnickinnic, and the Milwaukee. Each one is lined with promenades for biking or walking, and all are capable of being explored by kayak or boat from numerous rental slips. Milwaukee even turns its river green, not for St. Patrick's Day, as Chicago does, but for its championship NBA team, the Bucks, when they make the playoffs. (Good Land green is the team's official hue.)

The Milwaukee River is even more beautiful at night.

Independent merchants sell baked goods, cheeses, meats, and prepared foods at the Milwaukee Public Market.

Step foot in Milwaukee and you'll discover a city eager to engage with visitors, especially over a beer mug. Public tours are a favorite pastime at breweries, from craft makers like **Lakefront** to megasuppliers like **Miller**. And travelers will soon discover that elbowing up to a local tavern's bar often leads to an invitation to join a table of Milwaukeeans sampling local suds like Spotted Cow, a popular farmhouse ale. In **Walker's Point** the tavern **Fat Daddy's** maintains a sandy volleyball court for teams to practice into the night beneath the watchful Polish Moon, the locals' nickname for the face of the **Allen-Bradley Clock Tower** rising above the neighborhood.

Milwaukee likes its food tasty and in big portions. Downtown's **farmers market** and its local suppliers are fun to explore. Much of the produce finds its way onto plates in local restaurants. Expect local beer on tap and make sure to order Milwaukee's favorite local treat: deep-fried cheese curds. **Third Street Market Hall**, on West Wisconsin Avenue across the street from the Bradley Symphony Center in the heart of downtown, has a beer hall and 17 local vendors selling imaginative fare like arepas, artisanal custards, and potato donuts.

Hotels to consider include **Saint Kate—The Arts Hotel**. Its downtown location, behind the historic **Pabst Theater** and across from the ornate **City Hall**, can't be beat. The playful rooms sport graphic art prints and expressive lighting. **The Iron Horse Hotel**, a boutique hotel adjacent to the **Third Ward**'s bars and restaurants, is heavily beamed and sports a Harley in the lobby. Housed in a 1907 mattress factory, its rooms are handsomely appointed in rich brown and slate blues that emphasize the industrial setting. Another newcomer, **The Trade**, near the Bucks' home court, features two floors for visiting NBA players, with rooms that include special touches like 12-foot-high (3.7 m) showerheads.

The Wright Stuff

Any city would eagerly tout its collection of Frank Lloyd Wright buildings. Milwaukee is no exception. On the **2700 block of Burnham Street** on the city's south side is a collection of the architect's Usonian houses that the notoriously imperious Wright designed for the average man. Since this is Milwaukee, a city that does not put on too many airs, one owner proudly clad his historic abode in vinyl siding. But this isn't the only neighborhood boasting Wright's architecture. America's Dairyland, in fact, is chockablock with Wright buildings. If you're eager to see more examples of the architect's work, explore Wisconsin's **Frank Lloyd Wright Trail**. Wright designed 40 buildings in total throughout the state, and this self-guided driving tour takes you through southern Wisconsin to visit eight of those landmark structures. Top picks include the iconic **S.C. Johnson Wax** complex in Racine; **Taliesin**, Wright's Wisconsin vacation retreat; and **Monona Terrace**, a civic structure in the college town of Madison.

For a Hilly Tech Town
Pittsburgh, Pennsylvania, U.S.A.

Gravity-defying houses on steep hills gaze down on waterside esplanades filled with bicyclists and pedestrians. Sidewalks are lined with brick warehouses populated with tech start-ups and a can-do attitude. A downtown area is packed with thrusting skyscrapers and bounded by water on three sides. Restaurants are equally comfortable welcoming a banker's pin-striped suit or an artist's tattoos. Thinking San Francisco? Think again. This isn't the hilly 415, it's the hilly 412—a town otherwise known as Pittsburgh. The former industrial city has cleaned up and greened up and is looking ahead. And it's very much worth checking out.

As headquarters for Andrew Carnegie and a host of other industrialists, Pittsburgh was the Silicon Valley of the 19th century—a place where huge fortunes were made and spent. Like San Francisco's financial district, Pittsburgh's version—called the **Golden Triangle**—affords watery views. Instead of a bay, you'll see where the Allegheny and Monongahela Rivers meet to form the Ohio River. This confluence of waters is memorialized by **Point State Park**'s fountain as well as the remains of **Fort Duquesne** and the **Fort Pitt Museum**. The **Kimpton Hotel Monaco Pittsburgh**, housed in a classic stone 1900-era law office, makes a good stay to explore downtown.

Beyond downtown Pittsburgh are its hills, some of which sport record-breaking inclines. Case in point: **Canton Avenue** in the city's Beechview neighborhood. Short and sweet, it holds the record for the steepest street in the country, with a 37 percent grade. Maybe the altitude affects one's attitude, for Pittsburgh's neighborhoods (there are 90 in all) exude a profound sense of place. You could spend far more than a weekend exploring them. Some, like **Shadyside** and **Squirrel Hill**, are well known, but there are several others to visit to give you the flavor of the city.

Catch a ballgame at PNC Park, home of the Pittsburgh Pirates.

Pick up a Pittsburgh-themed souvenir at Wildcard, one of the charming shops on Lawrenceville's Butler Street.

The **Strip District** sports no red lights. This strip of land along the Allegheny River northeast of downtown was where Pittsburgh's early innovators gathered, making everything from Revolutionary War cannons to ketchup. The city's manufacturing history can be glimpsed at the **Heinz History Center**, housed in an old ice company warehouse. The Strip also supported a number of grocers, many of them Italian, and some survive to this day along **Penn Street**. It's an avenue to nibble and nosh your way down. You'll join an increasing number of employees of the tech and robotic firms ensconced in the bright jumble of glass offices, restored warehouses, and loft apartments lining the river.

To soak up a 19th-century feel of the city, amble through the **North Side** and the **Mexican War Streets**, two historic neighborhoods (the latter so named for the generals and battles of the 1840s conflict between the United States and Mexico). Finish your day touring the edgy **Mattress Factory**, which encourages visitors to interact with its inspiring, frequently kinetic, and always novel installations created by rising young artists.

Lawrenceville, farther east of the Strip District, contains boutiques, patisseries, and cafés along **Butler Avenue** and exudes a decidedly bohemian vibe. Restaurants from Thai to southern barbecue draw people in droves, eager to taste something new. "Pittsburgh food is hunky," says celebrated hometown chef Richard DeShantz, with a cuisine heavily influenced by Hungarian, Polish, and Italian immigrants, and now newcomers.

And like San Francisco, there's even an Oakland. Pittsburgh's version is centered around the University of Pittsburgh and its beacon, the 42-story **Cathedral of Learning**, a 1920s Gothic skyscraper. But the museums are the draw: The **Carnegie Museum of Natural History**, the **Carnegie Museum of Art**, and the **Phipps Conservatory and Botanical Gardens** will consume a day.

A Dandy Warhol

Working-class Pittsburgh in the 1940s wasn't well known for accommodating pale and pensive gay boys like Andrew Warhola, nor his penchant for drawing. The child of European immigrants who came to America for a better life, Warhola showed an artistic aptitude early on. But to be a creative flower, you needed to blossom elsewhere, so in 1949 to New York City he went, transforming himself into a fashion illustrator. Andy Warhol (1928–1987), as the world would know him, was born. His journey from his hometown to art superstardom is documented at the **Andy Warhol Museum**, located in Pittsburgh's North Shore and stockpiled with 900 paintings and 2,000 drawings from the renowned artist and LGBTQIA+ hero. His famous silkscreen canvases are all here: Campbell's Soup cans, Jackie O, and Chairman Mao, along with less well-known works, like his sketchbooks and advertising posters—whimsical line drawings of shoes and hats that Warhol created as a commercial artist. The museum possesses a collection of videos starring a group of friends who collaborated with the artist at The Factory, as Warhol's studio was called, and longer films such as *Sleep* and *The Chelsea Girls*. These films capture the cultural ferment of mid-20th-century New York. The museum also holds a collection of photographs from across the decades that help flesh out the life of Pittsburgh's most celebrated artist, who was a pioneer of modern art.

For Star-Studded Glitz and Glam

Palm Springs, California, U.S.A.

Instead of Hollywood, California, U.S.A.

Palm trees and convertibles are quintessential elements of the Palm Springs lifestyle.

Hooray for Hollywood, but the famous destination's reality often disappoints visitors hoping to uncover more of that magical Rat Pack and Ray-Bans glamour. The Los Angeles neighborhood still has iconic landmarks like the Hollywood Walk of Fame, TCL Chinese Theatre (formerly Grauman's Chinese Theatre), and the romantic Hollywood Roosevelt hotel, but later development has brought nondescript shopping malls and a grittier edge. Golden State tourists eager to find elements of the old film colony should do their location scouting 100 miles (160 km) east—in Palm Springs and the surrounding desert communities of the Coachella Valley.

Chockablock with convertibles, canary palms, and scores of midcentury modern swankiendas, Greater Palm Springs is both a hipster hangout (famous as the site of the Coachella and Stagecoach music festivals) and an old Hollywood hideaway. Far from the prying eyes of the film studios, Palm Springs was where Clark Gable and Cary Grant cavorted, Sinatra played it cool in his piano-shaped pool, and Elvis honeymooned.

Visitors can soak up the glamour at a series of hotels that have preserved the flair and tail fins of that era along with its swimming pools. There are luxurious, social-media-friendly properties like the **Parker Palm**

Escape the heat with a dip in the Saguaro Palm Springs hotel's iconic pool.

Springs. The 144-room resort and 13-acre (5 ha) grounds—where Angelina Jolie and Brad Pitt once checked in under the names Jasmine and Bryce Pilaf—is furnished in an eclectic modern style that belies its former life as a 1959-era Holiday Inn. Also check out **Holiday House**, a jet age–inspired boutique, and the **Colony Palms**, an intimate oasis of glamour that could pass for the Beverly Hills Hotel's little sister. Both are within walking distance of Palm Springs bars and restaurants. There are more secluded accommodations, like Albert Einstein's favored retreat, now called the **Willows Historic Palm Springs Inn**, a Mediterranean inn that was also a favorite of Marion Davies, mistress of press baron William Randolph Hearst.

If you're still hungry for a connection to Hollywood's golden age, try dining at **Mister Lyons Steakhouse** (opened in 1945) or **Spencer's**, the restaurant at the Palm Springs Tennis Club (circa 1934).

There are plenty of other things to do in the Coachella Valley besides sunbathe. Take the **Palm Springs Aerial Tramway** over Chino Canyon and rise more than 8,500 feet (2,590 m) to the top of Mount San Jacinto, part of a rugged wilderness area and state park. Or trek to **Sunnylands**, the residence of billionaires Walter and Leonore Annenberg in Rancho Mirage. Landscaped with desert plantings, the 15-acre (6 ha) mid-century estate became a western Camp David for presidents and royalty and is now open to the public. Also worth perusing is the **Palm Springs Art Museum** and its **Architecture and Design Center**, housed in a 1950s bank building, which celebrates the region's connection with

modernist architecture. And don't miss the live-music venue **Pappy and Harriet's**, near **Joshua Tree National Monument**, where musicians such as Robert Plant, Paul McCartney, Rufus Wainwright, and Kesha have performed.

Palm Springs has become synonymous with music festivals, including country music's Stagecoach Festival (here) and the massive Coachella Valley Music and Arts Festival, one of the largest music events in the world.

Modernism Week

When it comes to historic architecture, Palm Springs is the mid-century modern version of Colonial Williamsburg. No American city is more closely associated with the 1950s and 1960s architecture—and nowhere else throws a bigger annual festival celebrating it. The futuristic style known for its low-slung, flat-roofed glass-and-brick buildings flourished in the California desert post–World War II when celebrities wanted their vacation homes to make a statement. Luckily, few houses were torn down when the town fell on hard times in the 1980s. By the turn of the century a wave of interest led to their restoration. Proud new owners decorated the houses with period furniture and organized **Modernism Week**, a February festival that offers tours of the restored homes. The festival now lasts two weeks and attracts more than 100,000 visitors, with a second event in the fall. The Mod Squad, led by local historian Kurt Cyr, showcases famous landmarks like the **Kaufmann Desert House** and even has a tour recounting the Rat Pack's history, with stops at the desert homes of Dean Martin, Sammy Davis, Jr., and Marilyn Monroe.

For Opulence and Ghosts

Natchez, Mississippi, U.S.A.

Instead of Savannah, Georgia, U.S.A.

Built in 1855, Natchez's Dunleith Historic Inn, now a national historic landmark, hosts events and overnight guests.

Twin cantilever bridges span the Mississippi River and connect Natchez with Vidalia, Louisiana.

OPPOSITE: The Towers mansion was constructed in three stages during the late 18th and mid-19th centuries.

S avannah, Georgia, seduces with its *Midnight in the Garden of Good and Evil* assemblage of eccentricities, walkable neighborhoods, and lilting antebellum homes. Natchez, Mississippi, offers a similar mix of southern Gothic ambience—think *Tiger King* meets *Gone With the Wind*—and extravagant architecture fueled by the roiling currents of Old Man River. Hurry before a tourist boom takes away all that makes this town so unique.

Natchez may be the hippest unhip city in America, the last in a line of architecturally significant southern towns still waiting to be restored. Commanding the bluffs above the Mississippi River, Natchez remains an arresting spot despite its small population. Walk through downtown's empty streets to feel a sultry, feline ambience mixed with the gentility of a garden club meeting. Indeed, it was the garden clubs that saved the town's opulent buildings. Starting in the 1930s the **Natchez Pilgrimage**, a festival that showcased house tours during the fall and spring seasons, played a significant role in adding more than 1,000 buildings to the National Register of Historic Places. However, the pilgrimage's perspective on the antebellum period, or Old South, which portrayed a glorified image of the past, only recently began to acknowledge the reality of slavery. It was through enslavement that Natchez's wealth was built, and it was the enslaved individuals who suffered as Natchez prospered.

It's a welcome change. Natchez was never an innocent southern belle. Founded by the French in 1716, it flourished as an early commercial hub for the booming cotton industry, with banks and stores lining Main and Franklin Streets on the city's high ground. Below the bluffs lurked a neighborhood called **Under-the-Hill**, where the flatboats that floated down the Ohio and Mississippi Rivers docked. It was a ramshackle collection of buildings, bars, and bordellos where gambling and drinking went on all hours. One madam kept a floating brothel on the river. At six feet eight inches (2 m), Annie Christmas was said to be able to wallop the roughest Kaintuck, as all boatmen were called. The strip is far quieter now, but there's fun to be had watching the tatted-up bikers congregate around their Harleys outside the **Under-the-Hill Saloon**, and in seeing an occasional armadillo as it scrambles to the river while the sun sinks over the horizon.

Today it's the architecture, not the sin, that draws visitors to Natchez. Builders erected many of the houses within sight of the great river. Christened with names like **Choctaw Hall** and **The Towers**, these mansions survived the Civil War and economic vicissitudes to become objects of history and house envy. You can tour them and even sleep in them. More than 36 historic bed-and-breakfasts are listed on the Visit Natchez website. One that's not is **Windsor Plantation**, an 1851 house burned to the ground 40 years later (a lit cigar started the blaze). Its surviving moldering columns are a remainder of an age of exploitation. There's even more Gothic sensibility in Natchez's **cemetery**. You'll see where a grief-stricken mother built stairs down into the earth to an underground chamber with a window from which she could view her dead daughter's coffin. An early morning walk along **Bluff Park** reveals stupendous views of the river below. With luck there'll be atmospheric mists, and the Mississippi's majesty and power will be unfailingly impressive.

Rhythm Club Fire

The joint was jumping. On April 23, 1940, the Rhythm Club on St. Catherine Street in downtown Natchez had booked Chicago swing band leader Walter Barnes and His Royal Creolians. Lying between Chicago and New Orleans, Natchez was a favorite one-night stopover for bands playing the Chitlin' Circuit, a collection of Black-owned nightclubs in the segregated United States.

By 11 p.m. more than 700 people were crammed inside. The one-story corrugated metal building was festooned with Spanish moss sprayed with FLIT, a mosquito repellent. The fire began by the front door. Its origin remains unknown. Fueled by the petroleum-based insecticide and the moss, the flames exploded. Most of the panicked crowd rushed to the back, only to find the exit locked. To stop people sneaking in, the back door had been nailed shut. Many of the 209 victims died there, the bodies piled shoulder high. The heat was so intense that when water from the fire hoses hit the metal building, it produced clouds of steam that scalded some of the victims. The Rhythm Club fire deaths decimated Natchez's Black community.

The event is memorialized in blues songs like "The Natchez Burning" by Howlin' Wolf and John Lee Hooker's "Natchez Fire." A marker in **Bluff Park** commemorates the tragedy, and stories are found at the nearby **Rhythm Night Club Memorial Museum**. The Rhythm Club fire is the fourth deadliest assembly or club fire in U.S. history.

Blowing Springs' trail system is located just outside Bentonville, the self-proclaimed "mountain biking capital of the world."

For Utopian Urbanism
Bentonville, Arkansas, U.S.A.

Instead of Boulder, Colorado, U.S.A.

Boulder's reputation as an outdoor-loving, fleece-wearing, eco-friendly town filled with cafés, mountain sports, and community-minded spirit is well known. But there's another town that can go Teva to Teva with that adventure-oriented mecca in Colorado. Bentonville, located in northwest Arkansas's Ozark Mountain region, is Walmart's global headquarters, and it is filled with craft breweries, James Beard–nominated chefs, and bike trails. Walmart, founded by Sam Walton in 1962, has been good to Bentonville, and Sam's descendants are transforming his hometown into a mini-Boulder, coffee pourovers and recycling programs included.

The town is filling up faster than a Sam's Club parking lot on Black Friday. From a population of some 35,000 in 2010, Bentonville has grown to 55,000-plus people as of 2023. Start exploring and the place seems like a traditional small southern town—the kind of place with ice-cream parlors on the downtown square (and a **Walmart Museum** showcasing the company's history). But you will also meet residents who have relocated to Oz, the trendy new sobriquet for the Ozarks, from places like São Paulo and Seattle. **Onyx**, a hip coffee roaster, a new **Walmart campus**, and the college town of Fayetteville—home to the University of Arkansas—some 30 miles (48 km) south add a youthful feel.

There's a six-story co-working office building where hybrid employees can reach every floor via bike, thanks to an innovative ramp system.

The Crystal Bridges Museum of American Art is most famous for housing Walmart heir Alice Walton's esteemed art collection.

Cycling trails string together various surrounding neighborhoods. These, among other trails, allow Bentonville to proclaim itself the "mountain biking capital of the world." It's a serious boast. There are more than 140 miles (225 km) of trails, 40 miles (64 km) of hard surfaces, and 100 miles (160 km) of single-tracks that draw travelers eager to conquer the Ozark hills and dales on two wheels. The trails are also graced with sculptures, including an 11-foot-tall (3 m) Sasquatch welded from recycled bicycle chains. Two trails to hit are **Park Springs**, which begins on the north side of town and heads up to the hills beyond it, and **Blowing Springs**, a path that leads to a large bluff featuring streams cascading down its rock face and to **Blowing Springs Cave**, a spot offering a cool respite on a hot day. Other outdoor adventures include kayaking or canoeing on the **Buffalo National River**, 70 miles (110 km) away, or the opportunity to shoot through some Class IV white water on the **Cossatot River** in Ouachita National Forest.

But Bentonville's biggest attraction lies indoors. The town is home to Alice Walton's (Sam's daughter) stellar collection of American art housed in the stunning **Crystal Bridges Museum of American Art**. Designed by celebrated architect Moshe Safdie, the museum sits in a spectacular wooded setting. There's even a classic Frank Lloyd Wright house relocated from New Jersey. And there's more culture to come: Crystal Bridges is planning to expand its building by 50 percent, with additional galleries and dining spaces opening by 2025.

Crystal Bridges is Bentonville's most famous museum, but it's not the only one. The town supports the **Museum of Native American History** and the **Scott Family Amazeum**, a children's museum founded by the family of Lee Scott, a former Walmart CEO. The Amazeum is known for its innovative exhibits including the Incredible Electric Technicolor Mockingbird, an interactive public sculpture. The youngest generations of Waltons are behind **The Momentary**, a 63,000-square-foot (5,850 m²) communal art space in an old Velveeta cheese factory. The redone building is filled with performance spaces and has an outdoor pavilion for live events.

Kids participate in hands-on learning experiences at the Scott Family Amazeum.

Some Like It Hot Springs

If you have kids and an affection for the hubble-bubble and ballyhoo of a classic American tourist haven, then Hot Springs National Park is another Arkansas destination worth a visit. At the turn of the 20th century Hot Springs was a boomtown, celebrated for its mix of health and wealth. The reason? The town's mineral-laden hot springs, which drew an assortment of colorful characters and remain an attraction today. Hot Springs' elegant **Bathhouse Row** features an array of elaborate 1900s-era facilities filled with pools and massage and steam rooms. While the focus remains the spas, the 5,500-acre (2,225 ha) park features a surprising number of trails and paths to explore. Downtown the attractions are more of the Niagara Falls family-fun variety, including a **gangster museum** and a waxworks filled with likenesses of Bill Clinton and Princess Di housed in the former **Southern Club**. Hot Springs has some upscale eateries and accommodations, too, like historic **Hotel Hale** (housed in one of the historic bathhouses), and **The Waters**, an elegant, terrazzo-floored hotel dating from 1913.

For Oktoberfest
Cincinnati, Ohio, U.S.A.

Instead of Munich, Germany

Twilight falls over Cincinnati's skyline, the Ohio River, and the Roebling Suspension Bridge.

B eer is the ballast for many a memorable party, and none are sudsier
or more fun than German Oktoberfest celebrations. The annual
autumn beer bust in Munich draws millions of people during a two-
week-long celebration. For an equally joyous kegger, but one that's maybe
a bit more manageable, consider attending an Oktoberfest in a historic
Ohio river city. Cincinnati boasts one of the biggest Oktoberfests outside
Deutschland—and the largest in the United States. Traditionally held during
the last weeks of September, Oktoberfest Zinzinnati usually has more than
500,000 participants, who consume upwards of 80,000 bratwursts and
16,000 pieces of strudel alongside four million fluid ounces (118,290 L) of
beer over its four-day run.

There's plenty of beer to quaff and some uniquely American events
including musical acts and silly competitions like the Running of the Wie-
ners, which pits 100 dachshunds wearing hot dog bun costumes in a race.
There's also a German costume show, Frocktoberfest, that features creative interpretations of dirndls and lederhosen and a stein-hoisting competition. For some reason there's a giant chicken dance. During the festival
100 kinds of beer, including those from a host of local breweries like Rhine-
geist, Braxton Brewing Company, and Fifty West, are on offer.

A patron of Oktoberfest Zinzinnati dons his
Alpine hat decorated with souvenir pins.

OPPOSITE: The Tyler Davidson Fountain, also
known as "The Genius of Water," was dedicated in 1871.

Cincinnati has always been a beer town. That history dates back to the early 19th century when thousands of German immigrants arrived in the Queen City to work in its meatpacking plants and iron foundries. Many of them settled in the Over-the-Rhine neighborhood. While the 20th century saw the familiar decline of Cincinnati's inner city, things are different now as knowledge workers (P&G is headquartered here, as are five other Fortune 500 companies) and young college graduates snapped up the historic housing stock. Today the city supports a host of attractions, such as the **Cincinnati Museum Center**, housed in its enormous Hollywood Bowl of a train station with brilliant murals by German American artist Winold Reiss. Its basement contains a scale model of the city as it was in 1940.

Visitors can grab a view atop the 49-story **Carew Tower**, Cincinnati's grandest skyscraper. Close to it is **Fountain Square**, the city's town square, which hosts ice skating and bumper cars in the winter and summer pop concerts. Along the Ohio River there's the opportunity to call on the **National Underground Railroad Freedom Center**, stroll the **Riverwalk** in **Smale Riverfront Park**, or walk to Kentucky across the now pedestrian-only **Roebling Suspension Bridge**. Similar in construction and looks to its more famous Brooklyn cousin, it is 17 years older, having been finished in 1866. The city also has the **American Sign Museum**, which displays an array of blinking and buzzing vintage advertisements in a rainbow of neon. Cincinnati sports a lot of hills, and an afternoon atop **Mount Adams** with its pubs and restaurants overlooking the downtown is a treat. Nearby are the **botanical gardens** and **Cincinnati Art Museum**.

Lastly, no trip to "the 'Nati" is complete without sampling two regional foods: Goetta, a fried sausage or meat mush favored by German immigrants, and Cincinnati chili, a meat sauce with spices like cloves, cumin, and cinnamon used as a topping for hot dogs or slathered on spaghetti. Both dishes are highly venerated in a town proud of its traditions.

Over-the-Rhine

The revival of Over-the-Rhine (OTR), Cincinnati's most vibrant neighborhood, is a success story and a model for urban communities everywhere. Visitors come to OTR for its rich history, architecture, and colorful music and arts scenes, but it was once a very poor neighborhood. OTR's story began in the 19th century as a destination for German immigrants. Its name came from the workers living there who would cross a canal, nicknamed "the Rhine," to get to their jobs in the industrializing city.

Thanks to its density and German inhabitants, OTR became home to many breweries. Today tours take you below the busy sidewalks to explore several old facilities whose subterranean cellars, used for keeping the beer cool, finally closed during Prohibition.

OTR is also the site of one of the largest preserved collections of 19th-century Italianate architecture in the United States. Self-guided walking tours are available to discover the many historic buildings including a stop at **Findlay Market**, Ohio's oldest continuously operating public market, with vendors selling fresh produce, meats, and other goods. There are also galleries, theaters, and music venues including the **Cincinnati Opera** and the **Cincinnati Ballet**. Visitors can catch a concert at **Music Hall** or the smaller **Memorial Hall**, which faces vegetation-rich Washington Park, recognized as one of the country's best urban green spaces.

For a Hipster Vibe

South Philadelphia, Pennsylvania, U.S.A.

Instead of Brooklyn, New York, U.S.A.

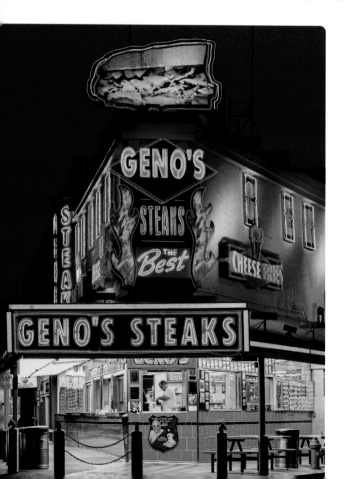

Well before dawn, chefs begin prepping cheesesteaks at the legendary Geno's Steaks in South Philadelphia.

Brooklyn is a place that became an attitude. Gritty yet sophisticated, New York's most populous borough developed a reputation for a certain hipster vibe and as a creative oasis for poets, painters, and pourovers. But a lot of wealthy migrants and new real estate development transformed the place, giving its downtown skyscrapers and brownstone houses multimillion-dollar prices that sandblasted away its affordable reputation. Just a short train ride away, however, is a diverse community where workers, artists, and writers can afford to live—and where they know your name at the corner bar. Visit South Philadelphia to recapture Brooklyn's former plucky and bohemian spirit.

Appropriately enough, **South Street** is the border between Philadelphia's downtown, called **Center City**, and South Philly. Stretching between the Delaware and Schuylkill Rivers, the avenue is lined with bars and restaurants to sample, but the heart of the neighborhood is below that in block after block of small row houses, some just 850 square feet (80 m²) in size. Such low-rise density fosters intimacy and community. Everyone feels free to share their opinion. Pick up a few cannoli on **10th Street** and you'll converse with fellow customers about the weather, the mayor, or how you're dressed. In South Philly, residents feel free to park their cars in the median of **Broad Street**, Philadelphia's great north–south boulevard. Why? "Because they can," is how one local put it.

Historically South Philly was Italian, with immigrants arriving in droves beginning in the 1890s. Their influence still permeates the neighborhood. Visit the famous **Italian Market** on Ninth Street, a collection of dozens of

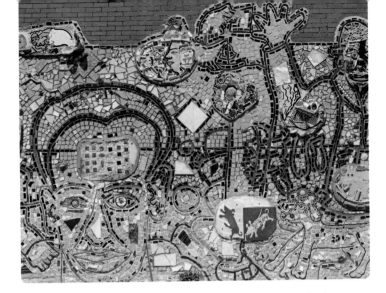

Isaiah Zagar's colorful mosaics cover the walls of Philadelphia's Magic Gardens.

family grocers and restaurants. The **Singing Fountain** at 11th Street belts out Sinatra hits over the vest pocket park's loudspeakers. Opera star Mario Lanza, '50s teenage heart throb Frankie Avalon, and Rocky's Sylvester Stallone all called South Philly home. So does the famed Philly cheesesteak, a cheese-and-beefsteak hoagie. Its two most famous purveyors—**Pat's King of Steaks** and **Geno's Steaks**—compete with each other from across East Passyunk Avenue, which runs diagonally from South Street to Broad Street.

Cheesesteaks and crooners aside, there are a lot of other attractions in South Philly. Mosaic artist Isaiah Zagar filled three city lots with galleries and an outdoor maze to create Philadelphia's **Magic Gardens**, a favorite of visitors and Instagram feeds. The **Mummers Museum** tells the colorful story of the country's oldest folk parade, while **Washington Avenue** hosts many Southeast Asian restaurants between 16th and Front Streets. The **Bok Building**, a former technical high school that looms over South Philly like a fortress, is now filled with restaurants, makers, and start-ups of all sorts. The massive art deco building features commanding views of the surrounding city from its eighth-floor rooftop restaurant. **Passyunk Avenue** hosts a proliferation of sophisticated eateries mixed in with everything from clothing boutiques to tattoo parlors and even a typewriter repair shop.

South Philly isn't known for its hotels, but there are short-term rentals in some of the area's trademark row houses. For those looking for something more upscale, Center City offers plenty of familiar brands including a new **Four Seasons Hotel** with spectacular city views from its 57th-floor infinity pool along with in-hotel restaurants headed by Michelin star– and James Beard Award–winning chefs.

The Southeast Asian Market

One of South Philadelphia's most popular attractions is its Southeast Asian street food market. Organized by Cambodian Americans and located in the neighborhood's Franklin Delano Roosevelt Park, the market grew organically when refugees from war-torn Vietnam, Laos, and Cambodia arrived in Philadelphia in the 1970s and '80s. Hankering for the flavors of home, the new immigrants congregated in the park. Soon enterprising vendors created an impromptu market selling Asian vegetables, barbecue, and familiar dishes like peppery steamed buns and papaya salads that were impossible to find elsewhere. Word spread fast and thousands of people came eager to sample and shop. Today the Southeast Asian Market in FDR Park is open on most weekends from April through November. Tasting tours are also available. **FDR Park** is filled with historic architecture and green spaces, and even has a golf course. Designed by the Olmsted Brothers, the famous landscape architects of the early 20th century, it also features a boathouse and skateboard park.

Visitors to Budapest's grandiose Hungarian Parliament building will only be able to glimpse a handful of its elegant rooms and hallways (page 206).

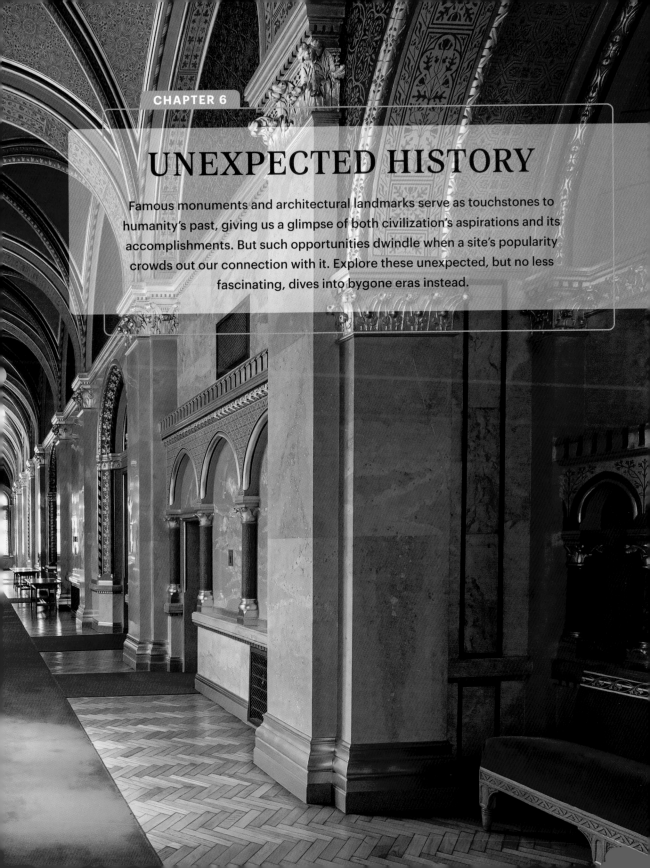

CHAPTER 6

UNEXPECTED HISTORY

Famous monuments and architectural landmarks serve as touchstones to humanity's past, giving us a glimpse of both civilization's aspirations and its accomplishments. But such opportunities dwindle when a site's popularity crowds out our connection with it. Explore these unexpected, but no less fascinating, dives into bygone eras instead.

Bell-shaped stupas decorate
Borobudur's Buddhist temples.

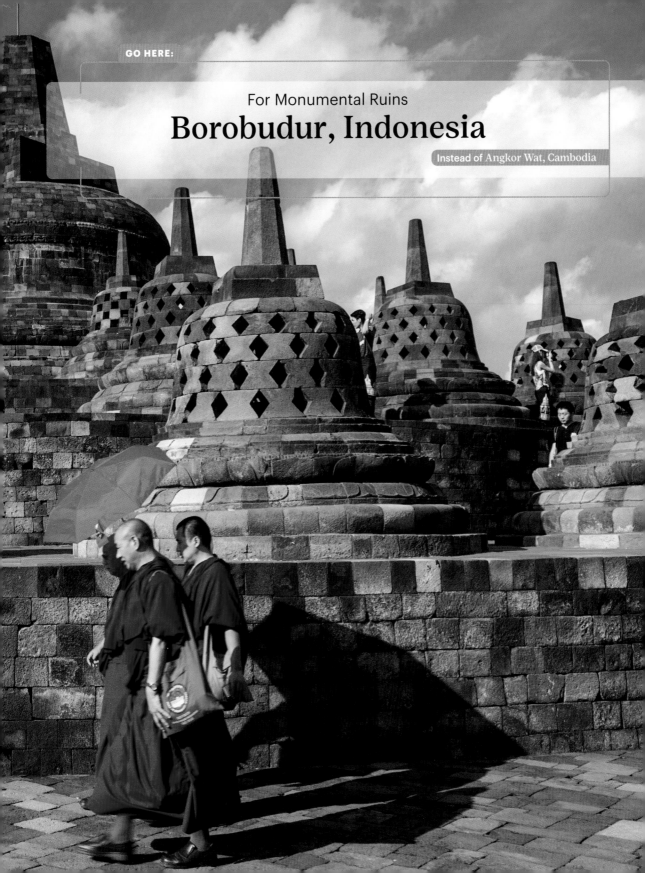

For Monumental Ruins

Borobudur, Indonesia

Instead of Angkor Wat, Cambodia

Thought to have been completed in the ninth century, Borobudur is now protected as a UNESCO World Heritage site.

W hen it comes to glorious monumental ruins, Cambodia's Angkor Wat gets a lot of attention. The remains of the 12th-century Khmer kingdom, near the modern city of Siem Reap, are both full of history and visually breathtaking—capable of stealing a scene even from Angelina Jolie, whose *Tomb Raider* used them as a moody backdrop. But Angkor isn't the only outpost of a vanished civilization to inspire wonder in Southeast Asia. On Indonesia's island of Java, the Buddhist temples at Borobudur are equally bewitching, if not equally well known. At least not yet. Consider putting this UNESCO World Heritage site on your bucket list.

Borobudur is thought to have been completed around the year 825 during the Shailendra dynasty, Buddhist royalty who ruled over parts of Java and Sumatra. Sometime between the 10th and 14th centuries Borobudur was abandoned. Covered in volcanic ash, then jungle, and finally anonymity, the temple complex at Borobudur slumbered until the ruins were rediscovered by Europeans in 1814, when English colonial bigwig Sir Thomas Stamford Raffles, then administrator of British Java, ordered it excavated. Over the next two centuries renovations of the 63-acre (25 ha) spiritual grounds proceeded at different points in time, from colonial rule to independence, with the most recent conducted by international groups and the Indonesian government.

Sitting in the mists that rise around the Kedu Plain, the main temple at Borobudur exudes both power and grace. It consists of a great three-tiered stupa (a commemorative monument filled with relics sacred to the Buddha) encompassing an entire hill and was built with two million stones. The massive building is crowned by 72 smaller bell-shaped stupas, each with a statue of the Buddha. There are two other temples to Borobudur's east that are also associated with the larger complex. The exact reason why the temple was built here and what it represents is still murky. One theory posits the buildings form a mandala and the structures are devoted to Buddhist cosmology. Carvings of the rising stages of human enlightenment are portrayed at each level of the complex.

Perhaps the best time to visit Borobudur is at sunrise or sunset when the stones glow orange and pink against the surrounding mountains like great jewels. Numerous hotels have sprung up nearby to accommodate tourists. One that stands out is the **Amanjiwo resort**, part of the Aman luxury brand, which offers varied Javanese cultural tours including the rare opportunity to experience the island by rail.

Borobudur is about a 90-minute drive from **Yogyakarta**, Central Java's largest city and a cultural center in its own right. The city (population 422,732) is celebrated for its crafts and performing arts, including the famous gamelan bands and Javanese puppet shows. The **Kraton**, an 18th-century palace and home to the sultan of Yogyakarta, is worth a visit. It features a museum with displays of Javan culture along with a plethora of royal artifacts. Other activities in the area include touring the **Jomblang Cave**; hiking past the rice terraces, hot springs, and geysers of the **Dieng Plateau**; and visiting the Hindu **Prambanan temple complex**, also a UNESCO World Heritage site. Adventure enthusiasts can even try a little white water rafting on the **Elo** and **Progo Rivers** that flow near Borobudur, a distinctly modern pastime in a place of timeless culture.

Rappel into Jomblang Cave and explore an ancient forest on a guided tour.

Java East of Krakatoa

On the far western tip of Java lies a lost world where some of the last remnants of Indonesia's wildlife—including gibbons, leopards, and monitor lizards—eke out a precarious existence in the lowland rainforests of **Ujung Kulon National Park**. Its 466-square-mile (1,207 km²) boundary abuts the remnant islands of Krakatoa, site of the stupendous 1883 volcanic eruption that set off a spell of planetary cooling. Treks and tours within the park can be arranged, and you may spy some of its rare creatures. The **Javan rhinoceros** is the most critically endangered and elusive. With only an estimated 60 left in the wild, it's possibly the rarest large mammal in the world. Once found throughout Southeast Asia, these one-horned rhinos are making a last stand in the park. Their habitat is at risk from tsunamis, and the rhinos aren't safe from diseases transmitted by domesticated cattle. Meanwhile, an invasive palm tree is crowding out the vegetation the rhinos eat. The World Wildlife Fund is attempting to establish a second population to increase genetic diversity and as an insurance policy against a tidal wave wiping out the survivors.

The Avebury stone circle sees fewer crowds than nearby Stonehenge and is free of charge.

 GO HERE:

For Mysterious Neolithic Ruins

Avebury, England, U.K.

Instead of Stonehenge, Wiltshire, England, U.K.

Why Silbury Hill—the largest artificial mound in Europe—was built and how it remains standing remain mysteries.

OPPOSITE: Brave travelers can explore West Kennet Long Barrow, a neolithic tomb built around 3650 B.C.

Why do some archaeological sites receive all the attention and others hardly any at all? Stonehenge, with its giant Jenga-like assortment of pieces, is one of the most instantly recognizable landmarks in the world and one of Britain's top five tourist attractions. Such familiarity breeds traffic jams, if not contempt. Stonehenge is usually mobbed, with cars frequently backing up on the nearby road as rubberneckers brake to get a better view of the ancient stones. It's so popular that the British government is considering a controversial plan to burrow a freeway beneath Stonehenge to manage the traffic. Yet just 28 miles (45 km) away lies a similar Iron Age site that's uncelebrated, uncrowded, and free of charge. When you're in England stop by Avebury for an encounter with a mysterious collection of stones considered to be one of Britain's most important archaeological sites. It consists of several parts including the enigmatic **Silbury Hill**, the largest such mound in Europe, and **West Kennet Long Barrow**, a Neolithic tomb that once held the remains of up to 50 people.

Like Stonehenge the purpose behind Avebury's stones and human-made landscapes remains unknown. Built some 4,500 years ago, the site is thought to have been religious in nature. Today the ruins serve as literal touchstones to a world of Neolithic pagans and their forgotten rites and rituals. The stones are arrayed in a series of rings contained inside a circular ditch that extends into Avebury village, a quaint collection of thatch-roofed English cottages alongside a pub. The megalithic rings, considered the largest of their kind in the world, are recognized as a UNESCO World Heritage site.

Unlike their more famous neighbor, where an intimate encounter with the megaliths costs 48 pounds ($60) per adult for a quick 45 minutes, Avebury's visitors can wander in the circles at will and at any time—including sunrise and sunset, a boon for any traveler's moody social media feed. However, West Kennet Long Barrow is on private property, and climbing Silbury Hill is not permitted in order to protect its archaeological finds.

Travelers who want to learn more about Avebury and its mysteries should consider signing up for a **National Trust guided tour** (5 pounds/ $6.20 per person). The **Alexander Keiller Museum** on the village's High Street contains some interesting displays including pottery and human skeletons found on the site. Also nearby is **Avebury Manor**. The house is a 16th-century time capsule of rooms kitted out with antiques stretching from the 1590s through the 1930s. After exploring Avebury's collection of prehistoric tombs and ruins, the **Avebury Manor Garden** returns visitors to the delights of English flowers. Consider disconnecting in the orchard, a designated silent space where visitors are encouraged to turn off devices and enjoy nature uninterrupted.

Foamhenge

Stonehenge's prehistoric stones have inspired a raft of imitators across the globe. As the land of the roadside attraction, America counts a half dozen "faux-henges" that function as giddy attractions to lure rubberneckers, including a version fashioned from limestone on the University of Texas Permian Basin campus in Odessa; a fiberglass replica called Bamahenge in an Alabama marina (the monolith is paired with several colossal dinosaur statues); a version in Maryhill, Washington, that serves as a memorial to soldiers killed in World War I; and a gearhead Stonehenge constructed from a collection of old cars in Alliance, Nebraska, famously known in those parts as Carhenge.

Perhaps the happiest of them all is Foamhenge, which stands in a field on Cox Farms in Centreville, Virginia, a 40-minute drive from Washington, D.C. Foamhenge is a full-size replica of the British version but carved entirely from Styrofoam. Originally created by fiberglass artist Mark Cline in 2004 and installed in Natural Bridge, Virginia, as an April Fool's joke, the piece was purchased in 2017 by the farm and each of the 400-pound stones moved and reassembled at the Fairfax County location. Originally used as an advertisement for Cox's annual autumn festival, the attraction is now open to the public on Saturdays from spring through fall and has achieved something of its own fame, starring in a GEICO insurance commercial and on the TV crime drama *NCIS*.

For a Lost Middle Eastern City
Jerash, Jordan

Shoehorned into the red rock canyons of southwestern Jordan is the world-renowned ancient city of Petra. Its spectacular buildings, carved directly into sandstone cliffs, have bewitched adventure seekers from ancient spice traders to Indiana Jones. Yet few of them know that just a few hundred miles north lies another photogenic collection of ruins that is just as historically significant and harks back to a time when Jordan was at the crossroads of a multicultural world. Welcome to Jerash, the classical city of northern Jordan so well preserved it's frequently called the Pompeii of the Middle East.

Locals play music at Jerash's South Theater, built around A.D. 90.

Jerash, only a 50-minute car ride from the Jordanian capital of Amman, is one of the Middle East's most captivating archaeological sites—and, overshadowed by the crowds flocking to Petra, it could be the region's best kept secret. The city flourished under successive civilizations: The Greeks, Romans, and Byzantines each ruled there before the Galilee earthquake of A.D. 749 led to its quick abandonment. Today the large number of magnificent and intact structures in Jerash, such as Hadrian's Arch, the hippodrome, the Oval Plaza, and the forum, speak to its glories as a center of trade in the classical world. There is also a museum and displays of traditional handicrafts to help provide visitors insight into the city's rich history and culture.

The first stop in Jerash should be the ancient Roman city. All structures here, including a number of temples, theaters, and colonnaded streets, date back to the height of the Roman Empire, when the Caesars' rule extended from the Middle East to the Scottish border. Visitors can explore the **hippodrome**, used for chariot races, and the **forum**, the once bustling city's administrative center. But the most impressive site is

The Romans held important meetings at the Oval Plaza, where many of the original columns remain today.

the **Oval Plaza**, Jerash's central meeting place, surrounded by a forest of still standing Ionic columns, arches, and, occasionally, local reenactors who appear in Roman gladiator and legionnaire gear to the delight of visitors.

One of the most well-known monuments in Jerash is **Hadrian's Arch**, built to commemorate the Roman emperor's visit on a whistle-stop tour of his realm in the second century. Hadrian was an irrepressible traveler who made numerous journeys throughout his empire. The impressive archway that honors him here is one of the best preserved Roman arches in the world, making for a natural selfie stop.

For those interested in delving deeper into Jerash's story, a number of museums in the city are worth a visit. The **Jerash Archaeological Museum** exhibits many artifacts that showcase the city's classical and Byzantine past, while the **Jerash Visitors Center** displays archaeological finds discovered after 2016.

Another nearby attraction is **Ajloun Castle**, just a short drive from Jerash. Built during the Ayyubid dynasty in the 12th century, the castle sits in a spot that offers commanding views of the Jordan Valley and the surrounding countryside. For those looking for a more adventurous experience, Jerash is close to the **Jordan Trail**, a 419-mile (674 km) route through the country—and the castle ruins are an easy stopover.

There are numerous hotels and guesthouses in Jerash catering to all budgets. The **Olive Branch Hotel** is a popular and affordable choice and features a rooftop terrace with city views. A top hotel choice in the capital is the **Four Seasons Hotel Amman**.

For anyone interested in history, culture, and adventure, Jordan's Jerash is a surprising and surprisingly accessible heritage site in a country that has stood at the crossroads of history for centuries.

The New Egyptian Museum

The antiquities of Jerash and Petra are not as well known as those in Egypt, where the government recently unveiled a new billion-dollar museum to house many of its treasures. Cairo's new **Grand Egyptian Museum** (GEM) reignited global interest in ancient Egypt and its treasures. Dramatic and modern, GEM is located in Giza. "It's the perfect museum in the perfect setting," says Fredrik Hiebert, former National Geographic Society archaeologist-in-residence. "It's going to become a destination museum and will change the way people visit Egypt."

Along with more than 5,000 treasures belonging to King Tut, the nearly 5.3-million-square-foot (492,390 m²) complex houses enormous collections of ancient artifacts—an estimated 100,000 pieces in all. But space could soon grow tight. Recent excavations have uncovered 250 mummies in Saqqara and a "golden city" built more than 3,000 years ago near Luxor. Such finds, and the recent restoration of Luxor's statue-lined Avenue of the Sphinxes, mean there's much to celebrate.

For a Praise-Worthy Parliament Building
Budapest, Hungary

The majesty of Britain's Houses of Parliament is hard to beat. But in Budapest, the Hungarian Parliament building flanks the Danube and is as spired and bespoke as its British counterpart on the Thames, rivaling Westminster's seat of government in grandeur and exceeding it in size.

With its ornate beauty and prime location, the Hungarian Parliament building draws a stream of daily visitors eager to take 45-minute-long tours conducted in a variety of languages. Tourists can climb the **Grand Stairway**, carved with gilded banisters and balustrades, and marvel at the assemblages of stained glass and carved wooden statuary. Made from light-colored limestone, the building was completed in 1896; politicians moved in in 1902. The 194,000-square-foot (18,020 m²) civic structure conceived by architect Imre Steindl is still the country's largest building, designed to reflect the greater Hungarian state (a territory that embraced parts of present-day Romania, Slovakia, and Ukraine). While the currents of fashion and politics may ebb and flow like the Danube it fronts, Budapest's Parliament building endures as a symbol of the city.

The Hungarian Parliament's centerpiece is a 314-foot (96 m) dome. A walk beneath the soaring cupola is the tour's highlight. Directly below the dome's ceiling is the national symbol, a crown given in A.D. 1000 to St. Stephen, the first Christian leader of Hungary, by the pope. The crown is guarded on all sides by statues of 15 kings and one empress (Maria Theresa) who ruled the country until the end of World War I. In a bow to democracy the adjoining room features statues of nonroyal Hungarians.

Inside are 10 courtyards, 29 staircases, and 691 rooms—some of which have scarcely been used since its opening. Divided between two equal chambers, the building features a lower and upper assembly. Membership to the latter was reserved for aristocrats and hereditary title

Completed in 1896, the Hungarian Parliament building wows in splendor and size.

The Hungarian Parliament building is the largest edifice in the country, towering over the Danube River and surrounding structures.

holders, so the handwoven carpet in the senate chamber's anteroom is blue to reflect the "blue bloods" inside.

But neither commoners nor royals had much of a chance to legislate thanks to the vagaries of history. Hungary, originally a part of the Austro-Hungarian Empire and allied with Germany, lost World War I. With the monarchy overthrown, the country achieved independence but lost most of its outlying territories. Hungary's modern parliament, the National Assembly, uses only one of the chambers, conducting the country's business in the old lower assembly. The former upper chamber is reserved for meetings and conferences.

At the tour's end the guide leads visitors to a small museum detailing the building's history that includes unexpected artifacts, such as a battered red glass star that crowned the spire during communist rule. Just outside, alongside the Danube's embankment, is another moving memorial: Dozens of bronze shoes mark the spot where Jews were executed by the Nazis and thrown into the river during World War II.

The building sits on the Pest side of the city, facing the Buda Hills—the ancestral home of Hungary's kings and currently the site of a massive building project. Surrounding it are neighborhoods stuffed with landmarks, including the **Hungarian State Opera House** and **St. Stephen's Basilica**, and surprises—bronze statues of former U.S. presidents Ronald Reagan and George H. W. Bush stand in a nearby park.

Budapest's accommodations often reflect its late 19th-century architecture. The restored **Anantara New York Palace Budapest Hotel**, formerly an 1890s American insurance building and still home to a famous literary café, provides echoes of old Budapest with waltz music wafting up its great atrium. It's a stone's throw from the hip "ruin bars," youthful drinking spots that sprout inside the run-down 19th-century tenements of the **Jewish Quarter**.

Restoring Old Budapest

Hungarians joke that they always pick the losing side in wars, but there was nothing funny about the damage inflicted on Budapest during the 20th century. Heavily bombed in World War II when the Nazis sacrificed the city in a pointless siege (an attempt to forestall the approaching Russian Army), Budapest was assaulted again by Russian forces during the 1956 Hungarian Revolution. Today, however, the city is undergoing a restoration boom. Netting and cranes are everywhere in historic sections of the city, none more so than the **Castle District**, the hilly historic neighborhood on the opposite side of the Danube from the Hungarian Parliament building. Momentum started in 1987 when Buda's historic core became a UNESCO World Heritage site, emphasizing the need for restoration. Preservationists repaired the bell tower of Matthias Church and installed 150,000 new roof tiles, following its distinctive multicolored pattern. By 2010 renovation of the Castle District was under way. Organized under the **National Hauszmann Program**, the effort aims to rebuild the popular neighborhood's vanished 19th-century palaces and buildings, restoring their facades and interiors to as they were before conflict or communist planners destroyed or disfigured them. Other buildings, such as Buda Castle's barracks, were rebuilt from the ground up. The reconstructed 1840s-era Chain Bridge linking Buda and Pest reopened to traffic in 2022.

For Lady Liberty

Statue of Liberty, Paris, France

Paris's Statue of Liberty, stationed just downriver from the Eiffel Tower, is a quarter the size of New York City's.

Colossal, inspirational, and oxidized, the Statue of Liberty is the Big Apple's most recognizable resident and an iconic symbol of the United States. It's also a victim of every cinematic catastrophe to hit New York, from the original *Planet of the Apes* to *Cloverfield*. Yet she endures, forever lifting her torch for the huddled masses who flock to visit her. No doubt many of them, feet sore from waiting to board sightseeing boats in New York Harbor, yearn to breathe free themselves. Well, they can: There's another Lady Liberty to see. This one's in Paris. Look her up the next time you're in the City of Light.

It may not be what Lady Liberty sculptor Frédéric-Auguste Bartholdi imagined, but a quarter-scale (37 feet/11 meters tall) Parisian copy of the copper-clad lady can be found in the middle of the Seine, standing on a pedestal on the **Île aux Cygnes**, or Isle of Swans. The Parisian Statue of Liberty, in fact, is in the heart of the French capital and a just short walk from the Eiffel Tower. She arrived here in 1889—three years after U.S. president Grover Cleveland's 1886 dedication of her older sister—as a gift from the American expat community to the French nation to honor the two country's shared republican ideals on the 100th anniversary of the French Revolution.

Dedicated on July 4, 1889, she originally faced east, affording a nice view of the then brand-new **Eiffel Tower** (travelers can conveniently visit that icon, too), but in 1937 Parisian authorities turned her westward, toward New York, her back to an outdoor workout station where Parisian boxing clubs and weightlifters gather. The smaller model is a mirror image of her New York sister, though the dates on her tablet differ, including not only July 4 (America's Independence Day) but also July 14, France's indepen-

Magnolia trees bloom at the Parc de Bagatelle, a botanical garden inside the Bois de Boulogne public park.

dence day (Bastille Day), commemorating when Parisians stormed the Bastille in 1789.

And this version of Lady Liberty isn't the only one in Paris. An expedition to find the others takes travelers on a satisfying tour past some of the city's most famous sights. There's a ⅟₁₆-scale replica, made by Bartholdi, on display inside the entrance to the **Musée d'Orsay**, itself a treasured collection of Impressionist and post-Impressionist paintings. A replica of *that* replica stands in the famed **Luxembourg Gardens**, a 56-acre (23 ha) green retreat in the 6th arrondissement. Lastly, the **Musée des Arts et Métiers** has two versions, including the plaster model originally used by Bartholdi to fashion New York's statue. A replica of the torch's flame outside the **Pont de l'Alma tunnel** has become a memorial to another iconic lady: Princess Diana died in a car wreck inside the tunnel while fleeing paparazzi in 1997.

After visiting Paris's main Lady Liberty, discover some other sites in the 15th and 16th arrondissements, near Île aux Cygnes. The 16th is full of classic postcard sights, from the **Trocadéro** (home of the Palais de Chaillot) to the **Bois de Boulogne** (a royal hunting reserve turned park), and a neighborhood accommodation: the 100-room **Shangri-La Paris**, a former palace. In the 15th arrondissement zip up the 60-story **Tour Maine-Montparnasse**, the Parisian answer to the Empire State Building, for a skyscraping view of the city. Peek into the apartment of vaccine pioneer, chemist, and microbiologist **Louis Pasteur** (it's now a museum), or visit **Marché du Livre Ancien et d'Occasion**, an antique book market. Consider a stay at the **Platine Hotel**, just one block from Paris's Lady Liberty. In a unique ode to the United States and another of its famous leading ladies, each of its 46 rooms features a photo mural of Marilyn Monroe.

Vive Las Vegas

If imitation is flattery, then Las Vegas, Nevada, lays it on thick at the **Paris Las Vegas Hotel & Casino**, where a half-scale copy of the Eiffel Tower rises out of the winking neon lights. Inaugurated in 1999—when French actress Catherine Deneuve flipped a switch to light up the complex—the 5,000-ton (4,535 t) tower was an engineering challenge, with three of its four legs planted inside the casino building itself. The 540-foot-tall (165 m) attraction serves as a beacon, drawing high rollers and slot zombies to wager their wallets or else check into the 2,914-room hotel. The casino features a Frenchified shopping mall as well as an imitation Arc de Triomphe. Atop the tower, its observation deck offers a 360-degree panorama of Sin City. Come nightfall, when the Strip blazes to gaudy life, the Eiffel does as well with its own light show. And like New York's Statue of Liberty, Vegas's imitation tower is irresistible to Hollywood, having been pulverized in *Godzilla* (2014) and serving as a roost for prehistoric pteranodons in the final credits of 2018's *Jurassic World: Fallen Kingdom*.

Visitors can walk the red-carpeted hallways of Bucharest's Palace of the Parliament on guided tours of the edifice's main rooms and basement.

For Glitzy Royal Digs

Palace of the Parliament, Bucharest, Romania

Instead of Palace of Versailles, France

The Palace of the Parliament houses Romania's parliament and governmental offices.

OPPOSITE: The Palace of the Parliament's Senate Hall has an intricately crafted glass ceiling.

"I am the state," proclaimed Louis XIV as absolute ruler of France. The man, known as the Sun King, proved it in 1661 by ordering the construction of the Palace of Versailles. While the monarch's suburban home became a top tourist draw, there's another even larger edifice in Bucharest, Romania, that qualifies for the motto *L'état, c'est moi*. It may not be as graceful as the French version, but it remains a fascinating symbol of iron will—and megalomania. Called the Palace of the Parliament, the gargantuan structure is an unintended memorial to the excesses of Romania's communist dictator Nicolae Ceaușescu (1918–1989) and his wife, Elena.

Set in the middle of Romania's capital, the palace's statistics are stupefying. Lit by 2,280 candelabras and 489 chandeliers using 3,500 tons (3,175 t) of crystal, the interior contains 400 offices, 30 ballrooms, three libraries, and two underground parking lots. Constructed with 700,000 tons (635,030 t) of steel and approximately 3,400 windows, it stands at 35.3 million square feet (3.28 million m²). Inside, you'll find 31.7 million square feet (2.95 million m²) of wood and parquet floors as well as 2.2 million square feet (204,390 m²) of wool carpet. Some rugs are so large that special machines were constructed to weave them on the premises. The building is listed as the world's heaviest by the *Guinness Book of World Records*.

It all started when the Balkan strongman Ceaușescu visited North Korean leader Kim Il-Sung in the early 1970s. Ceaușescu was captivated by

Pyongyang's huge boulevards and hulking socialist architecture. He wanted his own people to be awed by similar displays, and so began planning for what would become the planet's second largest administrative building (the biggest being the Pentagon in the United States). Its 1,100 rooms would house all ministries and administrative offices of the Romanian government as well as the dictator's enormous executive office. The boulevards leading to it would be made grander and longer than the Champs-Élysées.

A 1977 earthquake gave Ceaușescu the opportunity. Using reconstruction as an excuse, the communists bulldozed 2.7 square miles (7 km²)—approximately one-fifth of historic Bucharest—relocating some 40,000 residents to make way for this "House of the People." Ceaușescu laid the cornerstone in 1984, after an entire hilltop neighborhood with ancient churches, monasteries, and hospitals was leveled. Some 700 architects and 20,000 laborers worked in shifts to complete construction. They did so in vain. The building was so big many of the interior rooms remain unfinished to this day.

Ceaușescu did not live long enough to enjoy his palace. During Romania's 1989 Christmas Revolution, he and his wife were tried and executed as political criminals. Following the dictator's death, his building became one of the world's biggest white elephants. The structure was nearly torn down—a hated symbol of oppression—but was literally too big to get rid of. It now houses Romania's parliament and the **Muzeul Național de Artă Contemporană al României** (National Museum of Contemporary Art of Romania). The Palace of the Parliament is open to visitors, but as it is a functioning government building, they must be part of a guided tour. These are offered several times a day, seven days a week, throughout the year. Tickets can be booked by phone the day before arrival, or at the box office located at the **Constantin Brancusi exhibition hall**.

Bucharest in a Blink

Once called the Paris of the East, Bucharest is an eastern European capital that may be unfamiliar to many travelers but is worth exploring for the history etched into its old neighborhoods. With a population of 1.8 million people, it offers a layered fabric of Soviet government buildings, art nouveau palaces, art deco hotels, and intriguing neighborhoods. To get a sense of Romania, amble down Calea Victoriei (Victory Street). It's a prominent downtown boulevard filled with historic buildings, museums, and upscale boutiques that offers a mix of cultural landmarks and shopping opportunities. Explore the works of Romanian artists, including the sculptures of Constantin Brancusi, in the old royal palace, now home to the **National Museum of Art of Romania**. Bucharest's **Old Town** is the center of the capital's nightlife with restaurants, music venues, and nightclubs tucked into historic buildings. Travelers fascinated with the kitsch and grandiosity of Romania's socialist rulers will want to tour the 80-room **Ceaușescu Mansion**, where a self-proclaimed "man of the people" lived like a king. As an antidote to all the pomposity, take a stroll through King Michael I Park. Bucharest's largest park, named for a much loved monarch, surrounds a picturesque lake and features paths for walking and opportunities for other outdoor activities. While there, visit the open-air **Village Museum** for examples of traditional buildings and houses from Romania's provincial towns and villages.

For a Realistic Look at the Past
Whitney Plantation, Louisiana, U.S.A.

Instead of the River Road Plantations, Louisiana, U.S.A.

The Field of Angels monument commemorates the lives of 2,200 enslaved children who died within St. John the Baptist Parish.

Usually bucolic, often beautiful, antebellum plantations dot the southern United States. Those on Louisiana's River Road feature gracious houses surrounded by ancient oaks festooned with Spanish moss. They are aesthetically pleasing—all moonlight and magnolia, as the cliché goes—but these plantations are fraught places: Their grounds, buildings, and fields were constructed, maintained, and cultivated by enslaved African Americans. While other plantations are beginning to address the history of slavery, it is only at Whitney Plantation that enslavement is portrayed front and center as the brutal underpinning of a system built on subjugation. For a true understanding of the reality of plantation life and slavery, Whitney Plantation in Edgard, Louisiana, offers harsh truths and the opportunity to see the Old South for what it really was.

Whitney Plantation is located on River Road, a stretch of land fronting the Mississippi River between New Orleans and Baton Rouge where a number of antebellum plantation houses have been preserved and restored. Whitney Plantation's grounds have the usual attributes: Its main building, or Big House, is certainly gorgeous. With its wide galleries and porches, it is recognized as one of the best examples of Spanish Creole architecture in the country. Surrounding the house are 14 architecturally significant buildings, including the last surviving French Creole barn in Louisiana as well as two *pigeonniers*—a sort of silo where pigeons were housed and bred for both food and amusement.

The German American Heidel family purchased the first pieces of land that make up Whitney Plantation in 1752 and developed a successful indigo and sugar cane operation that eventually included more than 100 enslaved people. After the Civil War the plantation saw various owners including one who renamed it Whitney to distinguish the site from adjacent properties. In 1999 New Orleans trial lawyer John

Tours of the Whitney Plantation do not shy away from the darker parts of its history.

Cummings bought and restored the property, intent on documenting the reality of slavery. He opened the plantation to the public in 2014 and later donated Whitney Plantation to a nonprofit organization in 2019.

It's the open and honest story of the enslaved people who built and toiled on Whitney Plantation's land that resonates—and unsettles. The plantation's **welcome center** recounts the history of slavery to better prepare visitors for a tour of the grounds, which can be self-guided or walked with a docent.

"Your visit is designed so you experience the plantation from an enslaved person's perspective," says Susanne Hackett, a former docent. "What was it like to work there from dusk till dawn, never seeing your own home or family until nightfall? How could you maintain your dignity when you couldn't control your fate? Many visitors are moved to tears."

Such a perspective guarantees visitors will see plantations in a new light. They can understand the toll of such unpaid toil by stepping inside outbuildings devoted to cooking, sugarmaking, and blacksmithing as well as a 19th-century cell, or cage, that held people before they were sold as property. With little documentation recording the lives of the enslaved people, a simple list of names in a small outdoor monument beside the plantation's church bears witness.

Perhaps the most emotional exhibit at Whitney Plantation is the newest—the **Field of Angels**, a memorial dedicated to the 2,200 enslaved children who died in St. John the Baptist Parish between the 1820s and the 1860s. There were certainly more enslaved children who perished, but such records are often incomplete. No longer anonymous, their names are engraved on granite slabs, and a bronze angel sculpted by Rod Moorhead cradles a baby in her arms, preparing to ascend to heaven.

The Whitney Plantation is not a comfortable experience, but it is an unforgettable one.

Drayton Hall

Louisiana is not the only southern state grappling with acknowledging inhumane practices in its past. **Drayton Hall**, 15 miles (24 km) north of Charleston, South Carolina, on the Ashley River, is another antebellum site that has done something novel. The plantation house, built in the late 1740s in the Palladian style, has not been restored but rather stabilized—the former headquarters of oppression now a memorial to it and left empty in the middle of the estate's 600 acres (240 ha). Instead of showcasing the life of its white owners, Drayton Hall focuses more on the enslaved people who tended the property. Economic servitude did not end with emancipation. After the Civil War many formerly enslaved people, with little education or money, remained on plantations as sharecroppers—a form of indentured servitude. The families' hardships are documented in Drayton Hall's various outbuildings and exhibit halls, which tell the stories of African Americans who lived and worked on the plantation through three centuries. Tours of Drayton Hall should be booked in advance.

The Arena of Nîmes, which opened around A.D. 100, continues to hold concerts, special events, and historical reenactments.

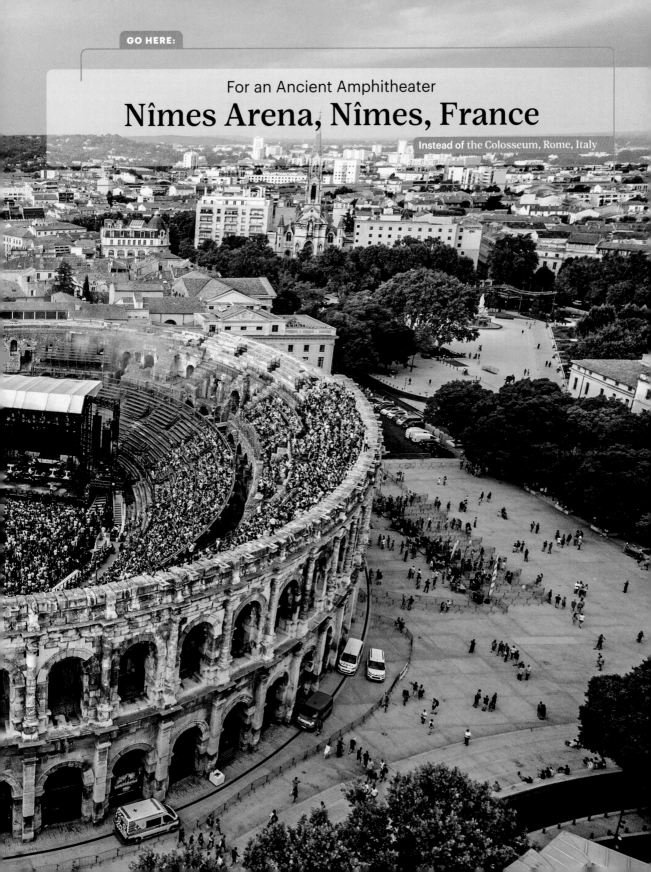

For an Ancient Amphitheater

Nîmes Arena, Nîmes, France

Instead of the Colosseum, Rome, Italy

Rome's Colosseum is as eternal as the Eternal City. Yet age has not been kind to the old amphitheater; during the Middle Ages it became a fortress and a marble quarry. It is still impressive, though a shell of its former self. But there's another ancient arena that's surprisingly intact in Nîmes, France, where travelers will discover not all the glory that was Rome was in Rome itself. And this amphitheater is still so functional it's used today for rock concerts.

Located near the Mediterranean Sea in the southern part of Provence, Nîmes (population 150,000) possesses so many examples of classical architecture that it's sometimes called the "French Rome." Founded by the army veterans of Julius Caesar's wars, Nîmes, then called Nemausus, prospered. Shortly after Rome's Colosseum was inaugurated, officials in Nîmes began planning their own version, opening it around A.D. 100, to display the wealth the city generated.

Designed to seat 24,000 spectators on 34 tiers of seats, the two-story amphitheater is located in the heart of the modern city. At 69 feet tall (21 m) and made from limestone, the elliptical arena is encircled by 60 arches with shaded arcades. Because of its excellent preservation the landmark gives modern visitors a real feel for how the original fans entered the arena, found their seats, and viewed the games. Gladiator shows continued until the Roman Empire's decline in the fifth century. The townspeople bricked up the

Canoe underneath the Pont du Gard, an ancient Roman bridge that was part of Nîmes's sophisticated aqueduct system.

OPPOSITE: The tombstone of Licinia Flavilla and Sextus Adgennius Macrinus is on display at the Musée de la Romanité.

arches and transformed the oval arena into a fortress from which to fend off invaders. Over the ensuing centuries the arena became a place of refuge, with people building churches and houses *inside* the structure. In the early 1800s the homes were demolished and the newly restored arena assumed its old function as a community entertainment venue.

Nowadays you can explore the Nîmes amphitheater by paying an admission fee and downloading an app that will take you on an 80-minute tour. Guides are also on hand to conduct tours during the summer months. The arena is open seven days a week, but check the schedule online, as it is frequently the host of special events, concerts, and occasional reenactments of ancient Roman spectacles. The colorful games feature a cast of hundreds including gladiators, charioteers, and wild animals—though without the blood sport.

As impressive as the amphitheater is, it is not the only Roman monument worth visiting in Nîmes. Make sure to visit the **Maison Carrée**, a small, intact temple recognized as one of the best preserved Roman buildings anywhere in the world. Also from that time period, two Roman-era city gates and other ruins are located in the **Jardins de la Fontaine**, a public garden. Across from the amphitheater is the **Musée de la Romanité**, which displays artifacts of Roman culture. The largest of the museum's three buildings is draped in a toga of glass tiles. The rooftop garden affords great views of the nearby arena and city. Perhaps the town's most famous ruins are those of the **Nîmes aqueduct**. The remains of the engineering marvel are located outside the city, with the most famous section, the **Pont du Gard**, 12 miles (19 km) to the northeast.

Accommodations within walking distance of the amphitheater include the **L'Imperator** hotel and **Jardins Secrets**, a boutique hotel in an 18th-century carriage house.

A Colosseum by the Sea

Nîmes isn't the only city outside Italy to have a coliseum to call its own. Rome built for the ages, and dozens of Roman amphitheaters survive in varying states of ruin across the Mediterranean, but the one in the Croatian resort town of Pula might have the most spectacular natural setting of them all. Like Nîmes's, this arena was built in the first century A.D. And just like modern developers jostling for beachfront views, Pula's ancient architects took full advantage of its dramatic location on the Adriatic Sea.

Similar in size to Nîmes's arena, the **Pula Arena** is the only surviving Roman amphitheater with all four sides intact. Quickly expanded after its original construction, the impressive structure could hold 20,000 people, who gathered regularly to watch gladiatorial contests and animal hunts before the emperor Honorius outlawed such blood sport throughout the empire in the fifth century A.D.

Today the amusements are far less violent. The modern amphitheater hosts reenactments of gladiatorial combat and other historic spectacles during the summer. It also serves as a venue for the annual local film festival and hosts numerous concerts, ballets, and sports competitions. Located on the southern tip of the Istrian Peninsula, Pula is also a good staging area to explore the nearby scenic **Cape Kamenjak nature reserve** as well as **Brijuni National Park**, an archipelago of 14 largely undisturbed islands north of the city.

For a Memorial to Love

Bibi Ka Maqbara, Aurangabad, India

Instead of Taj Mahal, Agra, India

With comparable domed silhouettes and traditional Mughal gardens, India's two most famous mausoleums, the Taj Mahal and Bibi Ka Maqbara, are strikingly similar.

Ornate artwork covers the walls inside the Bibi Ka Maqbara mausoleum.

The silhouette of the Taj Mahal is instantly recognizable, with a profile known to billions of people and a romantic backstory. Commissioned in 1631 by Mughal emperor Shah Jahan as an expression of eternal love for his deceased wife Mumtaz Mahal, the Taj is located in the city of Agra and remains one of the world's architectural wonders and a symbol of the country. A UNESCO World Heritage site since 1983, it's India's biggest tourist attraction, as evidenced by the swarms of daily visitors who crowd its courtyard, eager for a selfie in front of the iconic structure. But the Taj is not the subcontinent's only grand Mughal mausoleum. There's another testament to love and loss decked out in a similar intricate fashion and also crowned with an onion dome. By all means see the Taj Mahal, but if you want a little more solitude to ponder the power of undying devotion, put the Bibi Ka Maqbara on your itinerary.

Over the centuries the Taj and its symbolism has inspired many people to build their own monuments, including a miniature one built in 2021 by an Indian businessman as a home for his family. But none come close to the Bibi Ka Maqbara's scale and splendor. The "tomb of the lady," as the name is translated, is located in the city of Aurangabad, some 650 miles (1,050 km) south of the Taj, in the state of Maharashtra. Its 15,000-square-foot (1,395 m²) layout features four minarets, like the Taj's own, and a domed silhouette that's similar to its more famous cousin's. In fact, the resemblance is so strong that the Bibi Ka Maqbara is routinely called the "second Taj Mahal."

The two buildings are related. Jahan's son, the emperor Aurangzeb, commissioned the Bibi Ka Maqbara in 1660, three decades after the Taj's creation, and for the same reason—to memorialize the untimely death of his wife, Dilras Banu Begum. Dilras, an Iranian princess, gave Aurangzeb five children but died shortly after their youngest's birth. The grief-stricken emperor modeled his spouse's tomb after his mother's mausoleum. The construction was eventually overseen by his son Azam Shah, and the building's architect, Ata-ullah, was the grandson of the man who designed the Taj. His name, as well as that of the engineer, Hanspat Rai, who kept the massive dome from collapse, are inscribed on the building's main entrance doors.

The Bibi—in both structure and grounds—is smaller than the Taj due to that eternal source of family feuds: money. While Shah Jahan spared no expense outfitting his memorial, his son insisted that costs be contained for his. The result seems to have been a compromise: The Bibi Ka Maqbara has a marble (but smaller) dome, but the rest of the building is done in a mix of marble and high-grade plaster—this eventually earned it another nickname, the "poor man's Taj."

There are more similarities: The Bibi Ka Maqbara is set inside a traditional Mughal garden, called a *charbagh*, laid out in quadrants to reflect the four gardens of paradise. The grounds are also similar to those of the Taj: graced with reflective pools, ponds, and fountains as well as an enclosed mosque.

Emperor Aurangzeb built the Bibi Ka Maqbara as a sanctum for his deceased wife, Dilras Banu Begum.

India's Princely Hotels

What would it be like to live like a maharaja? Travelers to India have a chance to find out. Nowhere else in the world will guests encounter such a collection of former royal residences transformed into hotels. Examples include the 347-room **Umaid Bhawan Palace**, built for the royal family of Jodhpur. Their descendants maintain a private apartment—and a Rolls-Royce Silver Ghost—in the building. Indian colors and style fill the **Shiv Niwas Palace** in Udaipur. Its 19 suites, restored to their original grandeur, are festooned with Rajput designs, original furniture, and emerald- or amethyst-colored glass chandeliers. The white-columned, 60-room **Taj Falaknuma Palace**, high on a hill in Hyderabad, was once owned by the Nizam of Hyderabad, one of the world's richest men.

Why are so many palaces now hotels? India was once ruled by rajas and maharajas in 565 princely states. Following India's independence from Great Britain in 1948, the princes experienced a decline in income and an increase in taxes, forcing many of them to turn their expensive-to-maintain homes into hotels or museums.

For Inca Ruins
Choquequirao, Peru

Choquequirao, a lost city high in the Peruvian Andes, is challenging to get to and sees much sparser crowds than Machu Picchu.

The evocative ruins of Machu Picchu, the Inca cloud city in the heart of the Peruvian Andes, captivated the world when American explorer Hiram Bingham returned from its jungles in 1911 with the first photographs of the ancient citadel. Interest in the legendary site grew, and the arrival of mass tourism would eventually turn a trickle of visitors into a deluge. By 2019 local officials were recording some 1.6 million visitors a year making the high-altitude trek to this bucket-list destination. In turn, the opportunity to experience the site as Bingham did has vanished beneath a crush of humanity. On some days, up to 6,000 people wander its wonders. But there's another lost city, also high in the Andes, that remains mostly empty and off the beaten path—at least for now. Called Machu Picchu's sister city, Choquequirao reveals its mysteries to the few who put in the effort to reach it.

In contrast to overburdened Machu Picchu, only about 30 to 50 people visit Choquequirao on any given day. Not fully explored even now, Choquequirao (the name means "cradle of gold" in the Quechua language) blossomed in the 15th and 16th centuries before the Spanish conquistadores overran Peru. Filled with priests and aristocrats, the city served as a link between Cusco and the Amazon jungle before being abandoned. The ruins of its temples, plazas, and houses, 10,000 feet (3,050 m) above sea level, remain uncrowded due to the hardships of reaching them. The hike to Choquequirao Archaeological Park remains one for the physically fit. Those who make the trek must do so on foot, zigzagging up and down steep paths, from canyon to mountainside, then back again on the return. (Unlike Machu Picchu, there are no options of buses or trains to reach its wonders.)

A woman spins wool in front of the Monasterio, a historic hotel in Cusco.

The strenuous journey can take three to five days to complete and involves overnight stays in tents or modest lodges. Local guides are available through outfitters like Equity Global Treks, a mission-based mountain-trekking company focused on elevating women and Indigenous communities as well as supporting community-led tourism. Marinel del Jesus, owner of Equity Global Treks, suggests learning a few words of Quechua to show respect to the local people you'll encounter along the way.

Once you've made it to Choquequirao, the ruins are the reward for all the effort. "Exploring Choque can last for hours," says del Jesus. "It's a beautiful, gorgeous ruin that's not completely excavated. It might be even bigger than Machu Picchu, nobody knows."

The staging area for Choquequirao, like Machu Picchu, is Cusco, a city that's worth lingering in, if only to acclimatize to the Andes' altitude or recover after your trip. One place to do that in style is Belmond's **Monasterio**, a luxury hotel in the city's historic center. Housed in a 1592 monastery, it's full of art and antiques. Or consider overnighting in **Cachora**, where the trail to Choquequirao begins. The **CasaNostra Choquequirao** is a simpler lodge with hot showers.

Choquequirao's splendid isolation may come to an end, and that may even be someday soon. The Peruvian government announced it will spend $260 million to build a cable car to the almost two-mile-high (3.2 km) site. Development may draw more tourists and jump-start economic opportunities by creating jobs for locals as tour guides, porters, cooks, and hotel managers. But for now, Choquequirao feels like a sanctuary sheltered from the 21st century, and one that will stir any adventurer's imagination. So hurry.

Ciudad Perdida, Colombia

With even the most remote archaeological treasures made accessible by jetports and cable cars, it's reassuring to know some lost cities can still stay, well, lost. Such is the case for Colombia's Ciudad Perdida, or Teyuna, as it was called by the Native Tairona people. Founded around A.D. 800, it is hundreds of years older than both Choquequirao and Machu Picchu, hidden in the tangled vines and plants of the Sierra Nevada de Santa Marta mountains along Colombia's northeast Caribbean coast. The settlement was built on 169 stone terraces covering more than 80 acres (32 ha). Supporting a population of some 2,000 inhabitants, it flourished before the Spanish conquests in the late 16th and early 17th centuries led to its abandonment. Swallowed by the surrounding jungle, it was rediscovered by treasure hunters in the early 1970s. Archaeologists were alerted when gold objects, ceramics, and other artifacts cropped up on the local black market. A team with the Colombian Institute of Anthropology and History reached the site in 1976. This century, interest in visiting the lost city has grown along with Colombia's tourism boom. Accessible only by a multiday expedition with an approved guide, it's a 29-mile-long (47 km) hike to Teyuna and back. The scenic trail winds through the Indigenous lands of the Wiwa people, descendants of the Tairona. Like Choquequirao, Teyuna is a prize that rewards travelers who expend the effort to reach it.

For a Medieval Walled Town
Veliko Tarnovo, Bulgaria

Instead of Carcassonne, France

Modernist frescoes decorate the interior walls of the Ascension Cathedral in Veliko Tarnovo.

Most travelers imagine stumbling across medieval fortresses in western Europe. Maybe the walled town of Carcassonne in France, for example. Exploring its stonework and towers, visitors can imagine the Middle Ages returning to life. But an equally photogenic, if largely unknown, walled and ancient citadel lies in the Balkans. In northwest Bulgaria the redoubt of Tsarevets rises precipitously from the steep gorges formed by the Yantra River far below. The location might seem to be a set from *Game of Thrones*, but it's real. Tsarevets, and its hilly town, Veliko Tarnovo, the City of the Tsars, possesses a history to match its dramatic setting in a modern eastern European country that's off the typical tourist trail.

The site of the Second Bulgarian Empire capital that ruled the South Balkans for 200 years beginning in 1185, Tsarevets is beloved in Bulgaria as a symbol of a great national flowering. This period ended when the fortress was sacked, burned, and destroyed by the Ottoman Turks in 1393 after a ferocious three-month siege. The stronghold, surrounded on three sides by the Yantra River, lies just outside the modern city and is connected to it by stone bridges spanning the ravine below. Its thick, 12-foot-tall (3.6 m) stone walls and watchtowers were restored by Bulgaria's communist rulers. These protections enclose the ruins of the old city, which includes 470 structures, an A.D. 1235–era church, and the palace from which 22 Bulgarian kings ruled.

At the fortress's pinnacle is the **Ascension Cathedral**, destroyed by the Ottomans and restored in the 20th century to include, rather incongruously, frescoes in a 1980s style that were commissioned by the Communist Party. The **bell tower** offers expansive views of the surrounding region. After sundown a sound and light show tells the story of the fortress and other highlights of Bulgaria's his-

Surrounded on three sides by the Yantra River, the Tsarevets fortress lies just outside Veliko Tarnovo.

Rila Monastery

Greece is known for its Orthodox monasteries, but Bulgaria has them, too. The most spectacular of which, the Rila Monastery, became a symbol of the country itself. The assemblage of Eastern Orthodox buildings lies in the forests of the Rila Mountains southwest of Bulgaria's capital, Sofia. Rila was founded in the 10th century by a cave-dwelling hermit, St. John of Rila, and gradually grew over the subsequent centuries. Following its destruction by fire in 1833, the 300-room monastery was rebuilt and became a symbol of Bulgarian cultural revival. As Bulgaria entered the 20th century as an independent country free from the Ottoman Empire's domination, the monastery's image found its way onto the new country's stamps and banknotes. Today Rila is a UNESCO World Heritage site and is open to worshippers and visitors who come to admire the unique architecture and the monastery's museum. The church, with its black-and-white-striped porticoes, is done in an Egyptian-Mamluk style. Frescoes on the walls and ceiling and the monastery's priceless icons are a dizzying testament to faith.

tory. It's a tale few people know, but the country, now a member of both the European Union and NATO, is a modern one with a storied past. Travelers lucky enough to journey to the Tsarevets fortress will feel a thrill delving into that history and enjoy poking about the adjoining city of Veliko Tarnovo.

Set on three hills, the city is small enough to enjoy on foot, with narrow, cobblestoned streets lined by 19th- and 20th-century buildings rising above the horseshoe-shaped Yantra River far below. There's a good view of the city from a park where the kinetic 1985 **Asen Dynasty Monument** portrays the three brothers who founded the Second Bulgarian Empire astride rearing stallions. The statues mark the spot where the brothers allegedly plunged a sword into the earth to mark their empire's founding. Veliko Tarnovo's **Old Town** is a charming collection of whitewashed town houses, with the occasional vivid contemporary mural. Walk **General Gurko Street**, named after a Russian general who liberated the city from the Turks in 1877 during the Russo-Turkish War, to experience traditional Bulgarian architecture. For a stay in Old Town, consider Hotel Gurko, a bed-and-breakfast-style inn located on this beloved street. The stores along **Samovodska Carshiya** provide ample opportunity for watching busy artisans at work throwing pots, carving wood, and painting. It's a good place to find religious icons, silver jewelry, and antiques including Soviet-era kitsch like old military insignia. Also worth exploring are the traditional Bulgarian buildings in the nearby village of **Arbanasi**, which has an old monastery and several churches as well as houses featuring the stout walls and strong gates needed to repel the bandits who occasionally swooped down from the hills. Life in old Bulgaria was never easy.

Higher Town Bay's desolate beach in St. Martin's, part of England's Isles of Scilly, draws few crowds (page 256).

CHAPTER 7

INTRIGUING ISLANDS, UNCROWDED BEACHES, AND OCEAN VISTAS

The new shore strategy is simple: Think differently. Go where locals do or substitute one experience for a new perspective. Swap Bali, Indonesia, with its next-door neighbor Lombok, or salty Nantucket for the fresh water of Lake Huron's Mackinac Island. (Bonus point: Mackinac has banned cars.) It's not always the perfect ploy. Summer is crowded *everywhere*, but make that work for you by choosing spots your neighbors don't.

For a Tide-Accessible Island

St. Michael's Mount, Cornwall, England, U.K.

Instead of Mont-Saint-Michel, Normandy, France

I t can be confusing. Two small, rockbound islands with stone-slabbed causeways connecting them to the mainland, accessible only at low tide. Both are named for the same man, Michael, patron saint of fishermen. Each possesses a village and a medieval church, with a castle to boot. Mont-Saint-Michel in Normandy, France, draws the most crowds, but St. Michael's Mount off the coast of Cornwall, England, is no slouch.

At low tide, the brick causeway that leads up to the island of St. Michael's Mount becomes accessible.

It is a place you may well want to visit if you've got a yen for an island in a storied setting with a history stretching back more than 1,000 years. It is a package that is worth a gander.

For starters, St. Michael's is a very old place indeed. The island might have witnessed the Phoenicians reconnoitering the Cornish coastline for tin deposits well before the Roman conquest of Britain in the first century A.D. Appropriately for such a picturesque place, St. Michael's Mount is also home to inspired legends. As early as A.D. 495 tales surfaced of mermaids lounging on the rocks, as well as an appearance by St. Michael himself. The island was the centerpiece of a Cornish fairy tale, serving as the abode of Cormoran, an evil, cattle-gobbling monster who Jack the Giant Killer slew. In the Middle Ages, St. Michael's Mount forged close links with the Benedictine abbey on the French island Mont-Saint-Michel, and William the Conqueror deeded St. Michael's Mount to its French counterparts. Following the Hundred Years' War those ties were cut, leaving the two islands with a similar name but different fates. England's Mount was eventually sold to an English politician, Sir John St. Aubyn, 3rd Baronet, who erected a family castle. The island is still owned by St. Aubyn's

Sir John St. Aubyn, 4th Baronet, designed the Blue Drawing Room in his family's St. Michael's Mount castle in the 1750s.

Haji Ali Dargah, Mumbai, India

Far away from Europe lies another holy site with a tenuous link to its mainland. In the Arabian Sea, less than a mile (1.6 km) from the shore of Mumbai, is the Haji Ali Dargah, a site considered holy by Muslims and revered by other faiths. The building was constructed in 1431 as a tomb and tribute to a pious Islamic merchant from Uzbekistan named Pir Haji Ali Shah Bukhari, who eventually settled in Mumbai. He built a mission near the sea to promote Islam. His vow of poverty attracted followers, whom he asked, as he neared death, to build a shrine wherever his shroud would rest. Today the island's buildings are considered a masterpiece of Indo-Islamic architecture: The courtyard and mosque are made of pure white marble with pillars decorated in colored glass. Like at St. Michael's Mount, visitors must wait for low tide to cross the narrow causeway that links the shrine—visited by up to 80,000 pilgrims a week—to the mainland. In 2020 the Haji Ali Dargah was listed as one of the world's most visited shrines in the World Book of Records.

descendants. A fishing village was established, and at its peak in the 1800s the town held more than 200 people and 53 houses.

Today, with an admission ticket, travelers can explore St. Michael's Mount, including its gun batteries and the castle. Visitors can access the island by either walking across the granite slabs at low tide or by taking a boat from **Marazion**, the harbor town on the mainland. Access to the island is free during open hours October through April and by ticket only during the high season, May through September. The **hilltop castle** (tickets required) is accessible by the **Pilgrim Steps** leading up from the collection of cottages along the quay. A heart-shaped stone on the path is said to belong to Jack's giant. The castle, built on a series of crags, possesses two terraces with imposing views. Inside, the public rooms are filled with quirky souvenirs (QR codes will open information about the exhibits on your device) including a swatch of Napoleon's coat from the Battle of Waterloo, a mummified Egyptian cat, a samurai sword, and a couch on which Queen Victoria once sat sipping tea when she dropped in without warning and was entertained by a no-doubt-nervous housekeeper. Below the castle are **terraced gardens** featuring succulents, rosemary, and lavender (open during the summer, tickets required).

The island's other main landmark is the **Church of St. Michael & All Angels**, which dates from the late 1300s and was built on top of an original church constructed in 1135. The present-day building was mostly constructed in the late 14th century. A chaplain still conducts services here from May through September. Church highlights include an 18th-century organ, a 15th-century lantern cross made from Cornish stone, and a bronze figure of St. Michael defeating the devil.

For a Classic American Retreat
Mackinac Island, Michigan, U.S.A.

Moored off the Massachusetts coast, preppy Nantucket is a famous summer destination that's popular with powerful players from Boston, New York, and Washington, D.C. But farther west, dropping anchor in Michigan's Lake Huron, lies another island with similarly splendid scenery and traditions, tempered by its midwestern horse sense. Literally. For a classic resort destination that might be a model of a carbon-neutral future, there's no place quite like Mackinac Island.

Rent bikes on Main Street and cycle past historic homes on car-free Mackinac Island.

It takes 17 minutes to reach Mackinac via the fast-moving **Shepler's Ferry** from the mainland, but the voyage is less about speed and more about time travel. Step off the boat and onto the island—a world where automobiles have vanished. On Mackinac the only methods of locomotion are horse, bicycle, or one's own two feet. Cars have been illegal here since July 6, 1898, when the first ones terrified the carriage horses so thoroughly the island's council outlawed them.

With no cars, there's no need for stop signs, traffic lights, gas stations, parking lots, or Jiffy Lube. On Mackinac, the insistent, motorized thrum of the 21st century and its exhaust fumes vanish. The loudest noises are the *clip-clop* of hooves belonging to huge Belgian drays. These massive horses haul goods and luggage, rivet smartphone cameras, and act as equine Ubers for locals and day-trippers alike. The grassy aroma of their manure mingles with the sugary smell of baking fudge, the island's iconic treat, to give Mackinac a memorable, and altogether not unpleasant, fragrance.

During the high season (May through October) the best option for exploring the island's 3.8 square miles (9.8 km²) is by bicycle. Bikes can be rented along Main Street, where the ferries disgorge the day-tripping pas-

Fort Mackinac, established in 1780 by the British during the American Revolution, offers beautiful vistas of Lake Huron.

sengers (called "Fudgies" by the islanders for visitors' obsession with Mackinac's sweet souvenir), or you can bring your own bike on the ferry.

There's a lot of scenery to see—few summer resorts in America look as pretty. The island is a stately parade of Disney-like visuals: lawn concerts, croquet contests, and white rocking-chair porches of Victorian cottages fluttering U.S. flags. And flanking every house are rainbows of perennial flowers like daisies, black-eyed Susans, hollyhocks, and columbines.

While the island can be explored in a day, it's better to linger for a few to better absorb the rhythms of a car-free world. There's no shortage of accommodations in the shape of inns, B&Bs, and resorts. Two of the latter include the iconic **Grand Hotel**, a sprawling 388-room, white pillared palace sporting spectacular views of the Straits of Mackinac and a price tag equally as expansive, and **Mission Point**, a family-oriented resort (children's activities are free) on the island's eastern side convenient to, but away from, downtown.

Activities are simple and active: Rise early to watch the sunrise over **Robinson's Folly**, a popular lookout, or paddle a kayak out to **Arch Rock**, a natural rock formation. You can also circumnavigate the entire island by bicycle. It's an 8.2-mile (13.2 km) round-trip, and you're rewarded with startling intersections of lake and sky throughout. Visit **Fort Mackinac** and be treated to the island's fascinating and surprising history. Kids—and their parents—will love the cannon-firing demonstrations, which are held multiple times a day in the summer months. There is no shortage of restaurants and a few small grocery stores, too. Come night, the parties get going in the Main Street bars. One of the most popular is the Chippewa Hotel's **Pink Pony** and its buzzy porch where sailing crews, visitors, and locals gather to devour its harbor views and famous whitefish dip.

Indigenous History

Mackinac's roots as a multicultural, multiracial community are often obscured by the wealth of the mostly white summer population. But 20 percent of Mackinac Island's 580 or so permanent residents proudly acknowledge their Indigenous heritage. Some are descendants of Michigan's Anishinaabe, a tribal group that includes the Odawa (Ottawa) and Ojibwa who lived on the island. The tribes successfully avoided forced relocations to the mainland and remained on Mitchimakinak, their name for the island. Their engagement with white Europeans began in 1670 with the arrival of French Jesuits and fur traders, followed by the British, then additional European settlers.

Historian, author, and director emeritus of Mackinac State Historic Parks Phil Porter describes the late 17th-century period as "the six F's: faith, fort, fur, fish, fun, and fudge." Native Americans trapped and traded with the colonizers, gradually intermarrying and integrating with the white settlers. By 1900 Mackinac had become a tourist draw and a resort for wealthy Chicago and Detroit families. The prejudices of the time meant its Native American roots were downplayed. But today's visitors can find evidence of that cultural mash-up at **Biddle House**, a museum centered around tribal leader Agatha Biddle (1797–1873), who married an American fur trader. Her wooden house near the old fort tells the larger story of Mackinac's Indigenous communities.

Lombok is a year-round surfing destination.

For an Off-the-Beaten Path Island
Lombok, Indonesia

Instead of Bali, Indonesia

Trekking up and down Mount Rinjani, a 12,224-foot-tall (3,726 m) active volcano, takes several days.

"Bali" is a four-letter word for "paradise." This idyllic Indonesian island is famous for its mix of stair-stepping emerald green rice paddies, Hindu temples, and ingenious creators like the musicians, lithe dancers, and roadside wood-carvers whose ateliers churn out everything from dashboard charms to full-scale dining room sets. In fact, Bali's reputation as an artsy tropical Eden dates to the 1930s when Western celebrities such as Noël Coward, Charlie Chaplin, and Margaret Mead (who honeymooned there) visited and spread word of the island's delights. With the rise of mass tourism in the 1990s and 2000s Bali's visitor numbers exploded. Sadly, so did problems with traffic, pollution, and crowds. The pandemic hit Bali hard, and while it is recovering, the hiatus has given Asia-bound travelers time to ponder lesser known alternatives. If you're looking for an Indonesian island that's less familiar and less tame, head for Lombok, Bali's next-door neighbor.

The island sits in the Lombok Strait, to the east of its similarly sized but more famous neighbor. Most Lombok-bound travelers actually land in Bali before making an air connection to Lombok. (Another option is a six-hour ferry ride from Bali.) Being less well known, Lombok does not possess Bali's tourism infrastructure or its development. So, if you like bustling shopping malls or a big bumping nightlife in dance-till-dawn clubs, you are not going to like Lombok, which has far fewer of such attractions. What it possesses instead are uncrowded beaches and a spectacular national park surrounding an active volcano. It's a tropical island that suits both adventurous travelers who enjoy physical activity and beach blanket sun baskers. You'll sweat on Lombok, but the place is worth it.

A popular challenge is hiking to the top of 12,224-foot-tall (3,726 m) **Mount Rinjani**, the centerpiece of Lombok's **Mount Rinjani National Park**. Part of the Pacific Ring of Fire and an active volcano (the last eruption was in 2016), Rinjani is also a UNESCO Global Geopark, part of the United Nations' collection of parks with spectacular geological features. It usually takes several days to complete the round-trip Rinjani trek, and most hikers hire guides through local outfitters to make the overnight climb above the clouds. It's not a walk to be done lightly but, using the campsites by **Segara Anak** (a crater lake) as a base, hikers should be rewarded with a number of phenomenal views at sunrise and sunset.

Lombok is also a haven for sun seekers. Its coastlines are, as a rule, clean and uncrowded, and the plague of plastic waste that led Bali to organize shoreline cleanups is less severe here. Visitors can scrunch their toes in Lombok sand at the following spots: **Senggigi**, **Mawun**, **Mangsit**, and **Tanjung Aan**. Perhaps the most well-known beach on the island, **Segui** is famously called the Pink Beach for its rare, vivid hue. (Indonesia possesses two pink beaches, the other one being on Komodo Island, home to the famous dragons.)

Surfers have long made their way here. **Kuta Lombok** is the sport's epicenter, and the waves at **Desert Point** along the island's southwestern coast are considered some of the best in the world. The offshore coral reefs host spectacular collections of marine life, making Lombok a draw for scuba divers, too. The **Gili Islands**, a strand of tiny islands just off Lombok's northwestern coast, are known for their reef diving. Something of a backpacker destination, the islands are trying to protect their marine environments even as they draw more visitors. Lombok is changing as the world seeps in, but it can still evoke an era when Indonesia's islands seemed lands beyond time.

A harlequin sweetlips swims through a reef off the Gili Islands.

The Andaman and Nicobar Islands

The Andaman and Nicobar Islands are made up of 572 islands between the Bay of Bengal and the Andaman Sea. Just 40 of the islands are open to travelers. Indigenous islanders, known collectively as the Andamanese, occupy the others, and their privacy is fiercely protected by the Indian government. To travel around the Andamans and reach their numerous national parks, most visitors make use of private or government-run ferries. **Saddle Peak National Park**, located on **North Andaman Island**, is home to a variety of rare wildlife including monitor lizards. On **Great Nicobar Island**, **Campbell Bay National Park** has beautiful beaches and rare species like the crab-eating macaque.

On **South Andaman Island** lies **Chidayatapu Biological Park:** Small but beautiful, the park features rich biodiversity that includes giant geckos and flying squirrels. **Rani Jhansi Marine National Park** protects coral reefs and marine life including manta rays and sea turtles. **Mahatma Gandhi Marine National Park** is best experienced by snorkeling, scuba diving, or glass-bottom boat tours.

Marvel at the gushing waterfalls of Poço Ribeira do Ferreiro on Flores Island.

GO HERE:

For Warmth, Culture, and Beauty

The Azores, Portugal

Instead of Hawaii, U.S.A.

Rosais, a small village on São Jorge Island, overlooks one of the many volcanoes in the Azores.

OPPOSITE: Vendors at São Miguel Island's Graça Market sell fresh fruits, vegetables, meat, fish, flowers, and other local commodities.

What's the perfect island chain? The default has always been Hawaii: Its eight principal islands rising from the Pacific's deep are verdant and vibrant. But if you switch your gaze to the Atlantic, you will find a nine-island archipelago that's equally lush, with flowering landscapes, cascading waterfalls, black sand beaches, volcanoes, and marine wildlife refuges swarming with animals. Like the Aloha State, the Portuguese Azores are islands where the locals both nurture and protect their unique culture, determined to keep the natural beauty safe from overdevelopment.

And there's a lot in the Azores worth protecting. The islands are located in the North Atlantic, 2,390 miles (3,850 km) east of Boston and 870 miles (1,400 km) west of Lisbon. Colonized by Portugal in the early 15th century (the Vikings were rumored to have stopped by, too), today the Azores are an autonomous territory with a population of 242,796 (about two-thirds that of Honolulu). Thanks to the warm Gulf Stream and the archipelago's latitude, the temperature is usually mild throughout the year, ranging in the 60s to 70s Fahrenheit (mid-teens to 20s Celsius), though it does rain. The islands' many volcanoes are active, but so far fairly quiet this century. The last big eruption occurred in 1958.

Like in Hawaii, each of the islands of the Azores offers a distinct experience. The eastern part of the chain is home to **Santa Maria** with its numerous vineyards and white sand beaches. **São Miguel** is equivalent to the Big Island. Like the island of Hawaii, it exerts a strong influence over the rest of the archipelago and is a dynamic and geologically active place. Its landscape features geysers, volcanic lakes, and thermal hot springs. The central Azores consist of the islands of Terceira, São Jorge, Pico, Faial, and Graciosa. **Terceira** is home to the oldest city in the Azores, **Angra do Heroísmo**, a UNESCO World Heritage site. Its fertile soil supports numerous vineyards. On **Faial**, visitors can hike to the extinct Capelinhos volcano. **São Jorge** is celebrated for its cheese. Rugged, rough-hewn **Pico Island** is home to the highest mountain in Portugal, 7,713-foot-tall (2,351 m) Mount Pico. **Graciosa** is known for its iconic star-shaped pastries and red-peaked, Flemish-style windmills, brought by immigrants from Belgium. The western islands are **Flores** and **Corvo**. The former, known as the Island of Flowers, offers a rugged coastline, high cliffs marked by waterfalls (**Poço Ribeira do Ferreiro [Alagoinha]** being the most famous to see), and seven crater lakes. Flores's dramatic, verdant landscape and the surrounding turquoise waters often spark comparisons to Kauai.

As more travelers discover the Azores' allure, the future looks both bright and worrying. Luckily the islands have begun the task to ensure their biodiversity will be safeguarded for the future. In 2019 the Azores became the world's first archipelago to be named a sustainable tourism destination by EarthCheck, an Australia-based international advisory board. Four of the islands—Flores, Corvo, Gracioso, and São Jorge—are UNESCO biosphere reserves, and the government has established several marine reserves to protect seabirds, fish, sea turtles, whales, and dolphins. The fight to protect paradise is only just getting started.

The Amazing Flora of the Azores

Indigenous or imported, the flowering plants of the Azores play an important role in giving the islands their iconic Instagrammable look. Being one of the world's most isolated archipelagos, the Azores harbor many unique species, including one of the world's rarest flowers, *Myosotis azorica*. Called *não-me-esqueças*, or forget-me-nots, the purple flowers were considered extinct before a cluster of plants was discovered growing on Corvo, the Azores' smallest island, in 2014. Despite Corvo being a protected UNESCO biosphere reserve, these tiny flowers remain endangered thanks to the appetites of the island's insatiable goats and sheep.

In contrast, colorful hydrangeas are not native to the island chain. They are an invasive species believed to have been brought to the island by the Japanese in the late 19th century as decorative plants. Though they're imported, the flowers have become a symbol of the Azores and grow throughout the archipelago. Faial Island is often called the Blue Island for the azure hydrangeas that blanket its fields and roadsides. Their hue is due to the island's acidic soil, which deepens the hydrangeas' rich color. Volcanic eruptions in 1957 and 1958 only added to the fertility. And it was Azorean immigrants to the United States who are credited with popularizing the flower in America, especially in Massachusetts and Rhode Island, where many of these immigrants settled in the mid-20th century.

For an Island Buried in Ash
Montserrat, U.K.

All that remains inside a dilapidated church in Plymouth is covered in ash from the 1995–99 Soufrière eruption.

The volcanic eruption of Mount Vesuvius in A.D. 79 buried the Roman city of Pompeii in volcanic ash so completely it wiped the town from historical memory until its rediscovery in the 1700s. The ruins have attracted visitors ever since, making it one of Italy's biggest tourists draws—sometimes to its detriment, as the sheer number of visitors threatens the surviving artwork and archaeological remains. But Pompeii's not the only city to endure a trial by brimstone and pyroclastic flow. A similar volcanic event occurred within many readers' living memory in a British overseas territory. In 1995 the Caribbean island of Montserrat, in the Lesser Antilles, became a modern Pompeii when La Soufrière erupted and smothered the capital, Plymouth, in ash. The eruption killed 19 people and entombed churches, gas stations, and stores. The volcano remains active, but, depending on conditions, visitors can roam the ruined city (at a distance) and ponder nature's fearsome power.

Once known as the "Emerald Isle of the Caribbean," Montserrat cultivated a quiet existence as a tourist destination until La Soufrière's eruption forced the evacuation of thousands of people. The ensuing flows of mud, hot gases, and rock destroyed Plymouth and 20 other settlements, leaving more than half of the pear-shaped island an ashy landscape. The ruins are now part of a government-mandated exclusion zone where no one lives and travel is restricted.

Montserrat is determined to make the best of a bad situation—summarized by the local saying "From ash to cash"—with the goal of using the disaster to rebuild its economy. The island wants to exploit the volcano's geothermal energy to generate electricity. And sand mining has been developed in the exclusion zone, thanks to the volcano. When compared with other countries—and

Little Bay, a scenic port town, will be the future capital of Montserrat.

even the island's own past—tourism remains on a small scale. Any travelers arriving in Montserrat will be joining an exclusive club.

Montserrat is a find. From a population of 14,000 before the eruption, only some 5,000 remain. Its pace is not centered around the tourism culture that has consumed Montserrat's Caribbean neighbors. With the southern section off-limits, most of the population inhabits Monserrat's north, which retains the idyllic Caribbean vision as it once was and a local culture with its own rhythms. Ocean waters are vivid Caribbean blue, but most beaches are either black or gray, thanks to the volcano. The one white sand beach, called **Rendezvous Beach**, is hard to find but, maybe because of that, deserted and idyllic. **Hiking** is popular around the northern hills, which are covered in lush growth. **Turtle-watching** and **birding** are popular pastimes, too. More than 100 avian species inhabit the island. Keep a lookout for the yellow-and-black Montserrat oriole, the national bird. Places to stay include an inexpensive guesthouse, **Gingerbread Hill**, and **Tropical Mansion Suites**.

For most travelers, Montserrat's biggest draw is the exclusion zone and a chance to get a glimpse of this "Caribbean Pompeii." In living with an active volcano, island authorities are constantly monitoring its threats and permitting or limiting access based on geological activity. Check the **Montserrat Volcano Observatory (MSO)**, which lists current guidelines. A 0 or 1 rating permits controlled daytime visits to the exclusion zone. A higher rating will lead to visitor restrictions. Good views of the volcano are always available at the MSO's scientific and research center, while the **Jackboy Hill Visitor Centre** offers a view of both green hills and the gray, seemingly lifeless southern slopes where the airport once stood. Boat trips past the exclusion zone to view the ruined walls of the town are also available, as are helicopter tours.

A Snorkel in Atlantis

The legend of a city engulfed by the sea fascinates everyone. A real version of Atlantis can be found in the Gulf of Naples, Italy, where the underwater remains of a sumptuous ancient Roman holiday resort beckon visitors at the **Underwater Archaeological Park of Baia**. Accompanied by guides, divers and snorkelers are allowed to explore up to eight underwater sites, including ancient villas, baths, and the nymphaeum, a sort of shrine built by the emperor Claudius where they can ponder the mosaics and marble statues standing under the sea. In antiquity, Baia resembled a Roman Hamptons, a seaside resort town of luxurious villas built for wealthy tourists. Carefree and careless, Baia's social life scandalized more sober Romans. Once, to win a bet, the emperor Caligula ordered a three-mile (4.8 km) bridge of ships built to stretch from Baia to Pozzuoli so he could drive his chariot across it. Nero had his mother murdered here while everyone else indulged in food, drink, wellness, and love affairs. Never on sturdy ground, the city gradually sank beneath the waves, a victim of the region's restless tectonics.

For a French Tropical Experience

Martinique, Lesser Antilles

Instead of Bora-Bora, French Polynesia

Find peace at an uncrowded beach in the seaside village of Le Carbet in Martinique.

Find stunning Atlantic Ocean views on a descent of Mount Pelée, an active volcano.

OPPOSITE: Saint-Pierre's Depaz distillery sells colorful bottles of *rhum blanc*, an alcoholic beverage made from sugarcane.

ora-Bora's magical mix of striking landscapes, warm seas, and warmer smiles makes for a heady impact. The reality, however, is that for all its allure, Bora-Bora is a slog to reach for many—more than a 12-hour flight from New York via Los Angeles. From Paris it can be a journey of 20 hours. But a Bora-Bora stand-in, infused with the same francophone flair, swaying palm trees, and croissants, is only a few hours from Florida in the Caribbean Sea. Try Martinique, a French-speaking island paradise without the jet lag.

One of the Windward Islands in the Lesser Antilles, Martinique is only a 3.5-hour flight from Miami. Martinique's connection to France began in 1635 when French explorers proclaimed the island a colony. Today the so-called Island of Flowers remains part of France, enjoys special status in the European Union, and uses the euro as its currency.

A mountainous 436-square-mile (1,129 km²) landmass rising between Dominica and St. Lucia, Martinique has a hilly south end featuring rugged rock coasts and white sand beaches, while the north is marked by the volcanic Carbet Mountains as well as lush rainforests and beaches of volcanic black sand. Most Martinicans live in the island's middle, where the capital, **Fort-de-France**, is located. But the island may be best known for 4,428-foot-high (1,350 m) **Mount Pelée**, an active volcano that made international headlines in 1902 with a massive eruption that destroyed the town of Saint-Pierre and killed up to 30,000 people.

To ensure Martinique remains unspoiled, two-thirds of the island is protected land. In 2021 the entire island became a UNESCO biosphere reserve, recognized for its rich assortment of plants, landscapes, and marine reefs. For visitors this translates into plenty of hiking, with 80 miles (130 km) of trails; two of the more rigorous climbs take you to the top of Mount Pelée or the Carbet. Easier hikes are found along the Atlantic coast or by exploring the **Jardin de Balata**, a popular botanical garden near the capital. There's even a museum devoted to one of Martinique's principal agricultural products, the banana (aptly named **Musée de la Banane**). Other active pastimes in Martinique include scuba diving, kayaking, and horseback riding both along the island's scenic coast and into its hinterlands.

Regarding accommodations, Martinique's offerings are more European, with smaller, boutique-style hotels boasting outdoor cafés and restaurants. Two to consider are **Apolline Martinique**, a Creole mansion with panoramic views of the Caribbean Sea, and the **Aqua Lodge** floating villa.

Plan on bringing a healthy appetite. Martinique is celebrated for its cuisine—a mix of African, French, Asian, and Creole. Anyone familiar with a Louisiana menu might recognize some similar fare: boudin (sausage), seafood, and fried fritters made even more flavorful with Caribbean spices. Martinique's iconic dish is *colombo*, a South Asian curry served with lamb or chicken, lentils, and vegetables. Of course, there's also French wine. And Martinique has a reputation for distilling some of the best rum in the Caribbean, used in signature drinks like planter's punch and Ti' punch, made with local white rum, cane syrup, and limes. Many of Martinique's rum distillers offer tours of their estates, or else try a self-guided tour along **La Route des Rhums** with stops at 10 tasting rooms (designated driver not optional).

New Caledonia's Marine Reserve

New Caledonia is a French outpost thousands of miles from Paris. Located in the southwest Pacific Ocean, some 700 miles (1,130 km) east of Australia, the territory is a fusion of Melanesian and French cultures—a mix that gives a flourish to the local cuisine and architecture. But what may be most notable is the island's leadership in protecting its biodiversity: New Caledonia has created one of the world's largest marine reserves, protecting more than 9,300 species. The territory is blessed with an encircling 1,000-mile-long (1,600 km) lagoon system that nurtures one of the world's largest networks of coral reefs. Declared a UNESCO World Heritage site in 2008, the protected waters ballooned in size in 2014 when the government established the 500,000-square-mile (1.3 million km²) **Natural Park of the Coral Sea,** which as of 2017 is one of the largest protected areas in the world. Already a sanctuary for sharks, turtles, whales, and dugongs, the territory has recently taken additional steps to protect more of its species by banning fishing, nautical sports, and larger passenger ships from much of the park. It also established a coral farm to restore parts of its reefs that have been damaged by overtourism. Steps are afoot to expand the park again to reach the boundaries of Australia's **Coral Sea Marine Park.** The combined refuges would provide a vast protected buffer of critical habitat for resident and migratory marine species.

The wilderness on the shore of
Georgia's Cumberland Island
National Seashore

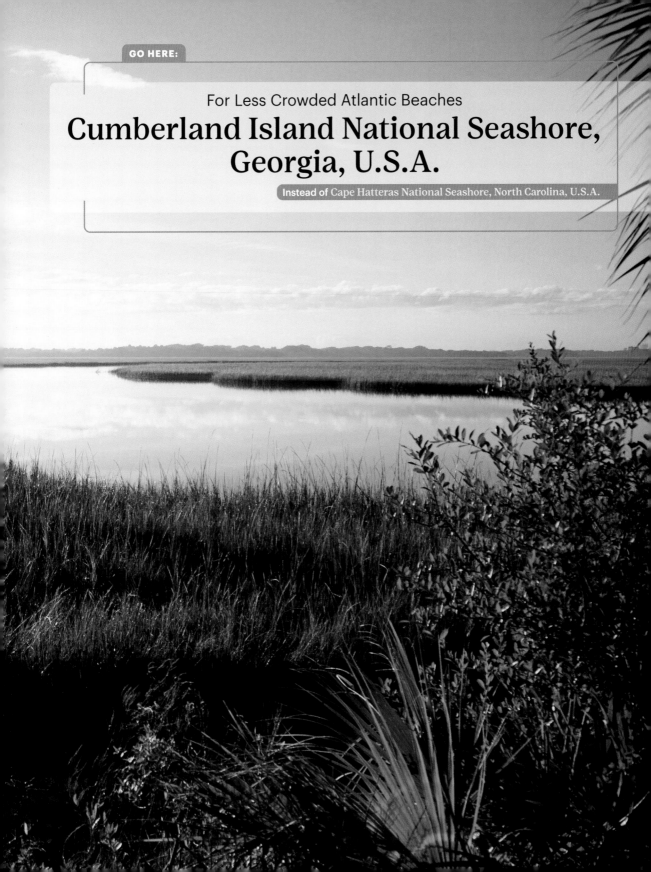

For Less Crowded Atlantic Beaches

Cumberland Island National Seashore, Georgia, U.S.A.

Instead of Cape Hatteras National Seashore, North Carolina, U.S.A.

Wild horses graze near the ruins of a deteriorating mansion built by a member of the Carnegie family.

The Atlantic barrier islands conjure dreams of flat beaches populated with more plovers than people. In reality, they may be windswept, but they are no longer empty. Take Cape Hatteras, North Carolina. In 2020 more than 2.6 million beachcombers walked on its stretch of sand, according to the National Park Service. Yet farther south, near the Florida-Georgia line, lies an island visited by just 37,295 people that same year. Those lucky few could walk beneath live oaks stirring with Spanish moss, unhurried to wander beaches with plenty of elbow room. Cumberland Island National Seashore is a place of isolation, splendidly preserved.

Cumberland's allure lies in its inaccessibility. Only a few people, plus wild horses, bobcats, and alligators, call the island's 57 square miles (147 km²) home. With no connecting bridges, visitors need to book a 45-minute ferry ride, with only two departures daily from a pelican-festooned pier in St. Marys, Georgia. Reservations are recommended: Camping is popular on Cumberland, and seats fill up fast. Anyone intent on snagging a tent site on the island's five campgrounds will need to do so well in advance.

Heed the park rangers' admonitions before boarding the boat. They'll remind you to pack food, water, and bug spray for the gnats, or "no-see-ums." They'll also share the best place to find sharks' teeth. (Pro tip: Forget the beach; look along the graded paths or dredged docks instead.) The ensuing ferry ride past salt marshes is scenic and relaxing. Progress is marked by startled heron wing flaps, and maybe a dolphin as an escort.

On shore, Cumberland's sights, both natural and human-made, beguile. More than **50 miles (80 km) of hiking and walking trails** lace the island's maritime forests. Exploring them can mean an afternoon or several days, depending on your ambition. Many trails are littered with horse apples—souvenirs from the herd of feral horses descended from the stock now-vanished property owners raised here. Keep your distance: They can kick. You'll frequently see them grazing on the lawn of the **Dungeness Historic District**, one of four historic districts on the island. The vast lawn contains the remains of an 1885 mansion built by Andrew Carnegie's brother, Thomas Morrison Carnegie. First expanded, then abandoned, the Italianate ruins resemble a Gilded Age Angkor Wat, with only a few intact outbuildings scattered around the periphery.

Biking is also popular on the island. For $10 you can bring yours on the ferry to explore the island's modest unpaved roads. Or you can simply follow the trails through the dunes to the island's ocean beaches, which offer 17.5 miles (28 km) of flat sand beaches that also serve as a nursery for endangered loggerhead turtles. If encountered, do not disturb them.

The island's north end is wilder but has buildings such as the **First African Baptist Church** (John F. Kennedy, Jr., married Carolyn Bessette here in 1996); **Plum Orchard**, another Carnegie family manse; and the upscale **Greyfield Inn,** which holds 15 guest rooms and abundant charm. The **Riverview Hotel** on Osborne Street in St. Marys is directly across from the ferry dock and is cheaper and furnished with antiques and thrift store finds. The bar is a popular local watering hole. The **St. Marys downtown** is charmingly drowsy, but the slumber may not last. Camden County is set to host a controversial new spaceport that may draw more development.

Hike or bike beneath Cumberland Island's many old-growth live oak trees.

The Gullah-Geechee Corridor

For travelers interested in exploring the unique culture of once enslaved West and Central Africans along the Atlantic coast, the Gullah Geechee Cultural Heritage Corridor knits together historic sites, attractions, and parks that both preserve and celebrate the Gullah-Geechee culture. The corridor covers 80 barrier islands and coastal counties between Wilmington, North Carolina, and Jacksonville, Florida. Historic sites include South Carolina's **Charles Pinckney National Historic Site**, the **Gullah Museum of Hilton Head Island**, and the **McLeod Plantation Historic Site.** Cumberland Island, too, was a Gullah-Geechee cultural center. Traces of this culture linger on the part of the island known as **the Settlement**. This was where most of the freed plantation workers settled after the Civil War and today forms the heart of the island's Gullah-Geechee community. In poignant contrast to the ruins of Thomas Morrison Carnegie's grandiose mansion, 26 chimneys and hearths are all that remain of a settlement of enslaved plantation workers.

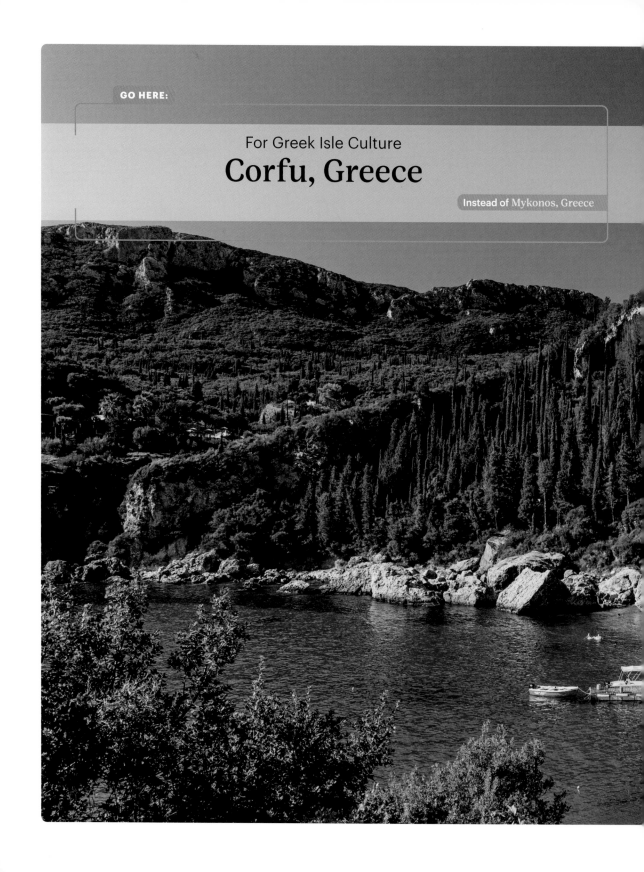

GO HERE:

For Greek Isle Culture
Corfu, Greece

Instead of Mykonos, Greece

Soak up the sun on Corfu's north-west coast at Liapades Beach, or explore an inland village just up the hill.

Cafés and shops line the cobbled streets of Corfu's charming Old Town.

OPPOSITE: Try classic Greek comfort foods like chicken *pastitsada*, a pasta dish served with chicken cooked in tomato sauce.

There's the usual image of the Greek islands—filled with bone-dry landscapes and bleached white towns crowded with tavernas and discos. That may be a portrait of Mykonos or Santorini, both part of the Cyclades archipelago in the Aegean Sea. But they aren't the only Greek islands that matter. There's another cluster, the Ionian chain, found along mainland Greece's northwest coast, that is green, lush, and influenced by centuries as the crossroads of great empires.

The chain counts seven principal islands: Corfu, Paxos, Lefkas, Ithaca, Cephalonia, Zante, and Cythera. **Corfu**, at 226 square miles (585 km²), is the second largest. While its history makes it familiar to the British, it is off the beaten path for many North Americans, who usually jet straight to Athens and, from there, launch themselves into the eastern Aegean. Forty miles (64 km) long, Corfu is defined by a hilly interior dense with trees (the island has more than three million olive trees) and beach resorts along its coasts.

With cobalt and turquoise waters set against golden sand or white pebbled shorelines, Corfu's beaches are one of its biggest draws. Generally, the shores on the east coast, facing the mainland, are calmer and good for swimmers. Popular sites include **Dassia Beach** and **Ipsos Beach**. Those on the west coast are long and sandy, attracting visitors to places such as **Halikounas Beach**. Perhaps Corfu's most photogenic beach, judging by social media posts, is **Paleokastritsa**. It's also on the west coast and is graced with a mix of dramatic rocky outcroppings and sapphire water. A short way away, the hilly village of **Lakones** is a good place to catch a sunset. But perhaps the best way to experience unspoiled Corfu is walking the **Corfu Trail**. Its 137 miles (221 km) take hikers into the heart of the island, past its trademark cypress trees, along stretches of coast, and away from more developed sections.

There's a lot of history to encounter. Only a part of the Greek nation since 1864, Corfu was previously ruled by the Venetians, French, and British, who all left their mark. The overlay left Corfu with an international cultural mix: The British sport of cricket is popular on the island; its food is influenced by Italy (a popular Sunday meat stew, *pastitsada*, derives from a similar Italian dish, *spezzatino*); and the Venetians bestowed their architecture. **Corfu Town** possesses two ancient Venetian fortresses. The massive stone structures served as a first line of defense against the Ottoman Turks. The Old Town, with its pastel buildings and narrow streets built between the 17th and 19th centuries, is a UNESCO World Heritage site. Its highlights include the **Archaeological Museum of Corfu**, with its scary gorgon statue from the Temple of Artemis that dates to classical times, and **St. Spyridon Greek Orthodox Church**, built in the 1580s. In the late 19th and early 20th centuries Corfu was a popular destination for European royalty. So it's no surprise to discover Corfu has several ornate piles like the **Palace of St. Michael and St. George**, built for the British colonial administrators and now the **Corfu Museum of Asian Art**. The **Achilleion Palace**, near Gastouri, was built in 1890 as a holiday getaway for an Austrian empress. It was later bought by Germany's Kaiser Wilhelm II of World War I infamy, then became a casino. It's now a museum—its layered story is a symbol for an island with a sophisticated and international pedigree.

The Durrells of Corfu

For English speakers, Corfu's most recognizable personalities are two brothers: Author **Lawrence Durrell** (1912–1990) was a serious novelist, but it was his brother **Gerald** (1925–1995), a celebrated conservationist, who popularized the island as the setting for his books. The two lived on Corfu from 1935 to 1939, along with their widowed mother, a sister, and another brother. Both brothers produced works about the island, and Gerald's Corfu trilogy (*My Family and Other Animals*; *Birds, Beasts, and Relatives*; and *The Garden of the Gods*), with its richly drawn characters based on the Durrell family, became the basis for the PBS TV show *The Durrells in Corfu*, introducing new audiences to the island's unique and breathtaking beauty.

Gerald was one of the first zoologists to realize captive-breeding programs could help save species from extinction. In 1959, on the English island of Jersey, he started a zoo to breed threatened animals, including the lowland gorilla. Several species have been named in his honor, including a mongoose-like creature from Madagascar, Durrell's vontsira, and a freshwater crab (*Ceylonthelphusa durrelli*) from Sri Lanka. The **Jersey Zoo**, operated by the Durrell Wildlife Conservation Trust, is a popular attraction and remains an important center for breeding endangered species. A park in Corfu Town honors both Gerald and Lawrence with monuments.

St. Mary's Island, the largest in the Scilly archipelago, is a hub for boating.

For Balmy Summer Days

Isles of Scilly, England, U.K.

Instead of the Bahamas

Which islands speak with an English accent, are warmed by the Gulf Stream, and take just minutes in flying time to reach from a much larger mainland? You might guess the Bahamas, and you'd be right. The independent nation is historically British and located just off Florida's coast. But there's also an island group a stone's throw from England with sandy beaches, palms, and those captivating accents. Meet the Isles of Scilly (pronounced "silly").

Spoiler alert: The archipelago off Cornwall is not quite as balmy as the Bahamas. Like the rest of the British Isles, the Scillies get wet and windy in the winter. But visit in the summer, between June and September, and you'll be treated to mild temperatures between the 60s and low 70s Fahrenheit (about 15°C–22°C), and the warmest average temperature in the United Kingdom (52.7°F/11.5°C).

The refreshing seasonal weather means the five main islands—St. Mary's, St. Martin's, St. Agnes, Bryher, and Tresco—are beguiling enough that their permanent population of 2,100 swells each summer when visitors take advantage of the mild climate. They can get there via air from three English cities, including Exeter. Flights arrive at St. Mary's/Isles of Scilly Airport near Hugh Town. Other visitors opt for the **Scillonian Ferry** for a two-hour 45-minute ride from the Penzance ferry terminal on the Cornish coast to St. Mary's Harbor. The ride includes occasional sightings of seals, dolphins,

Around 2,000 plant specimens not commonly seen in England live and grow at Tresco Abbey Garden.

and seabirds like cormorants. Interisland ferries, called tripper boats, carry people between the inhabited islands.

The Scillies' big draw is the variety of tropical plants imported to the islands by Victorian-era collectors and amateur horticulturalists. Norfolk pines, New Zealand veronica, and South African agapanthus flourish in the mild climate and give the islands much of their exotic feel. A variety of such flora is on display at **Tresco Abbey Garden**. The garden, originally planted by a lord proprietor, showcases tropical species like bananas and palms. Arriving birders appreciate that the Scillies' avian life, like their plants, are very different from those found on the mainland. Flocks of seabirds include the roseate tern, one of Britain's rarest. The islands also remain the only British breeding site for the Manx shearwater.

There is no shortage of activities in the Scillies. Shoppers will appreciate perusing the small galleries and boutiques, but most of the islands are geared toward exploring the outdoors via abundant hiking trails. The highlight is the **St. Mary's Island Coastal Path**, which takes trekkers on a 10-mile (16 km) shore trail that circumnavigates the island. The trail passes a site of moss-covered Bronze Age tombs known as **Innisidgen**. The islands were settled by Neolithic period adventurers around 2500 B.C., and there are more than 80 of these ancient grave sites scattered across the area. Other Scilly musts include visiting the westernmost edge of England off the coast of **St. Agnes**. The **Bishop Rock Lighthouse**, built in 1858 on a small rock ledge in the Atlantic, replaced one washed away in a storm. Regular boat tours to the lighthouse depart from St. Mary's Harbor. Lastly, on warm days the island of **St. Martin's** draws sunbathers and snorkelers to its legendary white sand beaches, where they might encounter Atlantic gray seals competing for the same patch of ocean real estate.

Where to stay in the Scillies? Two suggestions include Tresco's **Thatch** across from the island's church and minutes from Old Grimsby's beaches. **Star Castle Hotel** and its five-acre (2 ha) garden on St. Mary's has 38 rooms in a 16th-century star-shaped castle.

Atop a rocky ledge, the Bishop Rock Lighthouse towers 144 feet (44 m) above the Atlantic Ocean.

Conch Town in Miami

A haven for immigrants from across Latin America and the Caribbean, Miami shelters an enclave of 21,000 Bahamians. Travelers will find them settled in the neighborhoods of Coconut Grove and Coconut Grove Village West, a historic Black community known as Little Bahamas or Conch Town. Bahamians began immigrating to Miami as early as the 1870s, drawn by job opportunities and the city's proximity to their home islands. Black Bahamians endured the racism of that era, including a 1921 attack by the Ku Klux Klan on the community. But Bahamian Americans persevered, prospered, and contributed to their new country. Little Bahamas' landmarks include the **Mariah Brown House**, named for an early Bahamian pioneer, as well as the **Stirrup House**, owned by a Bahamian immigrant, E. W. F. Stirrup, who became a millionaire. Time a trip in conjunction with the colorful twice-yearly carnival known in the islands as Junkanoo, and in Miami as the **Goombay Festival**. The parties occur in July and December, with music and Bahamian street fare like conch fritters and Johnny cakes giving Coconut Grove a joyful explosion of music, color, and food.

For a Wildlife Adventure
Channel Islands, California, U.S.A.

Instead of Galápagos Islands, Ecuador

Like a schmear of cream cheese on crusty toast, thick white mist fills the nooks and crannies in the crags of Santa Cruz Island, one of five that make up Channel Islands National Park (three others in the island chain remain in private hands). Serene, unpeopled, and separated from the mainland by 32 miles (52 km) of Pacific Ocean, these Southern California islands became, by geographic accident, laboratories of evolution. On windy slopes and hiding above dramatic seaside cliffs and sea caves (**Painted Cave** on Santa Cruz is particularly notable) are almost 150 endemic animal and plant species found nowhere else. This unique biodiversity and isolation led this dramatic archipelago to be called the "North American Galápagos."

Comparisons between these two aren't exact. No marine iguanas swim in the Channel Islands, and those lumbering hunks of Instagram candy, Galápagos tortoises, are nowhere to be found, either. Instead, on the Channel Islands, lizards, foxes, and birds have evolved into separate species distinct from their mainland relatives. So, with Ecuador restricting access and raising fees to visit its most popular tourist destination, an alternative trip to the Channel Islands, just a few hours from Los Angeles, offers travelers the opportunity to play Charles Darwin and enjoy the islands' great and lonely beauty.

Getting to the national park requires planning and reservations. Because of their proximity to the mainland, **Anacapa** and **Santa Cruz** are popular, being only a one-hour boat ride from Ventura, California, where visitors can book passage on a regularly scheduled ferry. **Island Packers Cruises**, the park's concessionaires, run year-round boats to both islands. Ferry service to the park's other three islands—Santa Barbara, Santa Rosa, and San Miguel—runs from April to November.

A pair of western gulls rest atop a bush.

Inspiration Point offers stunning Pacific vistas from Anacapa Island.

Offering little in the way of amenities, the Channel Islands can be considered a fairly adventurous place to visit. With no food or supplies available, what you bring is what you will have for the length of your stay. On some islands this can mean water, too. To frustrate the clever foxes and ravens that learned how to unzip and pilfer food from untended backpacks, park rangers installed a number of "fox boxes" where visitors can store food and supplies, protecting them from hungry mouths. Suitably prepped, you'll be able to roam carefree, enjoy the stupendous vistas, hike along seaside cliffs, and gaze eastward across the water to where the coastal mountains rise like a theater curtain across California proper. There are camping and kayaking opportunities as well. Snorkeling and diving can be done mostly in the kelp forests along Anacapa and the eastern part of Santa Cruz.

The park's waters are full of life. The **Santa Barbara Channel** is one wet meetup for some of the world's most popular cetaceans, including gray and blue whales, orcas, dolphins, and porpoises (one-third of the world's total species swim off the islands). Sea lion– and seal-watching are on offer throughout the park. **Santa Rosa** and **San Miguel** host titanic elephant seals, and the latter is also a refuge for northern fur seals and two rarer species: Guadalupe fur seals and Steller sea lions.

Where to overnight? **Ventura** and **Oxnard**, just 11 miles (18 km) south, make great base camps, with plenty of lodging options for visitors and their own sights worth seeing. The latter's unique **Channel Islands Maritime Museum** features miniature sailing ships carved from bone by Napoleonic War POWs and a gallery of seascape paintings from the 17th to 19th centuries. You can easily imagine yourself on Darwin's H.M.S. *Beagle*, striking a blow for scientific inquiry.

An Elephant's Tale

While the Channel Islands are celebrated for flora and fauna found nowhere else in the world, their most unique animal, sadly, is gone for good. Only its bones remain, and they tell an interesting story. The extinct pygmy mammoth, or Channel Island mammoth, was a miniature version of its much bigger cousin, the 20,000-pound (9,070 kg) Columbian mammoth that trod over much of North America. Weighing just 2,000 pounds (910 kg) and only half as high as the 14-foot-tall (4 m) mainlanders, the little mammoths descended from Columbians that arrived on the islands when ocean levels sank during the Ice Age.

When the waters rose, the cut-off mammoths gradually shrank in size and thrived until their extinction, an event estimated to have occurred only 10,000 to 12,000 years ago. Why did they disappear? The jury is out. But there is one suspect: humans. With no natural enemies the tiny pachyderms would have been easy targets for hunters who arrived by boat to end one of nature's most unique evolutionary experiments.

Channel Island mammoth remains were first discovered on Santa Rosa in 1873. Later excavations revealed large populations of the elephant-like creatures throughout Channel Islands National Park, particularly on Santa Rosa and San Miguel Islands. The first complete skeleton was found on Santa Rosa in 1994. You can learn more about this fascinating creature and its evolution—and extinction—at the **Santa Barbara Museum of Natural History**.

For a Less Crowded Hawaii
Molokai, Hawaii, U.S.A.

Instead of Oahu, Hawaii, U.S.A.

Relax on Molokai's pristine Kawakiu Beach and experience a paradise unspoiled by overtourism.

The playground of Oahu, home to epic waves on the North Shore, luxury beach resorts in Honolulu, and the natural beauty of the Waimea Valley, is the Hawaiian island of popular imagination. But Oahu gets crowded—it receives the most tourists of all the Hawaiian Islands—and it can be expensive. Why not seek out a more unique experience in the Aloha State? Set your sights on the state's peaceful and placid Molokai. Hawaii's fifth largest island attracts fewer than one percent of the state's visitors. If you're looking for something different, Molokai is a Hawaiian adventure unlike any other in North America's Pacific outpost.

First, it needs to be said: Molokai is not for everyone. There's no Target nor Starbucks. No elevators or stoplights. (It has, as of this writing, just installed a school crosswalk with flashing lights.) Nor does it cotton to sprawling resorts with their luaus, leis, and pupu platters. Instead, Molokai exudes a feeling that can best be described as "old school," an independent, pioneer spirit that harks back to Hawaii in the years before mass tourism. Tourists learn that on Molokai residents don't cater to travelers expecting to be amused or entertained. Molokai requires you to both lean in and lean back. Listen, observe, and be respectful. You're a guest in someone else's home.

Some 38 miles (61 km) long by 10 miles (16 km) wide with just 7,345 inhabitants, Molokai, located between Oahu and Maui, is more rural than other Hawaiian islands. Do your homework before booking flights and rooms. There is one hotel on the island, **Hotel Molokai**, and it is frequently booked. Alternatively, there are a handful of homestays and other overnight accommodations, like the Polynesian-themed condos at **Molokai Shores**. Much of the island is privately held, so you'll need to think about hiring excursion guides who have access to places of interest. But with a little planning, your reward is a unique experience with a glimpse of the rhythms and traditions that seem to have vanished on other islands.

Molokai contains lush and beautiful landscapes such as **Halawa**, a privately owned valley with two waterfalls (**Moaula** and **Hipuapua**) on the island's eastern side, thought to have been settled in A.D. 650 by Polynesian voyagers. You'll need to hire a guide to reach the falls, but the views are worth it. Also nearby is the golden sand **Papohaku Beach**.

Perhaps Molokai's most resonant cultural landmark in the post-pandemic era is connected to a debilitating disease. In 1866 Hawaii's King Kamehameha V banished his subjects afflicted with Hansen's Disease, aka leprosy, to the dramatic Kalaupapa Peninsula in the shadow of the world's tallest sea cliffs, which rise up to 3,900 feet (1,190 m) on Molokai's north coast. Some 8,000 Hawaiians lived, suffered, and died there. In 1980 the peninsula became a national historical park, and a handful of former patients still reside there.

A good way to experience the island is through voluntourism, a practice strongly encouraged by the **Molokai Land Trust**, a nonprofit organization restoring native habitat on 1,700 acres (690 ha) of coastal and dune ecosystems along with ancient Hawaiian archaeological sites along the island's northwest coast. Volunteers must register ahead of time. Helping restore such landscapes imparts an understanding of the island's unique environment and is a reminder of the unchanging nature of Hawaii's "friendly island."

A gentle ocean breeze rustles leggy palm trees in Molokai.

Niihau, Hawaii's Tiny "Forbidden" Island

Just off the southwestern coast of Kauai, Niihau—Hawaii's "forbidden" island—is even more remote than Molokai. Though scuba and snorkeling charters can skirt the coast, the only way to visit Niihau is by invitation or on a helicopter tour. Aside from the occasional invited guest, the island is exclusive to its 170-or-so full-time residents.

The arid island's inaccessibility is largely thanks to its ownership by a single family who trace themselves back to Elizabeth Sinclair. Sinclair, an enterprising Scottish woman, purchased the 70-square-mile (180 km²) island for $10,000 from Hawaii's King Kamehameha V in 1864. Her descendants control access to Niihau to this day. It's an unchanging, simple existence. The island's electrical power comes from solar. There are no stores, and many of the 170 residents still speak the Hawaiian language, making Niihau one of the few places in the state where the ancestral language predominates. The island is best known for its Niihau shell leis, strung together from the tiny shells found on its beaches. The necklaces are now considered collectibles and can fetch upwards of $20,000 per piece.

For Colorful Coastal Towns
Ischia, Italy

Instead of Capri, Italy

Colorful shops and buildings fringe the Mediterranean shoreline of Lacco Ameno.

Treat yourself to a platter of freshly caught fish, lobster, and squid at a local restaurant.

OPPOSITE: Explore the natural side of the island on a trek up Mount Epomeo.

N o one ever named a pair of pants after Ischia. Capri's fame was such that when Audrey Hepburn sported mid-calf trousers in the late 1950s it seemed natural to attach that jet-setting island's devil-may-care moniker to them. But Ischia's name is obscure to many non-Italians, and the island likes it that way. Measuring 18 square miles (47 km²), it's larger than Capri but part of the same Campanian archipelago anchored in the deep blue waters of the Bay of Naples. Ischia seems content to let its neighbor get star billing (and the notoriety that comes with it) while it just concentrates on being gorgeous.

That's not to say Ischia doesn't get crowded. It can, and does, fill up in the summer. But it hosts more Italians than Americans or Brits, helping the island retain a local feel far more than places like Capri or the Amalfi Coast where, come June, English seems the native tongue. A volcanic island, Ischia's thermal waters and spas make it a destination for wellness and relaxation more than showing off, though it has enjoyed its share of glittery celebrities. The seductive landscape has drawn visitors for decades, and Ischia's beguiling combination of sea, pines, pastel-colored villas, and inlets made it the perfect backdrop for the 1963 Hollywood epic *Cleopatra*. Elizabeth Taylor, as the Egyptian queen, sails her luxury barge into the same port where visitors disembark the Naples ferry today.

Getting to Ischia is relatively easy. It's about an hour's trip via the fast hydrofoil from the port of Naples at the base of Castel Nuovo, the enormous castle welcoming passengers to the city since 1279. Landing at **Ischia Porto**, visitors can hire a taxi or take a bus to get around. Cars are allowed on the island, but traffic and parking are a nightmare. And who needs that? The lucky ones have a hotel minibus to meet them. And there's no end to accommodations, with hotels and resorts like the **San Montano Resort & Spa**, located high above the town of **Lacco Ameno**, with nine pools filled with thermal waters from the island's famous springs and spectacular views worthwhile of a splurge.

While many visitors will be content to lounge by the pool soaking up the sun, Ischia offers some notable adventures. For active visitors a hike up **Mount Epomeo**, at 2,589 feet (789 m), rewards the effort with terrific views. Cultural attractions include the **Archaeological Museum of Pithecusae** and its Neolithic and Greek pottery, along with the **Villa Arbusto** and its gardens. **Villa la Colombaia** is a museum devoted to 1960s filmmaker Luchino Visconti. Another worthwhile stop is **Giardini la Mortella** (La Mortella Gardens), designed by Susana Walton, wife of Sir William Walton, a 20th-century British composer. **Castello Aragonese d'Ischia**, built on a promontory of rocks, can trace its defenses back to 474 B.C. when a series of colonizers—first Greeks, then Romans, and, finally, in 1441, Spaniards—occupied the castle to protect the islanders from pirates.

The island is also large enough to produce its own wine, with Ischian reds and whites noted for the flavor imparted by the volcanic soil. A good time to visit the island is in the autumn, at the end of the tourist season, when crowds are lighter and room prices are usually lower than in peak season. It doesn't have the glitter of Capri, but Ischia imparts a real sense of place.

A Palatial Museum Worthy of Your Time

Naples, Italy, is known for its pizza and bumper car traffic as well as its proximity to Pompeii and Herculaneum on the other side of its well-known bay. However, many tourists who trudge off to those famous sites don't realize that some of their best treasures are back in Naples inside the **Naples National Archaeological Museum**. Called MANN, an acronym for its Italian name, Museo Archeologico Nazionale di Napoli, the museum is inside a sprawling, pink-colored palace. Its exhibits feature priceless ancient frescoes, mosaics, and ordinary household goods that give visitors a sense of the religion and daily life in the two doomed towns. Also here: the infamous "secret room" where frescoes and sculptures of a sexual nature were once hidden away. They're now just part of the collection.

The museum adjoins the increasingly hip **Rione Sanità** neighborhood, once known as a place of extreme poverty. Today it's sought out for its crowded, colorful street life, with a number of *pensiones* (boardinghouses), short-term rentals, and B&Bs. Within walking distance of the museum, the **Atelier Inès** sports nine guest rooms and a New Orleans–style courtyard with trees. The owner is a furniture designer, and guests are occasionally treated to a tour of his studio and insider recommendations on where to eat, drink, and shop.

Cruise Highway 101 and stop at Cape Perpetua headland for panoramic views of the rugged Oregon coast (page 294).

CHAPTER 8

TRACKS, TRAILS, AND ROADS LESS TRAVELED

Not all travel is about a destination; sometimes the journey to get there is the real adventure. From a Texas-size road trip to a Spice Islands sail off New Guinea, here are some fresh and unusual alternatives to well-known hikes, treks, and drives.

For a Railway Adventure

Copper Canyon, Mexico

Instead of Amtrak's *California Zephyr*, U.S.A.

The cliffs of Copper Canyon are especially eye-catching in the early morning light.

El Chepe transports riders through Mexico's red rock Copper Canyon.

Training across the Rockies on Amtrak's *California Zephyr* is a terrific way to experience the mountain majesty of the United States without a case of road rage. The three-day, 51-hour journey tootles from Chicago to the San Francisco Bay. (Spoiler alert: The train drops travelers in Emeryville, across the bay from San Francisco.) For those with time to spare, it's a leisurely amble across a chunk of the Old West. But there's another North American railroad journey that also crosses a steep mountain range and rumbles past enchanting towns and dramatic scenery, embracing waterfalls and forests of pine and oak. For anyone looking for a new superlative railroad adventure, think about heading south and boarding a train through the Sierra Madres and Mexico's magnificent Copper Canyon.

The name should be plural: Copper Canyons, like the Spanish Barrancas del Cobre. Six large, distinct canyons are found in this 25,000-square-mile (64,750 km²) region located in the state of Chihuahua. The canyons—estimated to be some 30 million years old—were formed by six rivers that merge into the Río Fuerte and flow into the Gulf of California. Their reddish, copper-colored walls give them their name. Collectively, the Mexican canyons are deeper, steeper, and up to seven times larger than even Arizona's Grand Canyon, and some even say the views are more gobsmacking.

And it's not just the landscape that is colorful—so is the region's history. Settled by the Native Tarahumara people, the canyonlands later attracted European explorers who discovered rich silver deposits during Spanish colonial rule. Exploitation of the land and Indigenous peoples followed soon thereafter. In 1880 American investor Albert Kimsey Owen of New Harmony, Indiana, sought to create a socialist colony in Mexico and won the right to develop a railroad through the region. However, it was another entrepreneur, Arthur E. Stillwell, who finally opened a line in 1900, but the combination of rough terrain, funding, and the Mexican Revolution prevented its completion until 1961.

The Copper Canyon Train Tour is actually part of a longer, 16-hour route beginning in the city of Chihuahua, crossing the Sierra Madres, and ending in Los Mochis, a town near the Pacific port of Topolabamba. The Copper Canyon run is a 220-mile-long (355 km) subsection, and the preferred direction is west to east, starting in Los Mochis and heading to the town of Creel. That's because the route originating in Chihuahua crosses the most scenic portions in the middle of the night. A trip on *El Chepe*, or the *Chepe Express*, is a popular choice; it allows travelers to get on and off the train. Other trains on the route do not. There are three classes of cars on *El Chepe*—first, executive, and tourist—with various amenities for each. Experienced riders advise sitting on the right side for the best views.

Those sights would include **El Fuerte**, a colonial town with quaint buildings and cobblestone streets. At **Divisadero**, the journey's highest point, a Swiss-made cable car takes visitors to the canyon's bottom (there are also zip lines for the daring). There's also a diversion to see **Basaseachic Falls National Park**. A three-hour drive by car from Creel, the park contains towering cliffs and the second tallest waterfall in Mexico.

Biking, horseback riding, and hiking are all popular ways to explore the region, but it's the train that remains the preferred way to see the wild and romantic landscape of Copper Canyon and the surrounding country.

Street food stalls in Divisadero, a village at the highest point of the Copper Canyon train route, offer delicious tostadas full of vegetables and meat.

Mexico's Silver Towns

High in the Sierra Madres, western Mexico's silver cities are as impressive for their urbanity as Copper Canyon is for its physical beauty. Lying 200 miles (320 km) northwest of Mexico City, the towns of Querétaro, Zacatecas, San Luis Potosí, San Miguel de Allende, and Guanajuato are colonial-era time capsules celebrated for their food, artisanal crafters, and welcoming climate. The towns, with their narrow, cobblestoned streets, retain most of the Spanish colonial architecture of the 1500s. Each town has a similar but different assortment of plazas, churches, municipal buildings, and historic neighborhoods. **Querétaro** is known for its monuments, numbering more than 1,000. **San Miguel de Allende**, probably the most famous, is full of expat Americans. **San Luis Potosí**, a university town, has a variety of noteworthy museums and plazas. **Guanajuato** hosts the **Museo de las Momias**, or Mummy Museum, which displays a number of mummified former townspeople. **Zacatecas** is celebrated for its ornate 17th-century cathedral with a stone facade resembling lace.

For a River Cruise Dotted With Islands

Thousand Islands,
New York, U.S.A., and Ontario, Canada

Instead of the Rhine or Danube Rivers, Europe

A handful of the Thousand Islands have waterfront cottages.

float down Europe's Rhine or Danube River, drifting past fairy-tale castles and picturesque villages, is the dream river cruise. These cruises can be expensive, however, with prices often starting at more than $2,000 per person. For those who want to find comparable inspiration for less cost or who simply want to explore an underappreciated corner of North America, the St. Lawrence River offers a similar opportunity to cruise past pastoral countryside and a passel of castles.

Stretching from Lake Ontario to Lake Champlain, and marking the border between New York State and Ontario, Canada, the St. Lawrence River contains some 1,800 islands scattered across the water like puzzle pieces. They are befitting of the title Thousand Islands, ranging in size from islets no larger than a backyard shed to one that's 40 square miles (105 km²). A St. Lawrence tour offers constantly changing scenery on both sides of the border, with miles of parklike riverbanks, forests, and fields, and dotted with villages along the way.

Most boats depart from the towns of **Clayton** and **Alexandria Bay** on the New York side, or **Rockport** in Ontario. The nearby **Thousand Islands Bridge** connects the United States and Canada via **Wellesley Island, New York**. These are half-day or leisurely daylong cruises, offering different themes. Tours include wildlife- and bird-watching, vintage speedboat rides

With deciduous trees changing their colors, autumn is the ideal time to visit Boldt Castle.

OPPOSITE: Camp right next to the St. Lawrence River in Thousand Islands National Park.

from Clayton's **Antique Boat Museum**, and even a visit to the sunken ships in the St. Lawrence's channels. The most popular trips are those that wind through the islands with stops at various castles and the river's famous 1848 **Rock Island Lighthouse**.

The St. Lawrence River castles were built at the turn of the 20th century by wealthy industrialists inspired by romantic visions of Europe. Set mostly on the river's islands, the castles mimic the turrets and spires from across the pond. None more so than **Boldt Castle**, a 120-room edifice that was the dream of hotel tycoon George Boldt, who commissioned the six-story building for his wife, Louise. Louise died in 1904 before its completion, and a heartbroken George halted construction. Restored now, Boldt's dream home is open to visitors. So, too, is the 28-room **Singer Castle**. The mansion and its five-story clock tower were inspired by the abodes of Scottish lairds and built by a CEO of the Singer sewing machine company. The castle contains hidden passageways. There's also a "royal" suite that sleeps six and is available for overnight stays for those lucky enough to secure a reservation. Other lodgings can be found on **Millionaires' Row**, a collection of Victorian-era mansions and cottages dotting the islands. **Thousand Island Hart House**, on Wellesley Island, is now an antiques-filled bed-and-breakfast featuring eight rooms with private decks. Island campsites are available at various parks including Canada's **Thousand Islands National Park** as well as New York's **Canoe-Picnic Point**, **Cedar Island**, and **Mary Island State Parks**.

Travelers can also navigate the river by car, driving the National Scenic Byways **Great Lakes Seaway Trail**, which skirts the St. Lawrence. The trip starts at Sackets Harbor, on Lake Ontario, and heads north, past Ogdensburg, New York, site of the **Frederic Remington Art Museum**, which features works by the Old West artist. The byway ends near Massena, New York.

New Zealand's Bay of Islands

On the other side of the world and a hemisphere south of the St. Lawrence islands lies another cluster of islands worth putting on your bucket list. Just off the coast of New Zealand's North Island between Cape Brett and the Purerua Peninsula, and a three-hour drive from Auckland, lies the Bay of Islands. The archipelago of 144 islands is famous for its subtropical climate, excellent fishing, unspoiled beaches, and pretty towns, including the old whaling port of Russell, the country's first capital.

The region has strong links to Native Maori culture and history. One of the country's most significant sites lies here: the **Waitangi Treaty Grounds**, where New Zealand's founding documents were signed. They established the country's multicultural heritage and affirmed Maori rights to forests, fisheries, and other resources. The agreement also became the basis for future redress of grievances. Here you can also see the world's largest Maori ceremonial war canoe and take in a cultural performance.

From the towns of **Paihia**, **Kerikeri**, and **Opua** travelers can book a kayak or boat to explore the shore and stop for a swim or picnic on islands such as twin-lagooned **Motuarohia** or **Urupukapuka**, which, at 514 acres (208 ha), is the largest in the Bay of Islands. Other activities include reef diving (marine life includes dolphins, marlins, whales, and penguins) and hiking. Overnight camping is also available on Urupukapuka Island.

For a Retro American Drive
Highway 90, Texas, U.S.A.

Instead of Route 66, Illinois to California, U.S.A.

On your trip down Highway 90, see an old windmill and yucca plants outside the Judge Roy Bean Visitor Center in Langtry.

Part declaration of independence, part joyride, a pedal-to-the-metal western road trip is a quintessentially American adventure—offering anyone the opportunity to experience the continent's vastness while following in the footsteps of explorers from Sacagawea to Jack Kerouac. Though the "Mother Road" for all such wanderers is Route 66, which "winds from Chicago to L.A.," according to the song, there are other less traveled but equally memorable drives to make. One of the most exhilarating is the stretch of Highway 90 from San Antonio to the Lone Star State's arid mountains and Big Bend National Park. Don't get all your kicks on Route 66; try driving Highway 90 through Far West Texas.

Opened in 1927, Highway 90 originates in Jacksonville, Florida, and heads west through the Deep South, skirting the Gulf Coast. Christened the Old Spanish Trail by regional boosters eager to attract tourist dollars, the highway was planned to reach California and the Pacific Ocean but only made it to Van Horn, Texas. Nevertheless, it attracted plenty of drivers, who patronized its souvenir stands, small restaurants, and motor courts, the latter a precursor to the modern motel. By the 1960s the newly built Interstate 10 had diverted most of the traffic to the freeway, but the romance stayed on 90.

Begin the trip in San Antonio, Texas. Highway 90 continues west, not far above the Rio Grande. The road offers heady spectacles with sightings of roadrunners, pronghorns, and javelinas among the agaves and ocotillos. And the sky-sweeping vistas of western Texas dazzle the eye and imagination.

Highlights of this road trip include **Hondo**, a town with a speeding sign warning "This is God's Country. Please don't drive like hell through it." Outside **Del Rio** the dizzyingly tall **Pecos High Bridge** spans its name-

Pick up fresh baked goods at Judy's Bread & Breakfast in downtown Alpine.

sake river. Highway 90 hits **Langtry**, home of legendary frontier justice dispenser Judge Roy Bean, followed by the town of Sanderson. However, the biggest draws of the far horizon are the three small towns of Marathon, Alpine, and Marfa in the mountainous regions near Big Bend National Park. Dotted with working ranches and vacation retreats, the area is becoming known as "Austin's sandbox." Like an island archipelago, the outposts are linked but distinct in attitude and architecture. All three feature historic hotels designed by the same pioneering architect, Henry Trost.

Marfa has been the most glamorous of the bunch since its landmark county courthouse became the model for Liz Taylor and Rock Hudson's mansion in the 1955 epic Western *Giant*. Later Marfa became the site of modern minimalist artist Donald Judd's **Chinati Foundation**, an artists' retreat that has since transformed the town into a bohemian playground for hipsters and wealthy techies. Two noted attractions include a roadside viewing area for the **Marfa lights**, a mysterious and sporadic nighttime phenomenon akin to St. Elmo's fire, and the **Prada Marfa** store, a conceptual art piece commenting on class and consumerism, erected west of town and Instagram bait for social media influencers. **Alpine** avoids sculptures and $400 hoodies, preferring work jeans and real cowboys, who are often seen buying canned goods at **Porter's**, the local supermarket. The biggest town in Far West Texas, Alpine is celebrated for **Kokernot Field**, a miniature version of Chicago's Wrigley Field built by a wealthy rancher in the 1950s to attract a minor league baseball team and now a beloved landmark. **Marathon** is the smallest of the three, but it is the self-proclaimed gateway to **Big Bend National Park** and its spectacular Chisos Mountains.

Roadside Attractions

In 1905 Toledo native Henry C. Trost (1860–1933) and his twin brother, Gustavus, opened their architectural firm, Trost & Trost, in El Paso, Texas. They equipped the growing cities and towns of Texas, Arizona, and New Mexico with schools and office towers, but especially with hotels celebrated for their flourishes, frequent use of colorful tile, and ironwork in the Spanish Colonial Revival and Mission Revival styles. The three Trost & Trost hotels in Marfa, Alpine, and Marathon remain the architects' most evocative, welcoming dusty travelers off Highway 90 eager to connect with the spirit of the Old West. The **Holland Hotel** (1928), previously a private residence, in Alpine is a popular draw following its sale by legendary owner Carla McFarland. The outspoken proprietor used to vacuum the hallways and 27 rooms wearing a tiara. Marfa's 41-room **Hotel Paisano** (1930) is filled with photographs of the cast and crew of *Giant* including James Dean, who stayed (or played) there during filming. The **Gage Hotel** (1927) serves as a social center for Marathon and features casitas and a pool.

For White Water Rafting
Ocoee River, Tennessee, U.S.A.

Instead of Snake River, Idaho, U.S.A.

The Ocoee Whitewater Center featured the first ever Olympic rafting competition on a naturally occurring river during the 1996 Atlanta Games.

The western region of the United States, with its many free-running rivers, is considered the center of white water rafting. Waterways like Idaho's Snake River and the Colorado River in Utah and Arizona draw visitors eager to experience an exhilarating ride. But there is another worthwhile rafting experience, this one in the Southern Appalachians in eastern Tennessee, just a few hours' drive from burgeoning cities like Nashville and Atlanta. If heading west seems a reach, consider grabbing an oar and paddling down the Ocoee River. It's a heart-pounding trip in some of the prettiest, greenest mountains anywhere.

The Ocoee River and its surrounding watershed have played a significant role in Cherokee history. A treaty signed between the Cherokee Nation and the United States government in the 1830s established the Ocoee as part of the boundary between Cherokee lands and those ceded to the United States. The treaty marked the beginning of a series of land cessions that would lead to the forced displacement of the Cherokee and other Indigenous peoples. That displacement, affecting more than 60,000 people, became known as the Trail of Tears.

"Ocoee" is a Cherokee word for apricot vine, aka purple passionflower, and the 93-mile-long (150 km) river's secret is that although it's a real river, its flow is regulated by the Tennessee Valley Authority (TVA), a government-run flood control and electrification project that maintains a series of hydroelectric plants and three dams across Tennessee and adjoining states. Thanks to its dams and flumes, the TVA can turn the Ocoee's water on and off like a faucet. When it's set to "on" the Ocoee's rapids run with the best of them, rated a Class III river, with Class IV rapids appearing throughout the year. Don't be fooled: Class III rapids can give pad-

Book a white water rafting trip down the Ocoee River in Cherokee National Forest.

dlers quite a ride—the Ocoee served as the location for the white water slalom events during the 1996 Olympics in Atlanta.

Excursions on the river are mostly half-day affairs, with no overnight or multiday trips needed. All floats down the Ocoee are accompanied by an outfitter's trained guide, or "river rat," and rafters must be at least 12 years old to join the fun. For families with younger children, the **Hiwassee River** in nearby **Cherokee National Forest** offers plenty of other recreational activities like canoeing, hiking, and fishing. Most Ocoee trips are done on the river's middle section, which features runs up to five miles (8 km) in length and navigates larger rapids with such colorful names as Cat's Pajamas, Diamond Splitter, Gonzo Shoals, and Hell Hole. The last one is rated Class IV.

The white water season on the Ocoee runs from March through October, with the summer months being the most popular time to go. From Memorial Day to Labor Day, the river runs every day except Tuesdays and Wednesdays (when water is redirected to the TVA flumes and power plants). Occasionally, strong rains may also close the river to rafting. Because of the river's popularity, advance reservations are highly encouraged by visiting TimeToRaft.com, a directory with links to all 23 licensed and active river outfitters. Outfitters provide parking; their buses pick up riders from the endpoint on the river and take them back to their vehicles.

After that, dry towels and a change of clothes will be in demand. So might food, and travelers can find several dining options in nearby Cleveland, Tennessee, celebrated for its "hot slaw," a spicy coleslaw that uses a mix of mustard and chili peppers. Afterward, visit the **Hiwassee River Heritage Center** to learn more about the importance of the region, its Indigenous Cherokee peoples, and its role in the Civil War.

The Chat Show

Known in the 20th century for the signature swing-era ditty "Chattanooga Choo Choo," the Tennessee River city (population 182,000) transformed itself in the 21st century from a lagging and rusty factory town into a tech and green industry leader. There's a railroad station hotel and attraction devoted to the famous 1941 Glenn Miller hit, but Chattanooga is now focused on its riverfront visitor attractions. Chattanooga's worth a stop to stroll its award-winning 13-mile-long (21 km) **Riverwalk** and the busy downtown it connects. Begin your explorations along the Tennessee in **Blue Goose Hollow**, the downtown neighborhood where blues queen Bessie Smith was raised. The nearby **Bessie Smith Cultural Center** is a touchstone for Chattanooga's African American community and honors the Jazz Age singer's contribution to the nation's musical legacy.

Need your own wheels? Rent a blue city bike share bike and follow the Lookout Mountain trail up to bluffs overlooking the city, with views up and down the Tennessee River. The 650-mile-long (1,050 km) Tennessee powers one of the world's largest hydroelectric systems. Take a breather at the **Hunter Museum of American Art** or bike over the river via the **Walnut Street Bridge** to enjoy some commanding panoramas of Chattanooga and the mountains of the Cumberland Plateau. Other sites include the **Tennessee Aquarium**, riverside **Coolidge Park**, and the **Creative Discovery Museum**, a well-regarded children's museum.

For an Eastern Mountain Adventure

Great Allegheny Passage, Maryland to Pennsylvania, U.S.A.

Instead of Appalachian Trail, Georgia to Maine, U.S.A.

An aerial view of Harpers Ferry, West Virginia, from Maryland Heights, an overlook above the town

For dedicated trekkers, walking some or all of the Appalachian Trail is a rite of passage. The 2,200-mile-long (3,540 km) hike marches up the East Coast, stretching from Georgia's Spring Mountain to Mount Katahdin in Maine. But for anyone intimidated by the length, time, and endurance required to hike the entirety of the Appalachian Trail (requiring an average of five to seven months), the Great Allegheny Passage (GAP) connecting Washington, D.C., to Pittsburgh might be a better fit. A hiking and biking trail running across three states, the GAP is another eastern mountain adventure and better for those without unlimited time. It can even be accomplished on bicycle in a week.

The GAP stretches from the fountain in downtown Pittsburgh's **Point State Park**, where the Allegheny and Monongahela Rivers meet, and continues east to Cumberland, Maryland, where the trail links up with the **Chesapeake and Ohio (C&O) Canal Towpath**. The route totals 335 miles (540 km) and ends in Washington, D.C. The key to the trail's appeal is that it is relatively flat with little elevation. Created out of abandoned railroad lines, the GAP has less than a 2 percent grade anywhere between Cumberland and Pittsburgh, making it a perfect trail for steady pedalers who can average up to 60 miles (97 km) a day on a bike.

The GAP Conservancy (the official trail organization) suggests either six- or nine-day trip itineraries, which allow plenty of time to explore the parks and towns along the way. Heading west from Washington, cyclists will start on the C&O as it follows the Potomac River north, go past the rush at the river's Great Falls, and then overnight in a series of trail towns spread about a

Travel 335 miles (540 km) from Pittsburgh to Washington, D.C., on the Great Allegheny Passage (GAP).

day's cycle apart. The first is **Harpers Ferry**, a West Virginia town at the confluence of the Shenandoah and Potomac Rivers. Next is **Hancock**, a precolonial trading post where George Washington once stayed. Busy **Cumberland**, Maryland, marks the C&O Canal's end and the official beginning of the GAP. You'll pass the **Cumberland Bone Cave**, named by workers in 1912 who discovered skeletons of Pleistocene-era saber-toothed cats and cave bears. They're now on display at the **Smithsonian National Museum of Natural History** in Washington. **Rockwood**, at the foot of 3,212-foot-tall (979 m) Mount Davis, Pennsylvania's highest peak, is a 25-minute drive from the **Flight 93 National Memorial**, which honors the air passengers of Flight 93 who died in the September 11, 2001, terrorist attacks. **Connellsville**, an old coal-mining town, has a tribute to its World War II–era canteen that honors 800 local women who served meals to troops passing through on the B&O Railroad.

While B&Bs are located in most of the towns cyclists will pass through, the C&O Canal Trust's innovative **Canal Quarters** project allows travelers to sleep in many of the historic lockhouse properties along the route. Try staying at **Lockhouse 10**, the circa 1830 building with furnishings reflecting the Works Progress Administration (WPA) restoration of the canal in the 1930s. **Lockhouse 49** in Clear Spring, Maryland, near the West Virginia state line, evokes a small canalside community from the 1920s.

While many bicyclists will take their gear with them, those who want to avoid lugging their stuff will be happy to discover that shuttle services can deliver bags from one overnight stop to the next. Once cyclists reach the end of their journey at either point, Amtrak's Capitol Limited train service will return them and their bikes to their starting point.

One Trail, Four Parks

The tristate Great Allegheny Passage begins and ends in two great U.S. cities, with a number of historic towns and more than 1,000 notable structures in between. Its route also passes through or near four worthwhile parks including **Rock Creek Park** in Washington, D.C. Created in 1890 it is small, at 1,754 acres (710 ha), and contains biking trails, colonial-era buildings, Civil War fortifications, a working mill, stables, and even a planetarium. The **Chesapeake & Ohio Canal** tracks the Potomac River for 184.5 miles (297 km) and once connected the Ohio River Valley to the East Coast. The canal operated from 1831 to 1924 and was later acquired by the National Park Service. It was established as a park on January 8, 1971. **Antietam National Battlefield** is adjacent to the C&O Canal Towpath and was the site of the bloodiest battle in the Civil War. On September 17, 1862, within the space of 12 hours, more than 23,000 Union and Confederate soldiers were killed, wounded, or went missing. Farther on, find **Harpers Ferry National Historical Park** at the site of John Brown's 1859 raid on a U.S. armory, which helped push the nation into civil war.

The posh *Queen Mary 2* cruise ship carries travelers on a trans-atlantic voyage.

For a European Crossing

Cunard's *Queen Mary 2*

Instead of a transcontinental flight

Dine in one of the 11 restaurants aboard the *Queen Mary 2*, such as the opulent Britannia Restaurant, pictured here.

OPPOSITE: Book a roomy twin cabin with a balcony.

The miseries of modern air travel are such that an opportunity to exchange a cramped seat on a Europe-bound jet for an ocean liner steaming in the same direction no longer seems like an extravagance but rather a legitimate alternative. Swapping security lines and crowded terminal gates for a transatlantic stateroom might be travel's equivalent of going from digital music to vinyl LPs. The trip isn't fast, but it is gratifying: seven days of fresh air, ocean views, and no jet lag with a journey that's an adventure in itself. Consider trading a Boeing for a boat the next time you're crossing the pond.

Cunard, the venerable British shipping line now owned by Carnival Corporation & plc, operates the last remaining ocean liner with regularly scheduled sailings between New York and Great Britain. The *Queen Mary 2* (pronouns she/her) was built for that reason in 2004. The ship and her crew of 1,250 can serve up to 2,691 passengers. She's impressive, rising to the height of a 23-story building. In fact, the *QM2*'s size was such that her builders needed to ensure the ship would clear the underside of New York's Verrazzano-Narrows Bridge.

The *QM2* makes 20 crossings (or 10 round-trips) between April and December (spring usually sees her depart on a world cruise, stopping in places like Dubai, Cape Town, and Hong Kong). She departs from her berth in Brooklyn and sails to Southampton, the English port where disembarking passengers board London-bound trains. Fares, which include meals and entertainment, begin at $1,200 one-way, on par with airlines' business class seats or even some in premium economy. Prices head north from there: One can book a two-story, apartment-like stateroom for $25,000 per person.

For the budget-minded, a freighter or a cargo ship crossing is worth investigating. These industrial ships, piled high with shipping containers, cross every five weeks with prices of about $140 a day to ride along. **Slowtravel**, a German company specializing in such ships, does bookings. Also on offer: masted sailing ships and South Pacific island-hopping mail ships.

Whatever the cost, what passengers get for their money is a return to leisurely travel. Before the 1960s this was how most people journeyed between the United States and Europe. A week at sea afforded the time to develop friendships or even a romance. Such opportunities still exist, but there are far more activities than shuffleboard and a deck stroll today. Borrowing from cruise holidays, the *QM2* features 11 restaurants, bars and lounges, modern fitness facilities, and a spa, as well as a planetarium, a library (including 200 audiobooks), lecture halls, and a kennel for dogs and cats. Some passengers opt to use the onboard Wi-Fi to work from sea rather than work from home, which may attract even more would-be travelers like director Wes Anderson, who used the crossing for collaboration with some of his colleagues for his film *Isle of Dogs*.

Southampton and New York aren't the *QM2*'s only destinations on the Atlantic run. Depending on the trip there may be additional stops in Cherbourg-en-Cotentin, France; Hamburg, Germany; and Halifax, Nova Scotia, Canada. Unlike on cruise ships, with their circuitous voyages of pleasure-seekers, transatlantic passengers travel with a purpose, and that intent changes the onboard mood.

Carrying Baggage

Like the lumbering *Brachiosaurus*, the seafaring luggage known as the steamer trunk has vanished from Earth. Named for their favorite habitat—the steamships that once crossed the oceans in large numbers—the trunks' extinction wasn't caused by a gigantic meteor but by the jet engine, which displaced commodious staterooms and cargo holds with jammed overhead compartments.

The stately luggage saw its heyday between the late 19th and early 20th centuries, when travel often took days. Previous evolutions included the Saratoga trunk, or, in the 1850s, the Jenny Lind trunk, named for a superstar Swedish singer who toured constantly. (One might call her the Taylor Swift of her day.) Constructed first out of pine and later from metal, and covered with canvas or leather, the steamer trunk featured bumpered edges to protect from jostling and padlocks to protect from thieves. Variations included hat trunks, popular with Edwardian ladies for storing elaborate headgear, and wardrobe trunks designed to be stood on end to hold voluminous dresses or an array of gentlemen's suits.

Most firms making steamer trunks died with them. Two that survived: Denver-based **Shwayder Trunk Company**, which eventually became the global brand called **Samsonite**, and French luxury leather goods maker **Louis Vuitton**, which still makes its own version of a steamer trunk, now carrying a retail price of more than $46,000.

Street vendors sell baskets, flowers, and produce at a market in Oaxaca.

For a Foodie Paradise
Oaxaca, Mexico

Instead of Burgundy, France

Learn how to roast ingredients for red mole at El Sabor Zapoteco, a cooking school in Teotitlán del Valle, near Oaxaca.

French cuisine is celebrated far and wide, and hungry foodies plot regular pilgrimages to rustic regions like Burgundy to sample a timeless food tradition that produces famous wines and dishes like coq au vin and beef bourguignon. But there are other places in the world as magically delicious, to paraphrase a cereal-loving leprechaun. One such region travelers might want to put on their menu is the state of Oaxaca in Mexico.

With 16 recognized Indigenous groups, including the Zapotec and Mixtec, the subtropical state is a fusion of taste and diversity that finds its way into saucepans and onto dinner plates. Oaxaca's enticing recipes such as *mole*, *tlayudas* (akin to street pizzas), and *tejate* (a maize and cacao drink) are increasingly popular worldwide, but there's nothing like making a pilgrimage to where they originated. An education might begin in the food markets of **Oaxaca de Juárez**, or simply Oaxaca, the state capital in the Sierra Madre foothills. A UNESCO World Heritage site, the city's center is celebrated for its colonial architecture, with many of its buildings erected using the region's native green stone. Its markets are a treat for the senses, offering visitors stall after stall of local gastronomy. The famous **Mercado 20 de Noviembre** is filled with vendors selling chilies of every sort and temperature, soups, and traditional prepared foods. Navigate the **Pasillo de Humo**, or Smoke Aisle, where the smell and sizzle of grilling meats will make any mouth water. A short walk away, **Mercado Benito Juárez** sells local specialties, meats, fish, cheeses, flowers, and even grasshoppers, as well as handicrafts like *alebrijes*—small, brightly painted fantastical animals carved out of wood. The Oaxacan capital also contains a number of cooking schools, where travelers can try their hand at sourcing and making classic but simple Oaxacan recipes such as shrimp or cactus tamales, squash blossom–filled quesadillas, and chicken with black mole sauce. Rural Oaxaca offers a kaleidoscope of tastes as well; it is a place to eat simply and well while doing a deeper dive into the surrounding landscape. Look for food stands or roadside restaurants dishing up delicacies such as *tamales Oaxaqueños* and *memelas*—fried or toasted corn cakes with fresh toppings.

While Burgundy is known for its vintage wines, Oaxaca is becoming famous for its mezcal. The capital features a number of *mezcalerias*, or tasting rooms, with many of them clustered within walking distance of downtown. The potent spirit is made from the agave plant, and the diversity of Oaxacan agave means distilleries produce a startling array of flavors. Try them in the local watering holes or at the many rooftop bars. Those who desire a deeper dive into mezcal and its production can tour distilleries and agave farms in the countryside.

Adventurers who want to combine hiking with good eats might enjoy the **Copalita Trail**, a five-day walk from the mountains of the Oaxacan Sierras to the Pacific coast. The guided journey sends hikers beyond the paved-road network and into nine remote Zapotec villages, where farmers make and share their meals. A chartered bus from Oaxaca City brings guests deep into the Sierra Madres. Over the next five days hikers descend through thick pine forests, past coffee and bamboo plantations, and into jungles before floating down the Río Copalita in rafts to the gold sand

beaches in Santa María Huatulco, on Oaxaca's Pacific coast. The trail's organizer, the Autonomous Group for Environmental Research, is a Oaxacan nonprofit that brings sustainable tourism to the isolated communities and returns 70 percent of its profits to participating villagers.

A donkey moves a stone wheel to grind agave as part of the mezcal distillation process.

Mexico City's Food Scene

In recent years, Mexico City's culinary riches have turned the capital into a required reservation for gourmands the world over, thanks to its wide and diverse offerings. "People from all over the country come to live in Mexico City, and bring their diverse cuisine with them," says travel journalist Bruce Wallin, who roams across Mexico with his family. "Whether it's plated in a fancy restaurant or handed to you from a street cart vendor, Mexico City's food is celebrated for its inventiveness." **La Merced Market**, with its range of traditional foods, is a good starting place for any eating tour. Local fare starts with corn and beans; the combination of *maís* and *frijoles* formed the basis for the ancient Aztec diet. The Spanish introduced their own foods, like beef and dairy, and later immigrants from China to Germany added their own flavors. Today new chefs compete in upscale neighborhoods like **Colonia Roma** to fuse Mexican tastes with international influences from New Delhi to New York. For most locals, the best food is found in neighborhood cantinas or taquerias, where an endless variety of tacos is on offer alongside sweet treats like churros.

For a Monumental Coastal Road Trip

Highway 101, Oregon, U.S.A.

Instead of Highway 1, California, U.S.A.

The western edge of Neahkahnie Mountain offers scenic views of Oregon's coastline.

Cannon Beach's dramatic Haystack Rock protrudes from the Pacific Ocean.

OPPOSITE: Sea stars cling to a rock in a tide pool at Cannon Beach.

When it comes to road trips, California's famed Highway 1, the Pacific Coast Highway (or PCH), is the seaside route everyone "must" do. But the fabled road is not the only scenic route along the Pacific coast. Look farther north: Highway 101 along Oregon's coast is another beautiful drive. Sometimes called the "People's Coast" for an innovative state law granting the public access to every inch of its Pacific shoreline, the 363-mile-long (584 km) journey features numerous pullouts, parks, and beaches to explore, plus picturesque seaside towns.

Technically one could do Oregon's 101 in a full day, but why? Wilder and less populated than California, Oregon's coast is a place to be savored. Four days seems the optimum number for exploring its coves and crannies. Depending on which way you come (let's assume from Portland), the journey starts in Astoria and heads south toward California. First stops: **Fort Stevens State Park** to see where the Columbia River meets the Pacific, or **Fort Clatsop**, where Lewis and Clark wintered. Continuing south, you traverse forests and cliffs to **Cannon Beach**, a town full of artisans, boutiques, galleries, and a view of iconic landmark Haystack Rock and its tidal pools. Farther on, **Tillamook Bay** offers opportunities for fishing, kayaking, and cheesemongering. The region is known for its cheddar, and the **Tillamook Creamery**, a farmer-owned cooperative, offers a cheesemaking tour.

Continuing south, drivers encounter the 240-foot-tall (75 m) sand dune at **Cape Kiwanda**—a challenge to anyone ambitious enough to try to climb to its peak. At nearby **Cascade Head Preserve** hike into and explore old-growth forests. With so many trees so close to the water, Oregon's Pacific shores can sometimes be dangerous, as big swells (aka "sneaker waves") can send the occasional downed tree tumbling onto the beach. Two more great places to explore are the 1871-era wooden lighthouse at **Yaquina Bay** in Newport and the tidal pools at **Otter Rock**, though the only opportunity to watch sea otters is actually in the **Oregon Coast Aquarium**. Hunted to extinction in the state, they have yet to be successfully reintroduced. For the chance to see marine life in the wild, get a view of the Steller sea lions that congregate at the **Sea Lion Caves** in Florence. Find a comfortable place for a snooze at the **Heceta Lighthouse B&B**; the historic residence of the former lighthouse keeper dates from 1894.

Entering **Oregon Dunes National Recreation Area**, the landscape becomes Saharan. For a 40-square-mile (105 km²) stretch to Coos Bay, the Oregon coast is essentially a dune-filled sandbox, punctuated with lakes and refuges of the Pacific Northwest's Roosevelt elk, plus foodies, who come to the southern Oregon coast to hunt for delicious wild mushrooms. Farther inland, vehicles are permitted around **Umpqua**, and a dune buggy tour is a favorite pastime. Others might prefer hiking through its vast stretches of sand, which inspired Frank Herbert's 1965 novel *Dune*.

The fishing port of **Coos Bay** is a safe harbor for Oregon's clamming and crabbing fleets. Driving south toward California, you'll pass temperate forests of redwoods and Sitka spruce, and a scenic 12-mile-long (19 km) coastal park, the **Samuel H. Boardman State Scenic Corridor**, dotted with sea stacks (tall, narrow islands) and scenic overlooks. The **Tu Tu' Tun Lodge** offers a rustic overnight experience along the Rogue River.

For a Fiery Finale to Summer

Zozobra, Santa Fe, New Mexico, U.S.A.

Instead of Burning Man, Black Rock Desert, Nevada, U.S.A.

Old Man Gloom, aka Zozobra, towers above festivalgoers before he ignites in flame, burning away the worries and fears of the Santa Fe revelers.

Each Labor Day in the arid heart of the American Southwest a communal event unfolds that astounds its attendees with eye-widening displays of artistic expression. It all culminates in a pyrotechnic blaze with the burning of a towering effigy. You might be forgiven if you conjure up Burning Man and its RVs filled with mushroom-tripping computer engineers and their ilk done up in body paint. But this end-of-summer holiday celebration assembles in Santa Fe, New Mexico, not the northern Nevada desert. Marking a century in 2024, the Zozobra festival rivals the better known technopalooza with its vibrant atmosphere, communal spirit, and transformative finale of fire.

Surface similarities aside, the family-friendly Zozobra (no nudity here) holds its own distinctive charms. Unlike Burning Man, Zozobra is deeply rooted in a historic town with deep Mexican and Native American cultural roots, though its birth was midwifed by Jazz Age bohemians. Zozobra was born in 1924 when Pennsylvania transplant and artist Will Shuster, a contemporary of Georgia O'Keeffe drawn to Santa Fe in the 1920s along with scores of painters and writers, constructed the first effigy. Influenced by Mexican and Native American traditions and myths, Shuster wanted to create a totemic figure that symbolized those communities' fears and worries (*zozobra* means "anxiousness" or "stress" in Spanish) and then set fire to it—literally sending the residents' collective fears up in smoke.

Held annually ever since, the Zozobra has evolved over the decades. The now 50-foot-tall (15 m) marionette, constructed of wire, wood, and cloth, has become an integral part of Santa Fe's identity, and its burning marks the unofficial start of the **Fiesta de Santa Fé**, the city's annual celebration of art, culture, and heritage.

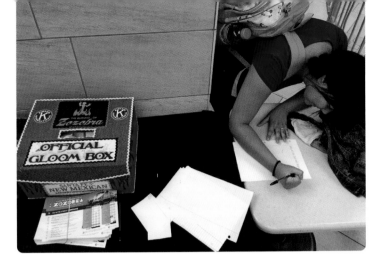

A festival participant writes down her fears and stresses to be placed inside the Zozobra effigy.

First celebrated in 1712 to commemorate the Spanish resettlement of Santa Fe, the fiesta is one of the oldest such gatherings in the country.

In the weeks before Zozobra's burning, residents write down their fears and sad thoughts on paper and drop them into boxes scattered across town. These are then collected and stuffed inside the giant puppet, making additional fuel for the conflagration. Sometimes people consign other unlucky totems like mortgage papers, hospital gowns, speeding tickets, and divorce decrees to the flames.

Nestled in the Sangre de Cristo Mountains, **Santa Fe** proves a stunning natural backdrop for the outdoor event and its fiery climax. A member of the UNESCO Creative Cities Network since 2005, Santa Fe has long honored artistry and creativity as a backbone of its culture. The festival's music, dance performances, and storytelling underscore this rich artistic tradition. By twilight on the day of the burn some 60,000 people converge on **Fort Marcy Park**, a five-minute drive from Santa Fe Plaza. They pass the time consuming refreshments or tossing beach balls while Zozobra raises his arms and growls at the crowd. As night falls, Zozobra's nemesis, the dancing Fire Spirit, appears. Armed with two torches, the figure proceeds to ignite the flammable giant to chants from the crowd of "Burn him!" Old Man Gloom, as Zozobra is often called, goes up in a blaze of flame and pyrotechnics.

While both Zozobra and Burning Man foster a sense of community, Zozobra's atmosphere appeals to both children and adults. Locals participate and run the festivities, giving everyone a role to play in this colorful tradition. Combining a rich heritage with such a collaborative and creative event, it is an authentic experience deeply intertwined with Santa Fe's identity. In a world of extraordinary celebrations, Zozobra shines brightly. Burn on.

A Global Burn

Burning Man's annual event isn't the only place to find a gathering of creativity, community, and radical self-expression. Sure, the famous fest garners the most press, but scattered across the globe are numerous other annual get-togethers that exude a similar countercultural vibe. In Europe look at northeastern Spain's **Nowhere festival**, held each July in remote Castejón de Monegros near Zaragoza. The intimate celebration has participants construct an ephemeral city replete with art installations, workshops, and musical performances. For something a little more humid, Costa Rica's week-long **Envision Festival**, usually held in March in the jungle of coastal Uvita, is an oasis of music and community. Adventure seekers might want to jet to South Africa for the annual **AfrikaBurn**, which unfolds in late April in Tankwa Karoo National Park. The inclusive festival is a mix of costumery, theme camps, and "mutant vehicles" (shades of *Mad Max*). Like Burning Man, all of these festivals advertise art, music, and creativity as transformative powers for goodwill and understanding.

For a Sailing Adventure

Eastern Indonesia

Instead of the Turkish Coast

Explore the healthy coral reefs of Raja Ampat in Indonesia's West Papua Province.

Enjoying a leisurely cruise with friends and family as you sail past exotic shores is a dream of many travelers. Most imagine such a trip unfolding in the eastern Mediterranean along the Turkish coast, perhaps, or the Greek islands. Yet there's a little-known region that beckons with the same idyllic promise, set in a far more exotic locale. Dream instead of navigating the islands and shores of eastern Indonesia. With more than 17,000 islands, Indonesia offers an endless variety of shipboard adventures to contemplate. In fact, increasing numbers of charter companies now offer passage on well-appointed boats that sail to places like Komodo National Park (home of the endangered and celebrated dragons) and the Spice Islands.

The **Raja Ampat archipelago** is a collection of 1,500 impossibly photogenic islands cloaked in jungles and flung like emeralds off western New Guinea's Bird's Head Peninsula in Indonesia's West Papua Province. Raja Ampat means "four kings," and the islands are certainly grand, set off by azure waters ringed with coral reefs where schools of tropical fish mass in such numbers that the Switzerland-size archipelago has become a prime destination for divers and snorkelers.

Just 88 miles (142 km) north of Raja Ampat, the **Wayag Islands** are celebrated for their beauty and remoteness. On shore, travelers can watch a sunset while soaking up some of the islands' cultural rhythms in a homestay in a traditional bungalow.

Local villagers pass a forest of palm trees on Halmahera Island in the Malukus.

OPPOSITE: A male Wilson's bird-of-paradise performs an elaborate display during mating season.

Komodo National Park is already famous. Its islands (there are three major ones, including Komodo Island, and 29 altogether) are, of course, home to some 3,380 "dragons," whose prehistoric looks and shambling ferocity have made the reptiles both fearsome and fascinating. The endangered dragons can grow up to 10 feet (3 m) in length and weigh up to 150 pounds (70 kg). They can be aggressive, they hunt in packs, and their bite is toxic, but they remain objects of wonder and living examples of evolution found nowhere else on Earth. A lure for scientists and travelers alike, the rugged and dry islands are protected by their national park status. With idyllic sandy beaches and cerulean surf, scuba diving and snorkeling off the islands' reefs are prime Komodo activities; bird-watching is another. But it's the dragons that remain the draw, and travelers will need an experienced guide to see them safely.

Once called the Spice Islands—made famous in medieval Europe for the fortunes people paid for their nutmeg, cloves, and peppercorns—today the **Malukus** (or Moluccas) offer visitors both history and scenery. The islands, comprising north, middle, and southern clusters, are located in Indonesia's northeast, between New Guinea and Sulawesi. They were the first places in the region to greet European sailors in 1519. Many of them still sport the ruins of fortresses built by adventuring Portuguese and Dutch entrepreneurs who gave up Manhattan for the chance to gain control of the lucrative spice trade. The northern Malukus, with their rainforests, are a growing ecotourism destination and contain two national parks. Diving and snorkeling are also growing in popularity, especially in the **Banda Islands**, the original source of nutmeg, as well as the islands of **Ambon** and **Ternate**.

Such unusual destinations give cruises a sense of real adventure. Indonesia's many islands offer an unequaled opportunity to roam a part of the world few travelers know but more are going to discover in the future.

Phinisi Ships

Cruising the islands of Indonesia is a thrilling experience for most travelers. It is even more adventurous when passengers clamber aboard traditional sailing ships called *phinisi*, or *pinisi*. Like Arabia's iconic oceangoing crafts, dhows, these twin-masted, seven-sail iconic vessels feature a design more or less unchanged since local sailors began using them to transport goods from Burma to Australia 200 years ago in an age when seafarers' fleets were powered by wind.

Originating in the 19th century, phinisi were adapted from the designs of traditional Bugis-Makassar vessels and more modern European and American ships to fit the needs of Indonesians and were perfected by the famed boatbuilders of Sulawesi, members of the Bugis ethnic group. Today phinisi are most likely to carry upscale tourists eager to explore the untamed coasts of eastern Indonesia's islands. Now shipbuilders are busy turning out phinisi for the carriage trade, creating vessels with all sorts of previously unknown creature comforts, such as room for Jet Ski docks, en suite cabins, air-conditioning, coffee machines, and fruit juicers. These days, it's not unusual for such vessels to feature a crew of 10 or more, including butlers, a master scuba instructor, and a chef—plus a captain, of course. Costs start at about $3,500 a day and spiral upward from there. But given the allure of eastern Indonesia's sapphire seas and jade-colored islands, for many eager sailors the price is a bargain.

For Beachy Southern Fun

The Space Coast, Florida, U.S.A.

Instead of Myrtle Beach, South Carolina, U.S.A.

The highly acclaimed Kennedy Space Center invites visitors to learn about space exploration.

Kayak past giraffes on the Expedition Africa kayaking tour at Melbourne's Brevard Zoo.

Parents debating a week with the kids in a seaside resort like Myrtle Beach, South Carolina, might want to reroute to Florida's Space Coast. Awarded its title because it serves as the location of NASA's rocket launches and the Kennedy Space Center Visitor Complex, the Space Coast possesses just the right combination of sun, sea, and, dare we say it, "educational" attractions.

The Space Coast is edifying, but you'd be hard-pressed to say it is boring, as it possesses a slice of all-American roadside exuberance. Cape Canaveral's **Golf N Gator** proclaims itself "so much more than Putt-Putt!" And there's **Cocoa Beach**, a quintessential, loud American shore town. But beyond the typical fried food and flip-flops, this stretch of Florida's Atlantic coast has a host of state and national parks, quirky museums, and cultural attractions.

Such attractions include the **White Sands Buddhist Center** in Mims, one of the biggest Buddhist sanctuaries in the United States. The contemplative 31-acre (13 ha) retreat with a temple and a teahouse features three gigantic white granite statues of the Buddha. In nearby Titusville, places of interest include the **Warbird Air Museum** and its collection of rare fighter jets and propeller planes, and the **American Space Museum**, staffed and put together by former employees of the country's space effort with material salvaged from everywhere, including NASA dumpster bins.

Of course, the Space Coast's biggest draw is the **Kennedy Space Center**, a Disney-style park with themed rides, shows, and science exhibits about the Saturn V rocket, space shuttles, Mars missions, and those all-American heroes—astronauts. It's all an IMAX-scale bustling tribute to America's space agency. A day spent here is a memorable one. Time your visit right, and you might witness a rocket launch or meet a living, breathing astronaut in the flesh.

In contrast, the only sound you hear at the **Merritt Island National Wildlife Refuge** is birdsong. Located northwest of the Kennedy complex on the same 35-mile-long (56 km) barrier island, the refuge is filled with subtropical plants and 500 species of animals including otters, endangered Florida scrub jays, and, of course, alligators. Look for one or two sunning themselves in the lagoon directly adjacent to the visitors center. There are six hiking trails in the refuge, but the seven-mile-long (11 km) **Black Point Wildlife Drive** serves as a good introduction to both the landscape and animals. **Cape Canaveral National Seashore** is accessible at Playalinda Beach down the road from the Merritt Island visitors center.

Anyone looking for more exotic animal sightings should try kayaking through the **Brevard Zoo**, Melbourne's spunky zoological garden. What it lacks in size it makes up for with enthusiastic staffers and keepers. Guides lead kayakers into the African exhibits, where paddlers can watch giraffes, rhinos, and lemurs from an entirely different angle. Come sundown there are all sorts of two-legged wildlife drinking destinations in **downtown Melbourne**, a walkable collection of mostly casual restaurants and bars along **East New Haven Avenue**. A few minutes north is the **Eau Gallie Arts District**, known for its antiquing and wall murals.

Come bedtime there's no shortage of hotels on the Space Coast. Cocoa Beach's retro **Beachside Hotel & Suites** is designed for families, with a fun serpentine pool and in-room kitchenettes. On the other end of the spectrum, the **Hotel Melby** is an upscale retreat in downtown Melbourne with a rooftop patio bar and restaurant incorporating terrific views.

Titusville's Warbird Air Museum showcases retired warplanes.

The Moores of Mims

Martin Luther King, Jr., helped inaugurate and lead the modern American civil rights movement, but before him came earlier crusaders who fought equally hard for justice and equality. Like King, they frequently paid for it with their lives. The Space Coast's **Harry T. & Harriette V. Moore Cultural Complex** in Mims, Florida, is an inspired testament to two Mims public school teachers, a husband and wife who taught in the small Brevard County segregated schools from 1926 to 1946. Harry organized the first NAACP chapter in the county in 1934. Together the Moores battled the racism of the day only to be murdered when Ku Klux Klan terrorists planted a bomb beneath their home on December 25, 1951. Harry died in the blast. Harriet died from her injuries nine days later. The future Supreme Court justice Thurgood Marshall spoke at their funeral. The museum and a re-creation of their bungalow home recounts the fight for civil rights in Florida and outlines the life and times of these two heroes.

An expressive mural outside a gallery in North Park, San Diego
(page 316)

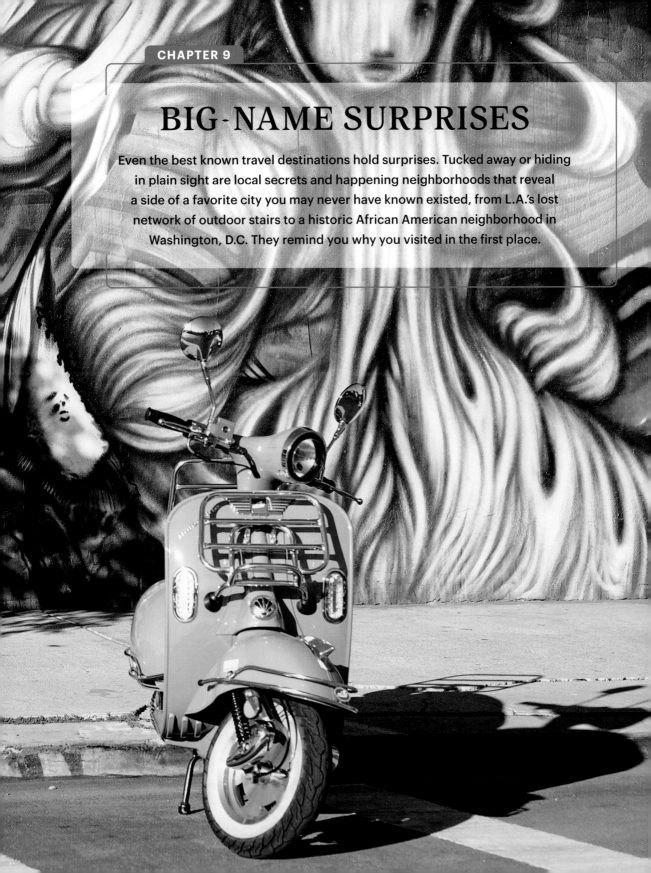

CHAPTER 9

BIG-NAME SURPRISES

Even the best known travel destinations hold surprises. Tucked away or hiding in plain sight are local secrets and happening neighborhoods that reveal a side of a favorite city you may never have known existed, from L.A.'s lost network of outdoor stairs to a historic African American neighborhood in Washington, D.C. They remind you why you visited in the first place.

For a Local Mardi Gras

Bywater and the Marigny, New Orleans, Louisiana, U.S.A.

"The Angry Mermaid" float travels down a street in the 'tit Rəx parade, one of New Orleans' wackier celebrations.

New Orleans' Mardi Gras is a party for the ages, but many visitors find Bourbon Street's focus on beer, beads, and body parts anything but family friendly. A far more personable version, one even kids can enjoy, unfolds approximately two weeks before Fat Tuesday (the calendar differs every year) in the picturesque and historic neighborhoods of Bywater and the Marigny (aka Faubourg Marigny), downriver from the French Quarter. Join New Orleanians to cheer whimsical sci-fi cosplayers and watch the world's tiniest floats roll through residential streets. These parades feel homemade and accessible and are much the better for it. An added bonus: They take place on streets graced with some of the best examples of the city's vernacular architecture—from Creole cottages to colorful shotgun houses.

Why are Carnival parades marching well before Fat Tuesday? It helps to understand that Mardi Gras is not actually just a four-day weekend party but rather a celebration that goes for weeks. It begins on January 6, the Feast of the Epiphany, and continues through the stroke of midnight on Ash Wednesday. The season feels like a second Christmas. New Orleans and the rest of southern Louisiana festoon homes and offices with flags and bunting in the trademark yellow, green, and purple and ready themselves for the merrymaking. While the biggest and most crowded parades conclude in downtown New Orleans near Bourbon Street, the city hosts a string of smaller, mostly weekend parades organized by marching groups called "krewes." These more intimate celebrations allow spectators a chance to get close to the participants who, as tradition allows, hand out small trinkets,

An army of Princess Leias, known as the Leijorettes, honors Carrie Fisher during the Chewbacchus Princess Leia Tribute Parade.

known as "throws." The two quirkiest parades are organized by the krewes of 'tit Rəx and Chewbacchus. Though the pandemic scrambled schedules, these two events are usually held on the same evening or close to it.

The first to "roll" (a New Orleans term for a parade in progress) is the krewe of **'tit Rəx**. The *tit* is short for "petite," and a clue to the organization's raison d'être. Each member must create a float no bigger than a shoebox to be hand-pulled through the streets of the **Marigny**. The little floats, often festooned with fairy lights, can be quite elaborate, usually using whimsical themes or making an observation on a current event. Many feature toys like stuffed animals or dolls. (Barbies have graced more than a few of them.) Along the route 'tit Rəx members hand out tiny, handmade throws, which can include thumbnail-size comic books, miniature lapel pins, or buttons.

With approximately 900 members, the **Intergalactic Krewe Chewbacchus** is a larger, noisier bunch. As the name implies, many of its costumes have been inspired by the Star Wars films, but homages to other sci-fi movies and TV shows appear, too. Some have become crowd favorites, like the drill squad of white-gowned Princess Leias, most sporting a space gun and Carrie Fisher's trademark Danish pastry hairdo. Chewbacchus is a green krewe and uses no internal combustion engines. Instead, floats are pulled by bicycles or pushed by hand. Marching through streets crammed with brightly painted homes, to the delight of the residents lining their porches, these two krewes hark back to an earlier time when Mardi Gras magic was local and could be celebrated from one's own stoop. These two parades exude that spirit of enchantment. Visitors will no doubt experience some of that happy New Orleans spirit as well.

Hotels Made for History

The past is everywhere in New Orleans, and that often includes your hotel room. The romantic **Hotel Peter & Paul**, located near the Marigny parade routes, is housed in a former 19th-century domed Catholic church, convent, and rectory and furnished in an airy European style. It offers 59 rooms as well as a bar and restaurant. Opened in 2021, the 75-room **Hotel Saint Vincent** is housed in a former 1861 orphanage reimagined as a hip retreat replete with a courtyard pool and plenty of outdoor spaces. Located on Magazine Street in a historic neighborhood of the Lower Garden District just below Coliseum Square, the Saint Vincent offers visitors a taste of what it's like to live and work in the historic city. For those who prefer the 1960s, the **Four Seasons Hotel New Orleans** opened in the city's former World Trade Center, built in 1967 by celebrated modernist architect Edward Durell Stone along the Mississippi in the Central Business District. Sleek rooms with river views and cool jazz in the lobby cocktail bar give a stylish twist to the skyscraper.

Ben's Chili Bowl is an iconic D.C. institution and played a role in the civil rights movement.

For Capital History
Shaw, Washington, D.C., U.S.A.

Instead of the National Mall, Washington, D.C., U.S.A.

Designer Pierre Charles L'Enfant—and the politicians and planning commissions that followed—built Washington, D.C., to impress. And they succeeded. The landmarks fringing that runway of fescue and Kentucky bluegrass called the National Mall are both grand and grandiose. Washington probably has more pillared piles per acre than London, more marble than Carrera, and beneath the Capitol dome, more hot air than Mauna Loa. But the District possesses a more human side. To experience it consider a visit to Shaw, a vibrant residential neighborhood north of D.C.'s traditional tourist spots. Its slender brick town houses flank tree-shaded streets and broad avenues populated by boutiques. Of-the-moment restaurants belie its centrality to African American history and its key role in the capital's political and cultural life.

Depending on how you define it—either by school district boundaries, historic preservation districts, or local opinion—Shaw begins at the city's **Convention Center** north of M Street. Its eastern border is Sixth Street. Its western one includes **Logan Circle** and trendy **14th Street** up to **Florida Avenue**, encompassing the **U Street Corridor**, the former Black Broadway and home to famous eatery **Ben's Chili Bowl**. The neighborhood is named after a junior high school that was itself named for Robert Gould Shaw, the white Massachusetts colonel of an all-Black Civil War regiment. Shaw (the

Try the grilled branzino, beef bourguignon, or warm shrimp salad at the celebrated Le Diplomate.

OPPOSITE: The African American Civil War Memorial commemorates the service of the more than 200,000 Black soldiers who served in the Civil War.

neighborhood) was where freed African Americans settled during and after the Civil War, finding jobs and building a new life. Many clustered in alleys where houses squeezed between liveries, grocers, and artisanal businesses. The varied, unplanned buildings gave Shaw an individualistic feel that's still evident in places like **Blagden Alley**, now filled with bars and restaurants with outdoor tables spilling onto the bricked alley itself.

African American history is everywhere, from the statue of Howard University dean **Carter G. Woodson**, the "father of Black history," to **Benjamin Banneker High School**, named for a Black colonial astronomer and mathematician who helped survey land for the new capital. Near the school is a **skatepark** that has been known to host Tony Hawk on occasion. The house at **1800 11th Street** once served as the headquarters of the *Afro-American*, a weekly newspaper founded in 1892. A stone's throw away are the **Whitelaw Hotel**, one of the first Black-owned hotels in the United States (now an apartment complex), and the **Lincoln Congregational Temple United Church of Christ**, where Martin Luther King, Jr.'s March on Washington was staged.

But these are only a few examples. Volunteer guides or private tour guides will walk visitors around the neighborhood and provide a deeper insight into Shaw's history. Discover more by googling "Historic U Street Walking Tour" or "History Through Street Art: Shaw and U Street Tour." As for where to stay, there are many short-term rentals available. **The Viceroy** on Rhode Island Avenue is a bright 178-room property with an outdoor patio and a fire pit for those who like hotels.

Fourteenth and U Streets stay busy late into the night. People cluster in bars sipping not inexpensive wines, catch a play at the **Studio Theatre**, or head into thumping music clubs. Perhaps the most well-known 14th Street establishment is **Le Diplomat** bistro. "Le Dip" serves presidents, Supreme Court justices, and senators the same *steak frites* the locals enjoy.

U Street

Shaw native Duke Ellington (who lived on 13th Street) found fame singing about the A Train to Harlem. But U Street in Washington, D.C., had a stronger hold on him, as well as dozens of other African American performers, during its heyday as the "Black Broadway" from the 1920s through the 1950s.

Black owned and operated, the music clubs, restaurants, and bars that lined U Street during the era of Jim Crow and segregation made it a world unto itself. An entertainment destination and a mecca of popular culture for an educated middle class who had transformed the surrounding neighborhood into a center for Black art, education, and intellectual debate, U Street was the liveliest corridor in a city known more for its bureaucracy than its nightlife. It drew an ever changing roster of stars including Cab Calloway, Sarah Vaughan, Billie Holiday, and Louis Armstrong. They performed at storied theaters such as the **Lincoln** and the **Howard**, both of which still showcase a variety of live performances today.

A decline after the 1968 riots, following the assassination of Martin Luther King, Jr., occurred before U Street's fortunes rose again with redevelopment beginning in the early 2000s. A Friday or Saturday night is likely to see crowded sidewalks and lines for dozens of restaurants and the surrounding rooftop bars, and a proposed redevelopment project would bring an outdoor amphitheater and a variety of arts and performance spaces to the neighborhood.

For More Than Beaches
San Diego's Inland, California, U.S.A.

Sun-kissed and knowing it, San Diego and a string of neighboring coastal communities such as Encinitas, La Jolla, and Del Mar deliver the classic California holiday of sandy beaches, fish tacos, and tan lines. But while the surf may be at the ocean, travelers shouldn't overlook San Diego's inland neighborhoods. They're percolating with diverse residents, farmers markets, boutiques, bistros, and bookstores. The lively atmosphere and buzzy streets make them worth exploring. Here are three neighborhoods to check out when you hit town.

Cut off from San Diego Bay by Naval Base San Diego, **Barrio Logan** is a primarily Latino working-class community shaped by the same aspirations that created modern California. Beginning in the early part of the 20th century, many Mexican Americans flocked to the area between Logan Hill and the bay to work in the canneries and shipyards that lined the waterfront. Decades later, development proved dangerous to the neighborhood's health. Interstate 5 created dislocations, and then a bridge to Coronado Island cut Barrio Logan in two, leaving a literal shadow on the community. The resilient residents reclaimed their neighborhood by creating **Chicano Park**. Its brilliantly hued and expressive murals are painted on the pillars supporting the freeway above. The colorful paintings both celebrate Chicano culture and welcome visitors of every background. More about the community is on display at the new **Chicano Park Museum and Cultural Center**. The neighborhood, especially along **Logan Boulevard**, is filled with small stores. It remains fairly quiet during the week, but the street comes to life on weekends as locals and out-of-towners arrive to frequent the coffeehouses, bookstores, and clothing boutiques; meet friends; and

San Diego's vibrant North Park neighborhood is known for its pubs and bars, such as the West Coast Tavern.

Under the San Diego–Coronado Bay Bridge, vibrant murals decorate Chicano Park.

inspect the goods from vendors who set up stalls to sell Mexican fashions, horchata drinks, and street food.

North Park lies, as its name implies, just north of Balboa Park, San Diego's favorite playground. Visitors usually head to **University Avenue** with its rich offerings of antiques, artisanal baked goods, breweries, and restaurants (from vegan to carnivore), along with several taquerias that have perfected the handheld and turned it into a gourmand's fast food. On Thursdays a farmers market sets up on North Park Way behind University Avenue that's a Californiacopia of fruits and produce—from eight different kinds of sprouts, organic citrus, and berries sparkling like jewels to vegetables of every description.

North Park is also home to the eccentric **Lafayette Hotel and Club**, a 1946 four-story colonial property on El Cajon Boulevard set around an Olympic-size pool, accessible to hotel guests as well as visitors (via a day pass). It can be a good base for independent travelers interested in exploring San Diego proper.

Just west of North Park is **Hillcrest**, the center of San Diego's LGBTQIA+ community. It's a colorful neighborhood, and a social one. The Hillcrest business association claims it invented the concept of "Sunday Funday," and to prove it Hillcrest's patio brunches are boisterous ones. The blocks along Hillcrest's University Avenue are filled with bars and brunch spots, with plenty of outdoor seating for people-watching. There's always something to see, especially on weekend nights when the bars and dance clubs go full tilt. But there's more to Hillcrest than parties. The neighborhood itself is worth walking around for a glimpse of historic California bungalows and adobe revivals, along with modern apartment buildings. Sunday's **Hillcrest Farmers Market** attracts shoppers from throughout the city to sample snacks, prepared foods, and produce from 175 vendors.

Balboa Park

Balboa Park is to San Diego what Central Park is to New York City: a front lawn, back patio, and playground all rolled into one. Located just south of the North Park and Hillcrest neighborhoods, the 1,200-acre (485 ha) park claims to be the largest cultural park in North America, with 17 museums and performance spaces, including some unique ones like the outdoor **Spreckels Organ Pavilion**, built for the 1915 Panama-California Exhibition that marked San Diego's arrival on the national stage. Many of the park's cultural institutions, including the **Fleet Science Center**, **Museum of Us**, and **San Diego Museum of Art**, are housed in ornate Spanish Colonial Revival pavilions from the 1915 fair. The park's gardens, including the **Japanese Friendship Garden**, are backdrops for quinceañera parties and scooter-riding hipsters. Balboa Park is also host to the new **Comic-Con Museum**, a 64,000-square-foot (5,945 m²) complement to the annual pop culture convention held in the city. Cosplaying fans might compete with the famous **San Diego Zoo** as Balboa's most popular attraction.

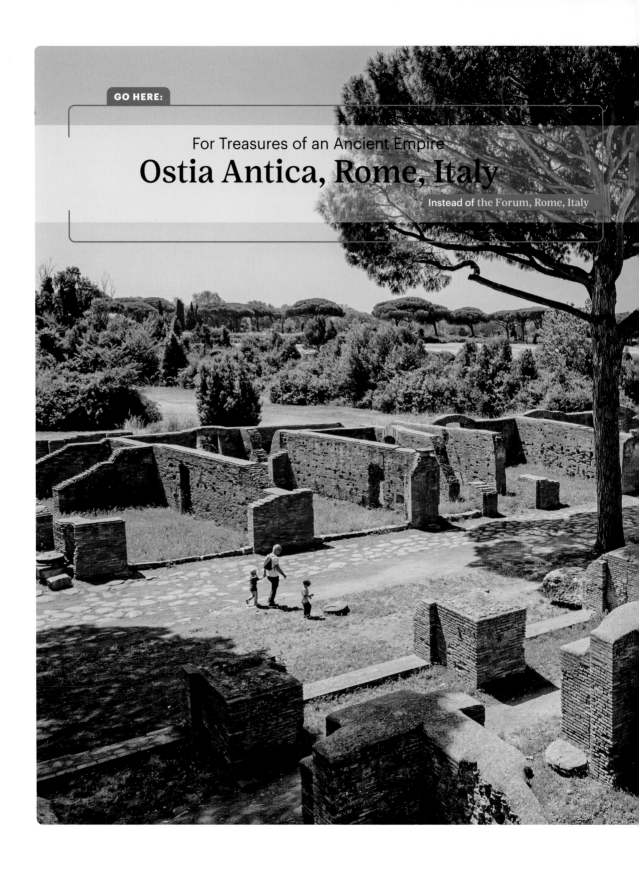

For Treasures of an Ancient Empire

Ostia Antica, Rome, Italy

Instead of the Forum, Rome, Italy

Ostia Antica, one of the best preserved ancient Roman cities, sees fewer tourists than other archaeological sites in Italy.

Explore an old theater to learn about ancient Rome's gladiator shows.

OPPOSITE: A black-and-white mosaic depicts grain measurers.

Tourists have flocked to Rome to see its sites since the days of Julius Caesar. But it's rarely been as crowded as today. Since the pandemic abated, the sidewalks on the Via dei Fori Imperiali, the wide Mussolini-era boulevard slicing through the ancient Forum to the Colosseum, have been mobbed with locals as well as tourists, counterfeit handbag sellers, and "Despacito"-playing buskers. Attempting to dodge and weave through the crush can seem like a battle worthy of *Gladiator*. But just 35 minutes and a three-dollar train ride away in the city's suburbs lies an often overlooked archaeological site displaying some of the best preserved ruins in Rome with far fewer people standing between you and history.

Located on the coast near Rome-Fiumicino Leonardo da Vinci International Airport are the ruins of Ostia Antica. In antiquity the city of 60,000 people functioned as the port of Rome. It was here that all the imported grain, wine, olive oil, marble, and luxury goods arrived to be transported up the Tiber to the capital. It was also a departure point, as Fiumicino Airport is today, where Caesars and plebeians alike boarded boats for journeys across the empire. When Rome declined and the Tiber changed course, Ostia was gradually abandoned and then ignored, leaving behind the temples, baths, mansions, and warehouses as both its graveyard and its memorial.

"Ostia is the place to see how ordinary Romans lived and worked," says classical archaeologist and author Darius Arya. "The city gives you more of a sense of daily life than the Roman Forum, which was built as a statement of imperial grandeur. And unlike Pompeii, which has Greek and Etruscan roots, Ostia is totally Roman, having been founded and built when Rome was already a growing power. To understand how real people lived during the imperial period, Ostia is the place to see."

Devoid of huge crowds, Ostia allows visitors to wander its ruins at will, exploring and entering many of the buildings on their own time. "It's like a treasure hunt," Arya says. A series of trading offices fringe the **Piazzale delle Corporazioni**. Fronting each one is a black-and-white mosaic illustrating the leaseholder's particular occupation: A measuring device proclaims an authorized grain dealer. An elephant indicates either an ivory or exotic animal importer, important given the demand for African animals to feed the games in the Colosseum. There are **26 bathhouses** in Ostia, many decorated with black-and-white mosaics with aquatic themes. Stairs take you up a multistory **apartment complex**, called an *insula*, for an overview of the town. (In an age without elevators the poorest tenants lived on the highest stories. Richer ones lived on the second floor.) There are even remains of Roman communal toilets. Look for the ones that can be sat upon, which never fail to amuse children (and some adults).

Ostia is accessible from Rome's Piramide train station and reachable from the city center via the Rome Metro or taxi. Piramide, named for a well-preserved pyramid, is actually an ancient tomb located across the street from Rome's ancient Aurelian Wall. Both landmarks are worth a look as well.

The (Early) Rise of Rome

The waits and lines to visit Rome's famous sites, ranging from St. Peter's Basilica and nearby Vatican museums to the Pantheon and the Colosseum, can defeat even the most patient visitor. But there's an easier solution for early risers in the Eternal City. If you get up and out of the hotel by 7 or 7:30 a.m., an early morning stroll through Rome's narrow streets will be both peaceful and crowd free. You'll be sharing your stroll not with tourists from Peoria or Busan but actual Romans walking their dogs, sweeping the streets, or getting a head start to the office.

"Morning is the time when you can easily see Rome's great sites free of crowds," says Isabella Calidonna, a Rome tour guide. "Plus the morning light is wonderful for pictures." Her company, **Archeo-Running**, leads private groups on early morning runs or walks through Rome's historic core. "To take advantage of the morning in Rome, stay right in the city's center, where you'll be steps away from the best sights. It's more expensive, but the convenience is unbeatable," says Calidonna. And you're guaranteed to find an empty café seat to enjoy a morning cappuccino.

Two hotel splurges in central Rome are the luxurious **Hotel Maalot**, just a squirt away from the Trevi Fountain; and the cozy, elegant **Hotel Vilòn**, tucked away behind the famed Borghese Palace. Both offer a quiet retreat from the tourists besieging Rome like the Hunnish hordes.

For the Unexpected

Parthenon,
Nashville, Tennessee, U.S.A.

Instead of Music Row, Nashville, Tennessee, U.S.A.

Nashville is Music City, and true to that sobriquet, Tennessee's capital sports legions of honky-tonks, breweries, and concert auditoriums where the hits just keep on coming (along with bachelor and bachelorette parties). But in an era before Garth Brooks or even Hank Williams, Nashville had an earlier nickname. Once called the Athens of the South, the city aspired to be a tasteful and learned metropolis. So much so that its inhabitants built an exact duplicate of the Greek capital's most famous landmark atop the Acropolis. Though it symbolizes Nashville's own glory, not Greece's, the world's only full-scale replica of the Parthenon is a fascinating landmark, and an unexpected, if unmusical, attraction in this tune-crazy town.

Set in Nashville's newly renovated **Centennial Park**, the Parthenon owes its creation to that most American of all enterprises: public relations. In 1897 a consortium of railroads and city business boosters eager to promote themselves and Nashville organized a grand fair, the Tennessee Centennial Exposition, to celebrate the city. Its main attraction was a wood-and-plaster replica of the Greek behemoth, and Nashvillians took to it immediately. After the fair closed, the re-creation stood for another 23 years before its rickety architectural details began to flake and crumble off. "In 1920 it was time to fish or cut bait," says Parthenon curator Wesley Paige. So the city erected a permanent replacement out of honey-colored aggregate concrete. Construction took 10 years, roughly the same number of years it took the ancient Athenians to build the original—and to the exact dimensions, too.

Built in 1897, Nashville's Parthenon is a full-size replica of the Greek original.

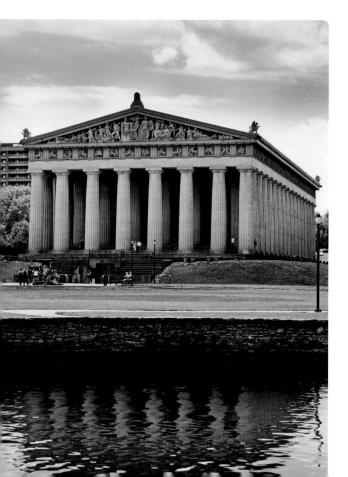

The Country Music Hall of Fame and Museum celebrates the history of the genre and its dazzling superstars.

Today, more than 65 feet (20 m) high at its apex, the temple has 46 Doric columns that create inviting shade for picnickers. On a recent Sunday afternoon Fisk University students posed for sorority pictures while children played hide-and-seek and enamored visitors lined up at the building's base to enter the three art galleries located on the structure's ground floor. The first holds a permanent collection of American painters, with works by Winslow Homer, Frederic Church, and Benjamin West. The others showcase changing exhibits. But the real treat is the rest of the building's vast interior, ruled by a 43-foot-tall (13 m) sculpture of the classical Greek goddess Athena. Created by Alan LeQuire, it took until 1990 to raise the money to install it. As gilded as an Oscar and shod in platform sandals, the gold Athena sports a pair of lips allegedly modeled after Elvis Presley's. The ancient deity even attracts the occasional modern pagan or two. People will sometimes leave offerings of flowers, maybe a container of Whole Foods olives, or dance and pray to the icon, says Paige.

Still, no trip to Nashville is complete without visiting the city's other, more musical, goddesses. Pay your respects along South Broadway at the **Patsy Cline Museum**, a country-and-western reliquary displaying the singer's costumes, highball glasses, and pine-paneled TV room removed completely intact from her Winchester, Virginia, home. Take a selfie with a bust of Dolly Parton 12 stories up on the patio of the Graduate Hotel's **White Limozeen** sky bar or genuflect in front of Ella Fitzgerald's leopard-skin coat in the **National Museum of African American Music**. Close your eyes at the **Country Music Hall of Fame** and conjure Minnie Pearl in her flowery straw hat with the dangling price tag yodeling her trademark "How-deee" to fans and acolytes. In Nashville, the goddesses come in all sizes, shapes, and octaves.

Triangulation Strategy

Nashville's not the only Tennessee town to copy a building from antiquity. Memphis, Tennessee, not only took the name of pharaonic Egypt's ancient capital for itself but also built its own 321-foot-tall (98 m) glass-sided pyramid as a downtown arena for musical acts and local sports teams, notably pro basketball's Memphis Grizzlies.

This, however, was Memphis's second go with a triangle. In 1897 city leaders constructed a wooden pyramid as a pavilion for the Tennessee Centennial Exposition. It stood alongside Nashville's Parthenon until the fair closed. Then, in 1991, local entrepreneur John Tigrett opened his new pyramid near the Mississippi River.

Despite hosting bands like the Rolling Stones and Phish, the Memphis Pyramid struggled to find both a purpose and a profit. After the Grizzlies abandoned it for the new FedExForum in 2004, locals began calling it the "Tomb of Doom." It found new life in 2015 as a Bass Pro Shops outlet. The sporting goods retailer now has a hotel, the **Big Cypress Lodge**, there.

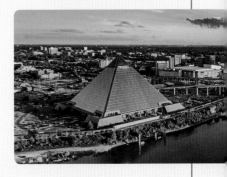

Charleston's International African American Museum is located on the hallowed ground of Gadsden's Wharf.

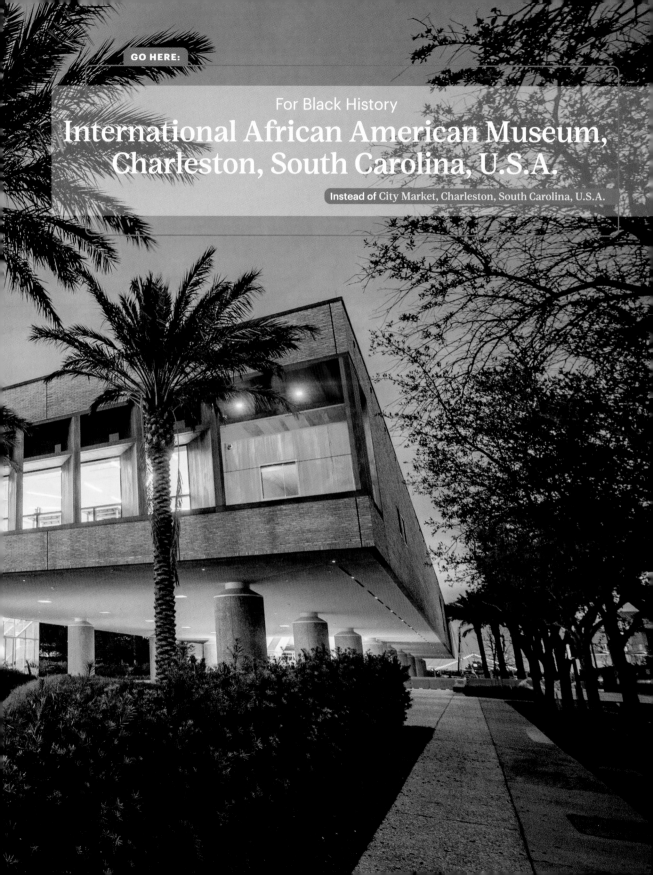

For Black History

International African American Museum, Charleston, South Carolina, U.S.A.

Instead of City Market, Charleston, South Carolina, U.S.A.

An exhibit displays Demond Melancon's "Jah Defender," a Mardi Gras suit that portrays Black Maskers, carnival revelers who wear costumes influenced by Native American ceremonial apparel.

OPPOSITE: Stone vertical monuments in the museum's courtyard date back to and are representative of prehistory.

Few cities enchant more than Charleston, South Carolina. Set shimmering on a peninsula lying between the Ashley and Cooper Rivers, the historic South Carolina port played key roles in colonial and antebellum America. But following the Confederacy's 1865 defeat in the Civil War, the city and its port took on a quieter role in U.S. history. That is, until the turn of the 21st century, when it came back on the map, ready to welcome an era of high-end tourism and culinary travel. Today Charleston is celebrated for its restaurants and an affluent allure epitomized by Lower King Street's expensive boutiques and the restored mansions along the city's legendary Battery. But visitors need to look deeper at Charleston to discover a city hidden in plain sight. They'll find one conceived, built, and energized by an African American community that was forced to the Holy City in chains only to birth a vibrant culture. Experience the real Charleston, not the one the T-shirt slogans hawk to cruise passengers in City Market, in a fascinating, if fraught, history that comes together at the new International African American Museum.

Opened in 2023 and built fronting **Charleston Harbor** on the abandoned ruins of Gadsden's Wharf, where enslaved Africans were marched ashore, the museum is part pilgrimage, part educational institution, part genealogical center, and a memorial to the people who died making the Middle Passage between Africa and the colonies.

The museum itself is raised on pillars above what is now considered a hallowed place. On the ground a line demarcates the original wharf, while around it are gardens and artist interpretations of the horrors of the slave trade. There's also a memorial to some 800 individuals who froze to death while detained in unheated cells during the winter of 1807–08.

Inside exhibits trace the 17th-century origins of the slave trade and its insidious tentacles, which stretched across the Atlantic. Other galleries document Africans' impact on the city and the United States. Some recount enslaved people's artistic contributions, which helped shape a rising American culture, including spaces devoted to the Gullah-Geechee people who, even now, live along the coast from the Carolinas to Florida. As South Carolina's biggest port, Charleston received huge numbers of human beings kidnapped and transported from their African homelands. The displays make use of the latest digital and interactive technologies to present an immersive experience of their stories, told with sound, images, and video, as well as moving and rare artifacts.

Visitors will encounter an extraordinary opportunity to delve into their own ancestries at the museum's **Center for Family History**. Historians estimate 49 percent of Black families, including that of former first lady Michelle Obama, can trace an ancestor back to Charleston's slave markets. To help interested visitors fill in their family trees, the center enlists the help of skilled genealogists and computer databases drawing from a host of resources, such as records from the transatlantic slave trade, plantation records, obituaries, and family bibles.

The International African American Museum may not provide a comforting view of Charleston's past, but it is a vital and affirming place for anyone interested in understanding the real history of one of the country's most popular cities.

Grit in the Grits

Charleston is rightly known as a culinary mecca, but what is not always realized by visitors is that the roots of some of the city's most iconic dishes can be traced back to the enslaved people who brought their own food cultures from Africa to the Americas. In the 18th and 19th centuries, great Charleston chefs like Eliza Seymour Lee, Nat Fuller, and pastry chef Tom Tully were African Americans. The resourcefulness and creativity of such chefs, along with their own cultural influences, fused with those from other immigrants to produce dishes like Low Country *pirlou* (a tasty rice pilaf) and barbecue, as well as regional crops such as Bradford watermelons and Carolina gold rice.

Shrimp and grits is a Holy City specialty. The traditional morning meal of stone-ground corn has been associated with Charleston's African American community since the days of enslavement. Grits were cheap and could feed a family, while shrimp, a valuable protein, could be easily gathered. Today the dish occupies a central place on restaurant menus from south of Broad Street to the top of King. And like the city's famous cluster of colorful Georgian town houses on aptly named Rainbow Row, the whole grain is polychromatic. Frequently made with heirloom corn, grits can come to the table in hues of pink, blue, red, yellow, or white. Each is different, and no one can imagine Charleston without its grits.

For a Wine-Tasting Adventure
The North Fork, New York, U.S.A.

Instead of the South Fork, New York, U.S.A.

Built in 1857, the Horton Point Lighthouse on the North Fork of Long Island is one of eight historic lighthouses in Southold.

New York State's Long Island stretches from Brooklyn to Montauk, a distance of 118 miles (190 km). Like a pair of scissors, at its eastern end the island splits into two blades becoming the North and South Forks, with Shelter Island and Peconic Bay as the watery landmarks in between. Until now, most travelers arriving at the literal fork in the road headed for the South Fork—flocking to the glitzy beach towns along the Atlantic collectively known as the Hamptons. Summer sets the region a-sizzle. Between Memorial Day and Labor Day the Atlantic shoreline fills with thousands of party-hungry Manhattanites competing for eye-watering hotel rates and $61 shots of Johnnie Walker. For travelers coming to New York City and curious about exploring eastern Long Island but not its frenzied social scene, choose the North Fork for a bucolic and slower pace.

The North Fork borders Long Island Sound, the great marine and tidal estuary that faces Connecticut and stretches for some 30 miles (48 km) from the town of Riverhead to Orient Point (where travelers can reach New London, Connecticut, via ferry and not the dreaded Interstate 95). The region cultivates a rural, agricultural feel. Its roads are lined with more than 100 active farms and farm stands, and even lavender fields, like those in Lavender by the Bay in East Marion. Considered one of the wine industry's most promising regions, the North Fork now supports more than 60 wineries, with an output that regularly wins both praise and awards. Such laudatory buzz around the North Fork's wines only increased as pandemic restrictions eased. More than three dozen tasting rooms now compete for visitor attention. New labels like **Rose Hill Vineyards** and **Lenz Winery**, as well as older ones, are seeing increased traffic as people arrive to sample the

Croteaux Vineyards in Southold is one of 60 wineries in the North Fork area.

vintages. The North Fork is further known for its oysters and scallops, particularly those harvested from Peconic Bay; Peconic scallops are considered a particular delicacy.

Drinking and eating aren't the North Fork's only diversions. There are cultural sites as well. In Southold, the town's **Historical Museum** comprises more than a dozen structures that showcase life on Long Island in the 19th century, when it was famous more for potatoes and oats than stylish resort communities. Riverhead's art deco movie palace, **The Suffolk**, has been refashioned into a cabaret-style theater with performances ranging from a cappella singing groups to rock and jazz. **Landcraft Gardens** in Mattituck showcases the region's wildflowers and is also a living laboratory for the 17-acre (7 ha) foundation's extensive plant collections.

There are outdoor recreational opportunities, too. The North Fork has excellent parks like **Wildwood State Park** on Long Island Sound; **Orient Beach State Park** fronts Gardiner's Bay at the tip of the fork. The North Fork is also the departure point to secluded **Shelter Island**, accessible by a 10-minute ferry ride from Greenport to Shelter Island Heights. The island is wooded and largely undeveloped, with more than one-third of it owned by the Nature Conservancy. Case in point, the organization's 2,350-acre (950 ha) **Mashomack Preserve** offers great hiking and kayaking opportunities.

The North Fork's lights are not as bright as those in the Hamptons, but for those who savor the good life, as defined by slow food and short sips, it's a great satisfaction. As Karl Kurka, an eastern Long Island native observed, "Discovering the North Fork is like finding fresh lobster at the Stop & Shop for $13 a pound instead of the $35 in East Hampton. You feel like you got a bargain."

The Finger Lakes

There's another underappreciated Empire State destination that should make any traveler's list—the Finger Lakes region located in upstate New York in a triangle between Rochester, Syracuse, and Elmira. These long and narrow lakes (Canadice, Cayuga, Canandaigua, Conesus, Hemlock, Honeoye, Keuka, Otisco, Owasco, Seneca, and Skaneateles) are not only beautiful but also productive, with a climate that makes them central to New York's winemaking industry. Many of the lakes feature wine trails showcasing local vineyards and tasting rooms. The region is also home to well-preserved 19th-century towns that contain surprising history. **Seneca Falls** was allegedly the model for Frank Capra's fictional Bedford Falls, the setting of his classic movie *It's a Wonderful Life*. The town is also home to **Women's Rights National Historical Park**, commemorating the 1848 gathering of people like Elizabeth Cady Stanton, Frederick Douglass, and Lucretia Mott. Local parks like **Taughannock Falls, Grimes Glen**, and **Watkins Glen** feature scenic gorges and multiple waterfalls, plus numerous walking and hiking trails.

For A-List Attractions and Authentic Flavors
East Los Angeles, California, U.S.A.

Instead of West Los Angeles, California, U.S.A.

Now located in Highland Park, the Bob Baker Marionette Theater is one of the longest running puppet show theaters in the United States.

The City of Angels remains a wildly popular destination, blessed with attractions sought out by travelers from around the world, who love strolling the Santa Monica Pier, hanging out at Venice Beach, and swanning through Beverly Hills (technically an independent city, not an L.A. neighborhood). Yet huge swaths of America's second city remain unknown to many visitors, and that's a shame. People eager to see a hidden Los Angeles, removed from the glitz of the Sunset Strip or Rodeo Drive, should explore the city's northeast corner pocket and its collection of residential neighborhoods. Mount Washington, Highland Park, and Eagle Rock harbor eclectic stores and lively restaurants, little-known museums, and even a collection of secret outdoor stairways.

These neighborhoods aren't the Los Angeles of a celebrity's TikTok feed, but the neighborhoods are distinctly L.A.—planted with the city's iconic palms and Seussian exotic shrubs. The canyons and steep hills sport Jenga towers of low-slung houses stacked in a jumble of historic styles from Arts and Crafts bungalows to mid-century split levels, all straining to catch a view. (Meander up **Mount Washington Drive** to glimpse some of the best ones.) Northeast L.A. caters to its residents more than tourists, who will be struck by its slower pace and the (relatively) calmer street traffic.

Explore museums and attractions like the **Los Angeles Police Museum**, which displays everything from officer badges to armored cars in an old Highland Park LAPD station. There's also the **Southwest Museum of the American Indian**, now part of the **Autry Museum of the American West**. It holds the country's second largest collection of Native American artifacts and resides in a Spanish-inspired castle in

Food trucks in East Los Angeles serve up tasty fare including carne asada tacos.

Mount Washington. Or scout out the city's **Historic-Cultural Monument #736**, a circa 1920 trailer park on Monterey Road.

The local flavor is tastiest, however, along the neighborhood's shopping streets. Spend an unhurried afternoon nosing and noshing among the vintage shops and pupuserias on **Figueroa Avenue**, and look for **Chicken Boy**, a 22-foot-tall (7 m) sculpture of a rooster-headed persona. The fiberglass fowl formerly graced an extinct downtown fried chicken joint before relocating to the roof of 5558 North Figueroa. Across the street, the **Highland Park Bowl**, a Depression-era bowling alley and bar, hosts bands and concerts. The buzz on **York Boulevard** is louder. The retail mix features one-of-a-kind boutiques, taquerias, and ice-cream shops as well as businesses offering typical California services like smog checks, skateboard repairs, and eyebrow threading. Window-shopping is most rewarding between **North Avenues 49** and **53**, an area that also includes the **Bob Baker Marionette Theater**. An Angeleno institution since 1963, the theater and its collection of 3,000 puppets moved to its Highland Park home in 2019.

Walking in car-crazed Los Angeles might seem absurd, but anyone wanting to combine exercise with sightseeing should consider exploring Northeast L.A. on foot via a series of paths and steps threaded throughout its hills and canyons. The stairs, built in the first wave of the city's development in the early 20th century, functioned as hillside shortcuts to schools, shopping, and streetcar stops when few Angelenos owned cars. Largely forgotten and mostly unmarked, they are a perfect way to penetrate the heart of the real L.A. A copy of *Secret Stairs: A Walking Guide to the Historic Staircases of Los Angeles* by Charles Fleming offers detailed directions to area climbs—including scenic steps in **Mount Washington** (4398 West Avenue) and in **Highland Park** (4836 Eldred Street)—as well as hikes throughout the rest of the city. "You'll discover parts of Los Angeles you never imagined existed," he promises.

Downtown Los Angeles

The perfect base camp from which to explore adjoining Northeast and East L.A., downtown Los Angeles is also a neighborhood with potent cultural pizzazz symbolized by the galleries and restaurants in the city's **Arts District** and important institutions like the **Disney Concert Hall** and **The Broad**, a contemporary art museum known for its collection of Lichtensteins, Basquiats, and Jeff Koons's "Michael Jackson and Bubbles," a 1988 porcelain sculpture of the infamous singer and his pet chimpanzee.

Out-of-towners who are more traditionally attuned to the sights of the city's west side should take an afternoon and sign up for a tour with the **L.A. Conservancy**, a group that offers guided walks devoted to downtown's important buildings and history from **Pershing Square** to **Union Station**. The hikes reveal a Los Angeles that is quite different than the sand, sun, and glamour of Santa Monica and Brentwood. Some tours even include a trip on the famed **Angels Flight** funicular, an antique cable car that hoists visitors up and down **Bunker Hill**.

There are all sorts of hotels here. One that exudes a contemporary style mixed with classic Spanish Revival details is the **Hotel Figueroa**. The "Fig," located across the street from the **Grammy Museum**, sports a busy lobby and details like a mysterious coffin-shaped pool and paintings by female artists, a tribute to the hotel's start as a YWCA women's hostel in 1926.

Bustling Yanaka Ginza is one of the best streets for shopping in the Yanesen district.

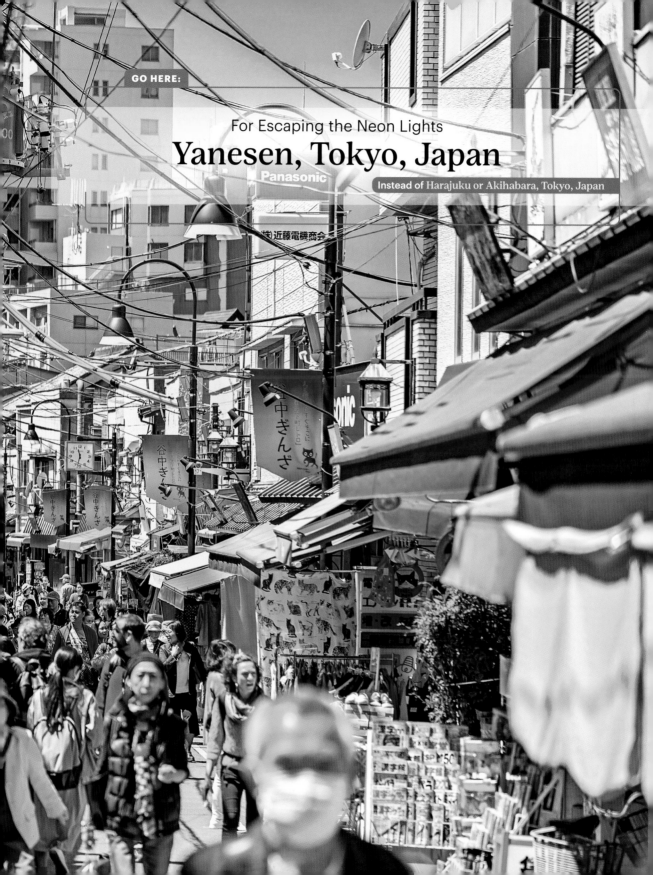

For Escaping the Neon Lights

Yanesen, Tokyo, Japan

Instead of Harajuku or Akihabara, Tokyo, Japan

Tokyo conjures images of Shinjuku's winking neon signs, painstakingly curated fashionistas in Harajuku, or stores stuffed with the latest electronics in Akihabara. After its urban reconstruction, Japan's capital can seem to many visitors an assemblage of modern and practical architecture festooned with technological touches. The older, classic Japan, it seems, is best found outside the capital. But it all depends on where in Tokyo you venture. Travelers who want to discover a Tokyo more connected to its past need to visit the Yanesen district, where older traditions still linger in an ever evolving city.

Yanesen is an acronym for Yanaka, Nezu, and Sendagi, a collection of neighborhoods located in Shitamachi, or lower Tokyo, east of the Imperial Palace. It's a section of the old downtown lucky enough to have survived many of the assaults visited on the city during the 20th century—both human-made and natural—like the 1923 earthquake, the bombings during World War II, and the urban modernization projects of the 1960s and 1970s. In contrast to downtown Tokyo, this part of the city is a pleasing jumble of narrow streets with a low-rise mix of shrines and temples, artisanal shops, and small bars and restaurants like those clustered along the pedestrian-only **Yanaka Ginza**. Outside many of Yanesen's wooden homes sit collections of flowerpots carefully arranged on entryways and

Visit the Yanaka district, known for its traditional temples and cemeteries, in the spring to catch the pink cherry blossoms.

stoops—the neighborhood's endearing visual trademark. Accommodations here are unique. Two hotels exude the low-key, community feeling of the neighborhood: The **Ryokan Sawanoya** is a traditional *ryokan*, or Japanese inn, with tatami mats, shared Japanese-style soaking baths, and bicycles to rent. In Nezu, the hip and minimalist **Hotel Graphy** features retro accommodations with a kitchen, a roof deck, and some shared bathrooms.

Also known for its local artisans and makers, Yanesen is a good place to scout for unique gifts and souvenirs. The shopping is particularly rewarding for items like wood carvings, pottery, jewelry, textiles, and ink prints. The district is also dotted with independent restaurants offering up unfussy, straightforward Japanese dishes like *menchi katsu*, a ground meat cutlet rolled in panko crumbs, deep-fried, and served with *tonkatsu* (a kind of Japanese Worcestershire sauce) and sliced cabbage. After a meal, visit a traditional coffee shop (called a *kissaten*) or try the special homemade candy, known as *amezaiku*, made from heated sugar syrup and sculpted on the spot by the candymaker into any kind of animal, Godzilla included.

Yanesen contains numerous cultural attractions, such as **SCAI the Bathhouse**, a contemporary art museum in Yanaka housed in a traditional bathhouse from Old Tokyo. Wander the cherry-tree bedecked **Yanaka Cemetery**, where dozens of famous artists and writers are buried. The cemetery's **Tennoji Temple**, with its large Buddhist statue, dates from 1274. There are other historic shrines as well: **Nezu-jinja**, or the Nezu Shinto shrine, is one of Tokyo's oldest and prettiest temples, with a passageway of red torii gates reminiscent of Kyoto's famed Fushimi Inari Shrine. A plum garden is the location of the **Yushima Tenjin Shrine**, beloved by students who pray here before their exams. There's also a cow statue. Stroking the bronze bovine is believed to cure disease.

With its smaller, neighborly atmosphere, Yanesen offers visitors the opportunity to discover a more intimate Tokyo with the rhythms of an earlier time.

Japanese women wearing *yukatas*, or more casual kimonos, shade themselves with parasols.

Seoul Reroutes Its Freeways

Inspired by the American freeway system, countries worldwide have overlaid their cities with strands of concrete spaghetti. But noisy expressways often hurt neighborhoods more than they help them. Seoul, however, did something different with theirs: Over the past 20 years South Korea's capital has torn down or repurposed at least 15 old freeways and transformed them into vibrant new parks, making central Seoul a more walkable city. Downtown's **Cheonggyecheon Stream** looks natural, but it was once the car-crammed Cheonggye Freeway. In 2003 Seoul tore it down and transformed it into a 5.5-mile-long (9 km) riverside park, breathing new life into the neighborhoods around it. Similarly, the city refashioned a train station overpass into a pedestrian-only garden called **Seoullo 7017**.

Other roadways have become bike or bus lanes, and one was transformed into a pedestrian bridge over the Han River. Inspired by a footbridge once built on the same spot, it provides stellar skyline views while allowing access to **Nodeulseom Island**, an arts and cultural center in the Han.

GO HERE:

For Modern Art in an Imperial City

798 Art District, Beijing, China

Instead of the Forbidden City, Beijing, China

The Center for Contemporary Art has presented more than 100 exhibitions and attracted more than four million visitors.

Bright murals and graffiti decorate Beijing's hip arts district.

OPPOSITE: A painted sculpture outside an art center in the 798 Art District

Beijing's sprawling Forbidden City preserves the power and glory of China's imperial past, but the Chinese capital has modern sections that are also worth exploring. By all means tour Beijing's centuries-old landmarks, but make room in your schedule to visit the city's 798 Art District, a lively new neighborhood devoted to celebrating urban China's creativity in a former industrial complex.

Beijing was once known for its traditional *hutongs*, or alleys, lined with low-rise courtyard houses. By the turn of the 21st century many of these old buildings and communities had been bulldozed out of existence. Like those vanished neighborhoods, the 148-acre (60 ha) Contemporary Arts District, located in the **Chaoyang District** in the northeast part of the city, is itself a jumble of roads and alleys interspersed with industrial-looking buildings. The 798 Art District, between Jiuxianqiao North Road and Jiangtai Road, is named after one of the numbered factories Communist planners working with Russian and East German counterparts constructed on these former farm fields during the first of China's "five-year plans" in the 1950s.

The buildings here were initially purposed as state-run manufacturing centers for military electronics. Built by East German designers schooled in the ways of the modernist Bauhaus style, with building materials imported via the Trans-Siberian Railway, the factories were planned to allow for luminous natural light. Such streamlined blueprints frustrated China's Russian colleagues, who wanted something more ornate like the Moscow sky-scrapers beloved by dictator Joseph Stalin. The Russians lost the argument. Though hailed for their futuristic forms, the inefficient factories were gradually shuttered as China modernized in the 1980s and '90s.

Artists began trickling into the area in the early 2000s, attracted by the buildings' architecture, cavernous empty spaces, and, of course, the copious amounts of light. Still adorned with Communist slogans and exhortations painted in large red Chinese characters, their empty hangars became studios and galleries. Gentrification soon followed, and the neighborhood is now filled with design studios, Sichuan and French restaurants, bubble tea lounges, and cutting-edge boutiques and shops. In some instances, the industrial goods became part of the allure—like an old steam locomotive parked outside a trendy coffeehouse. And the art is not confined to the interior of galleries: The district's brick facades and walls are splashed with vibrant and colorful murals as well.

Despite the flat white coffees and stores selling Mao T-shirts, the art scene remains the district's primary draw for both locals and tourists. There are plenty of galleries and changing exhibits here and on the adjoining streets to make for a full day out. Chief among them is the **Center for Contemporary Art** (UCCA), a three-building complex and exhibition space founded in 2007 by Belgian couple Guy and Myriam Ullens. Today it displays traveling art shows and works of contemporary Chinese artists. The nearby **Xin Dong Cheng Space for Contemporary Art** showcases both Chinese and Western artists. Other current contemporary art spaces include the **Triumph Gallery** and the **798 Art Factory**. Consider staying in the **Gracie Art Hotel**, a boutique property in the neighborhood, or **EAST Beijing** just south of it. The latter is a contemporary 369-room hotel.

Historic Tianjin

Shanghai's Bund, the iconic waterfront collection of imposing pre–World War II banks and sky-scrapers, is famous as a symbol of the city's global roots, but there's another Chinese metropolis with a similar architectural inheritance. The port city of Tianjin (population 11.2 million) is only 30 minutes from Beijing via China's famous high-speed trains. Tianjin offers visitors the opportunity to explore a city celebrated for both its Chinese roots (it was founded in 1401) and historic international neighborhoods built when China was forced to accept the presence of French, British, German, American, Japanese, and other world powers in the colonial era of the late 19th and early 20th centuries. Tianjin's Chinese heritage can be encountered in the theater museum at **Guangdong Guild Hall** and on **Ancient Culture Street**, an aptly named avenue of traditional Chinese buildings filled with food stalls, artisanal shops, and crafts-masters. Many of Tianjin's European buildings, like the **Tung Lai Bank Building**, line the Hai River on **Heping Road**, a commercial street also called Golden Street for its upscale shops and restaurants, now overshadowed by the skyscrapers of 21st-century China. More English-, German-, and French-influenced architecture is found along the **Five Great Avenues**, a neighborhood with numerous restaurants and many celebrities' homes. Close by is **Marco Polo Plaza**, surrounded by Italianate buildings.

Acknowledgments

To my family and friends: Firstly, my mother and father, who imparted the gift of curiosity. Then my siblings and their families, including Katrina and Lily, the newest inquisitive Nelsons. My friends who shared ideas, insights, dinner, and shelter across the world during this book's writing. In New York: Elissa Birke, Susan Block, Debi Dunn, Shawn Fitzgibbon, Paul Jebara, Tamara Loomis, Michael Martin, Christina Nickolova, and Ed Pittman. In Paris: Kimberly Charles. In London: Annie Fitzsimmons, Brendan and Andrea Murray, and Anne Nelson and her Notting Hill Nelsons. In Washington, D.C.: Chris Farmer, John Grant, Ilan Greenberg, Paul Hunt, Neil King, Shailagh Murray, Simone Rathle, Clay Smith, George Stone, Mike van Opstal, and the two Jaynes: Wise and Clark. In New Orleans: Edward Benfield, Sean Cummings, Wayne Curtis, Julie Ferriot, Ariana Ganak, Alex Geriner, Lisa Herman, Larry Lovell, Andy Myer, Patrick Owens, Kristian Sonnier, and the unquenchable Sue Strachan. In Texas: Stephanie Corley, Cristina and Vic Noriega, Laura Payne, and Chaney Tullos. In California: Jeremy Braud, Shannon Brooks, Bob Ciano, Chuck and Ally Finnie-Gervais, John Iglar, Joyce Khiel, Karena O'Riordan, and Biggi Vaughn. Elsewhere: Mike Alexander, Rebecca Chapa, Steve and Carmen Foster, Mark Guarino, David Haynes, Karl Kurka, Seth Maney, Matt and Sue Manley, Katherine and Tom Michael, Dana and Mike Murphy, the Sargents, and Wyatt Starosta. Also, those adventurers who are now somewhere but not here: Susan Cagann, Richard McKirdy, Doug Rockett, David Boyd Williams, and Martha Hume, an editor who reminded me to ask "what's not happening" rather than what was. You still light a path.

To my National Geographic circle: book editor Allyson Johnson, associate editor Gabriela Capasso, senior production editor Michael O'Connor, designer Nicole Miller Roberts, photo editor Meredith Wilcox, creative director Elisa Gibson, director of photography Adrian Coakley, and researcher Karen Carmichael. And my Traveler family: Meghan Aftosmis, Amy Alipio, Jenn Barger, Leigh Borghesani, Sheila Buckmaster, Kim Connaghan, Maria Coyne, Kris Davidson, Andrew Evans, Anne Farrar, Carolyn Fox, Heather Greenwood Davis, the undoubted Susanne Hackett, Nadine Heggie, Catherine Karnow, Emily King, Tom King, Andrea Leitch, Carrie Miller, Janelle Nanos, Susan O'Keefe, Norie Quintos, Jill Robinson, Krista Rossow, Brooke Sabin, Cat Salt, Jerry Sealy, Susan Seubert, Marilyn Terrell, Pandy Todd, Dan Westergren, Starlight Williams, Patten Wood, Heather Wyatt, and my late mentor Keith Bellows, the editor in chief who brought us together and was responsible for forging these extraordinary and enduring bonds.

To my fellow travelers: I was delighted to befriend such insiders as Cara Bongiorno, Kristen Bonilla, Vicki Bristol, Stephanie Brown, O'Shannon Burns, Mark Burt, Lauren Cason, Lucy Clifton, Victor De Vita, Dominika Dryjski, Vanessa Farquharson, Alessandro Ferrara, Joel Freyberg, Tom Garzilli, David Gonzalez, Kim Grant, Meagan Happel, Chris Heywood, Helen Hill, Jess Holt, Karna Hughes, Laura Hunt-Little, Kourtney Jones, Claire Koenig, Chris Moyer, Brad Packer, Angie Pappas, Scott Peacock, Julia Perowne, Diana Piktell, Dee Dee Poteete, Cathy Reynolds, Mark Romig, Eric Rosen, Brittany Rossi, Luke Sicard, Morgan Snyder, Dodie Stephens, Eleanor Talley, Marla Tambellini, Nick Urig, Nicole Vassallo, Liz Ware, Doug Warner, Nick Wayland, Amy Weirick, Anna Whitlow, and my ILTM kitchen cabinet: Bruce Wallin in L.A., Carlo Ducci in Florence, Bia Perna in flight, Jeremy Wayne in Westchester, Juliana Saad in São Paulo, and Martin Nahra in Buenos Aires. And lastly to the guides, river rats, pilots, flight attendants, flaneurs, publicists, chefs, hoteliers, bartenders, boulevardiers, baristas, waiters, drivers, and postal carriers whose tips and enthusiasm I welcomed. You are the sinew and soul of travel, and I shall continue to appreciate your suggestions and directions as to what lies around the corner, over the hill, or here not there.

Illustrations Credits

Cover, Karol Kozlowski/robertharding; back cover: (UP LE), Giovanni Simeone/Sime/eStock Photo; (UP CT), Bernd Rommelt/Huber/eStock Photo; (UP RT), Peter Kirillov/Getty Images; (LO LE), Nicholas Worden/Adobe Stock; (LO CT), Craig Jack Photographic/Alamy Stock Photo; (LO RT), Spring Images/Alamy Stock Photo; 2-3, Michele Rossetti/Sime/eStock Photo; 4, Bruno Morandi/Sime/eStock Photo; 6, Bruno Ázera; 7, chaney1/Getty Images; 8, Liam/Adobe Stock; 9, Wiskerke/Alamy Stock Photo; 10, sljones/Shutterstock; 11, Kristel Richard/Nature Picture Library; 12-3, Danflcreativo/Dreamstime; 14, Fotos593/Shutterstock; 15 (UP), Paolo Giocoso/Sime/eStock Photo; 15 (LO), ermakovep/Getty Images; 16, Zigres/Shutterstock; 17, Darren Robinson/Alamy Stock Photo; 18-9, f11photo/Adobe Stock; 20, Witold Skrypczak/Alamy Stock Photo; 21 (LE), Richard T. Nowitz; 21 (RT), Dori Lyn/Shutterstock; 22-3, Gunter Grafenhain/Huber/eStock Photo; 24, John Miller/robertharding; 25, Gaston Piccinetti/Shutterstock; 26, Domingo Leiva/Getty Images; 27 (UP), Mariana Greif/Reuters/Redux; 27 (LO), Ferrer & Sostoa/agefotostock/Alamy Stock Photo; 28-9, LongJon/Shutterstock; 30, rosinka/Stockimo/Alamy Stock Photo; 31, Nova Photo Works/Shutterstock; 32, Jon Chica/Shutterstock; 33 (UP), carlos/Adobe Stock; 33 (LO), JordiStock/Shutterstock; 34-5, Hal Bergman/Getty Images; 36, Claude Lapres/Getty Images; 37, Ed Jones/AFP via Getty Images; 38, warmcolors/Getty Images; 39 (UP), Paul Biris/Getty Images; 39 (LO), Hans-Georg Eiben/Huber/eStock Photo; 40-1, Luis Gutierrez/Norte Photo/Alamy Stock Photo; 42, Makasanaphoto/Dreamstime; 43, Chiara Salvadori/Getty Images; 44-5, P. de Graaf/Getty Images; 46, Sean Pavone/Getty Images; 47 (UP), aheflin/Adobe Stock; 47 (LO), Ian Cameron; 48, edb3_16/Getty Images; 49, edb3_16/Adobe Stock; 50-1, Colin Young/Dreamstime; 52, Jim West/Alamy Stock Photo; 53 (LE), tvirbickis/Getty Images; 53 (RT), blickwinkel/K. Wothe/Alamy Stock Photo; 54-5, Shane Pedersen/Alamy Stock Photo; 56, jamenpercy/Adobe Stock; 57, Pavel Dudek/Alamy Stock Photo; 58-9, Greg Vaughn/Alamy Stock Photo; 60, Spring Images/Alamy Stock Photo; 61 (LE), Terry Donnelly; 61 (RT), CSNafzger/Shutterstock; 62, flashhappymama/Stockimo/Alamy Stock Photo; 63, Karine Aigner/Nature Picture Library; 64, artitwpd/Adobe Stock; 65 (UP), Jing-Chen Lin/Shutterstock; 65 (LO), Stephan Gladieu/Figarophoto/Redux; 66-7, Migration Media—Underwater Imaging/Getty Images; 68, Airphoto Australia/Getty Images; 69, Blue Planet Archive/Franco Banfi; 70, Frans Blok/Shutterstock; 71 (UP), Nicolas Economou/NurPhoto via Getty Images; 71 (LO), Sergio Pitamitz/National Geographic Image Collection; 72-3, Jerry Whaley/Shutterstock; 74, Anthony Heflin/Shutterstock; 75, Allen Creative/Steve Allen/Alamy Stock Photo; 76, Paolo Giocoso/Sime/eStock Photo; 77 (UP), O. Louis Mazzatenta/National Geographic Image Collection; 77 (LO), Marc Dozier/Getty Images; 78-9, Bernd Rommelt/Huber/eStock Photo; 80, Patrick J Endres/AlaskaPhotoGraphics; 81, Brown W. Cannon III/Cavan Images; 82-3, Giovanni Simeone/Sime/eStock Photo; 84, George Rose/Getty Images; 85 (UP), Chuck Place/Adobe Stock; 85 (LO), Leonid Serebrennikov/Alamy Stock Photo; 86-7, rudi1976/Adobe Stock; 88, Gergo Csorba/Adobe Stock; 89, Peter Schickert/Alamy Stock Photo; 90, Martin Meehan/Dreamstime; 91 (UP), Adrian Davies/Alamy Stock Photo; 91 (LO), Christopher Nicholson/Alamy Stock Photo; 92, Reinhard Schmid/Huber/eStock Photo; 93, Gianfranco Vivi/Alamy Stock Photo; 94-5, Kevin Ruck/Adobe Stock; 96, George Rose/Getty Images; 97 (LE), Krista Rossow/National Geographic Image Collection; 97 (RT), Owen Franken/Getty Images; 98-9, Christian Heeb/laif/Redux; 100, Globepouncing/Adobe Stock; 101, Peter Treanor/Alamy Stock Photo; 102-3, Alfio Giannotti/REDA&CO/Universal Images Group via Getty Images; 104, Serenity-H/Adobe Stock; 105 (LE), Stephen Hughes/Alamy Stock Photo; 105 (RT), White Fox/AGF/Universal Images Group via Getty Images; 106, Alex Hinds/Stockimo/Alamy Stock Photo; 107, Mark Bolton Photography/Alamy Stock Photo; 108-9, Dennis M. Swanson/Adobe Stock; 110, Joanna Kalafatis/Alamy Stock Photo; 111 (LE), Chuck Place/Alamy Stock Photo; 111 (RT), Dee Jolie/Alamy Stock Photo; 112-3, Paul Panayiotou/Sime/eStock Photo; 114, Massimo Borchi/Sime/eStock Photo; 115, Anna Lurye/Adobe Stock; 116-9, Charlie Hamilton James/National Geographic Image Collection; 120-1, Paul Marcellini/Tom Stack & Associates; 122-3, Prisma/Christian Heeb/Alamy Stock Photo; 124, aheflin/Adobe Stock; 125 (LE), National Park Service; 125 (RT), Sean Pavone Photo/Adobe Stock; 126, Stephen Pingry/Tulsa World via AP; 127, Vineyard Perspective/Shutterstock; 128, Ventu Photo/Shutterstock; 129 (UP), Galyna Andrushko/Adobe Stock; 129 (LO), Greg McCown/Saguaro Pictures; 130, Ric Ergenbright/DanitaDelimont/Adobe Stock; 131, volgariver/Getty Images; 132-3, Olimpio Fantuz/Sime/eStock Photo; 134, Mauro Toccaceli/Alamy Stock Photo; 135 (LE), lorenza62/Shutterstock; 135 (RT), Polifoto/Adobe Stock; 136-7, Jordi Busque/National Geographic Image Collection; 138, John Elk/Getty Images; 139, Matt Williams-Ellis/SOPA/eStock Photo; 140, Bob Grabowski/Dreamstime; 141 (UP), Andy Williams photos/Shutterstock; 141 (LO), ImagineGolf/Getty Images; 142-3, Michele Hoffman/EyeEm/Adobe Stock; 144, Jon Reaves/Alamy Stock Photo; 145, VHcreations/Getty Images; 146, LukeandKarla.Travel/Shutterstock; 147 (UP), Michelle Laramore/EyeEm/Adobe Stock; 147 (LO), Deb Perry/Getty Images; 148-9, ricktravel/Adobe Stock; 150, Gary Crabbe/Enlightened Images Photography; 151, Art Wolfe; 152, Tom

Dempsey/PhotoSeek; 153 (UP), Jim Vallee/Adobe Stock; 153 (LO), National Park Service/Dunbar; 154–5, Blue Planet Archive/Doug Perrine; 156, Paul Marcellini/Tom Stack & Associates; 157, Francisco Blanco/Shutterstock; 158–9, Peter Essick/Cavan Images; 160–1, David A. Barnes/Alamy Stock Photo; 162 and 163 (LE), Melissa Farlow/Axiom Photographic/Design Pics Inc; 163 (RT), Nicholas Worden/Adobe Stock; 164, Jeffrey Isaac Greenberg 7+/Alamy Stock Photo; 165, Mark Kanning/Alamy Stock Photo; 166, James Kirkikis/Shutterstock; 167 (UP), rudi1976/Adobe Stock; 167 (LO), Sydney Dauphinais; 168–70, Wileydoc/Shutterstock; 171, Cynthia Mccrary/Dreamstime; 172, Bill Crnkovich/Alamy Stock Photo; 173 (UP), f11photo/Shutterstock; 173 (LO), Jim Packett/Shutterstock; 174, ivetakulhava/Adobe Stock; 175, Michael Henninger for the Washington Post via Getty Images; 176–7, Kimberly Genevieve/Gallery Stock; 178, Tom Ridout/Alamy Stock Photo; 179 (LE), Ken Howard/Alamy Stock Photo; 179 (RT), Tom Ridout/Alamy Stock Photo; 180–1, Steven Gaertner/Adobe Stock; 182, Jeremy Woodhouse/Getty Images; 183, Visit Natchez; 184–5, Marc F. Henning/Alamy Stock Photo; 186, picturelibrary/Alamy Stock Photo; 187 (LE), Tracy Godsey/Stockimo/Alamy Stock Photo; 187 (RT), Bram/Adobe Stock; 188–9, Anthony Heflin/Shutterstock; 190, Jeff Dean/AFP via Getty Images; 191, PapaBear/Getty Images; 192, Walter Bibikow/DanitaDelimont/Alamy Stock Photo; 193 (UP), Craig Jack Photographic/Alamy Stock Photo; 193 (LO), Yarvin Pennsylvania Journeys/Alamy Stock Photo; 194–5, mitzo_bs/Adobe Stock; 196–7, Eric Nathan/robertharding; 198, Adel Newman/Shutterstock; 199 (LE), Barry Kusuma/Getty Images; 199 (RT), Tobias Nowlan/Getty Images; 200–1, Richard Taylor/Sime/eStock Photo; 202, Julian Gazzard/Adobe Stock; 203, Denis/Adobe Stock; 204, Reinhard Schmid/Huber/eStock Photo; 205 (UP), A.J. Wilhelm; 205 (LO), Kenneth Garrett/National Geographic Image Collection; 206, mitzo_bs/Adobe Stock; 207, Stockbym/Adobe Stock; 208, Peter Kirillov/Getty Images; 209 (UP), Amy Toensing/National Geographic Image Collection; 209 (LO), Kit Leong/Shutterstock; 210–1, Walter Bibikow/Getty Images; 212, Cristina Ionescu/Adobe Stock; 213, MoiraM/Adobe Stock; 214, Michael Brooks/Alamy Stock Photo; 215 (UP), William Widmer/Redux; 215 (LO), Earth Pixel LLC/Alamy Stock Photo; 216–7, Ally Foster/Shutterstock; 218, eloleo/Adobe Stock; 219, Martin Thomas Photography/Alamy Stock Photo; 220–1, saiko3p/Adobe Stock; 222, ePhotocorp/Getty Images; 223 (LE), Frank Bienewald/Alamy Stock Photo; 223 (RT), Atlantide Phototravel/Getty Images; 224, Yuri Zvezdny/Shutterstock; 225, imageBROKER/Oliver Gerhard/Alamy Stock Photo; 226, mehdi33300/Adobe Stock; 227 (UP), Sergii Figurnyi/Adobe Stock; 227 (LO), Christian Kober/robertharding; 228–9, Neil McAllister/Alamy Stock Photo; 230, Steve Stringer Photography/Getty Images; 231 (UP), Gregory Gerault/hemis/Alamy Stock Photo; 231 (LO), Jon Hicks/Getty Images; 232, Gerard + Belevender; 233, Davslens Photography/Adobe Stock; 234–5, Konstantin Trubavin/Sime/eStock Photo; 236, Josh Owen/TandemStock; 237 (LE), Paul Sutherland/National Geographic Image Collection; 237 (RT), CRS Photo/Shutterstock; 238–40, Bruno Ázera; 241, Marija Krcadinac/Shutterstock; 242, Derek Galon/Getty Images; 243 (UP), Michael Runkel/robertharding; 243 (LO), Franco Banfi/Biosphoto/Alamy Stock Photo; 244–5, Matt Propert/National Geographic Image Collection; 246, Bertrand Gardel/hemis/Alamy Stock Photo; 247, David

Giral/Alamy Stock Photo; 248–9, Peter Frank Edwards/Redux; 250, Laura Liz Photography/Shutterstock; 251 (LE), jctabb/Shutterstock; 251 (RT), Peter Frank Edwards/Redux; 252–3, Frank Lukasseck/Huber/eStock Photo; 254, Greg Balfour Evans/Alamy Stock Photo; 255, Fanfo/Adobe Stock; 256–7, Westend61/Michael Runkel/Alamy Stock Photo; 258, Justin Foulkes/Sime/eStock Photo; 259 (LE), Michael Grant/Alamy Stock Photo; 259 (RT), Jeffrey Isaac Greenberg 5+/Alamy Stock Photo; 260, Spring Images/Alamy Stock Photo; 261, Ed Callaert/Alamy Stock Photo; 262–3, Blue Planet Archive/David B. Fleetham; 264, Blue Planet Archive/David B. Fleetham; 265 (LE), Douglas Peebles/eStock Photo; 265 (RT), HIPHO/Shutterstock; 266–7, Floriano Rescigno/Dreamstime; 268, Rainer Jahns; 269, Massimo/Adobe Stock; 270–1, Greg Vaughn/Alamy Stock Photo; 272–3, Jack Dykinga/Nature Picture Library; 274, Christian Heeb/robertharding; 275 (LE), Matt Mawson/Getty Images; 275 (RT), Luciano Leon/Alamy Stock Photo; 276–7, Panoramic Images/Les Palenik/Alamy Stock Photo; 278, Debra Millet/Alamy Stock Photo; 279, redtea/Getty Images; 280, Tosh Brown/Alamy Stock Photo; 281 (UP), parkerphotography/Alamy Stock Photo; 281 (LO), Lydia Schrandt/Alamy Stock Photo; 282, Archisto Library/Alamy Stock Photo; 283, Andre Jenny/Alamy Stock Photo; 284, Ali Majdfar/Getty Images; 285 (UP), Edwin Remsberg/VWPics via AP Images; 285 (LO), Walt/Adobe Stock; 286–7, eyewave/Getty Images; 288, Loic Venance/AFP via Getty Images; 289, imageBROKER/Guenter Graefenhain/Alamy Stock Photo; 290–1, Cathyrose Melloan/Alamy Stock Photo; 292, Wolfgang Kaehler/Getty Images; 293 (LE), Dante/Adobe Stock; 293 (RT), Patrik/Adobe Stock; 294–5, Feng Wei Photography/Getty Images; 296, Crin/Adobe Stock; 297, Vincent Louis/Shutterstock; 298, Tod Seelie/Getty Images; 299 (UP), AP Photo/Morgan Lee; 299 (LO), Lindsay Fendt/Alamy Stock Photo; 300–1, Blue Planet Archive/Reinhard Dirscherl; 302, Tim Laman/National Geographic Image Collection; 303, Tim Laman; 304–5, EWY Media/Adobe Stock; 306, John Coletti/Jon Arnold Images/Alamy Stock Photo; 307 (LE), James Schwabel/Alamy Stock Photo; 307 (RT), The Harry T. & Harriette V. Moore Cultural Center and Museum; 308–9, Craig Steven Thrasher/Alamy Stock Photo; 310, George H. Long; 311 (UP), Erika Goldring/Getty Images; 311 (LO), Serhii Chrucky/Alamy Stock Photo; 312–3, Mark Summerfield/Alamy Stock Photo; 314, Tom McCorkle for the Washington Post via Getty Images; 315, Randy Duchaine/Alamy Stock Photo; 316, Jon Bilous/Dreamstime; 317 (UP), Craig Steven Thrasher/Alamy Stock Photo; 317 (LO), Maurice Savage/Alamy Stock Photo; 318–9, Maxime/Adobe Stock; 320, Tony/Adobe Stock; 321, Jule_Berlin/Adobe Stock; 322, Pgiam/Getty Images; 323 (UP), Stephen Saks Photography/Alamy Stock Photo; 323 (LO), Kevin Ruck/Adobe Stock; 324–5, Greg Noire, Sony, courtesy International African American Museum; 326, Sean Rayford/Getty Images; 327, Tony Cenicola/The New York Times/Redux; 328, J. Conrad Williams, Jr./Newsday RM via Getty Images; 329 (UP), Katharine Andriotis/Alamy Stock Photo; 329 (LO), Paul Massie Photo/Adobe Stock; 330, Nolwen Cifuentes/The New York Times/Redux; 331, Bryce Bridges/Stockimo/Alamy Stock Photo; 332–3, kuremo/Shutterstock; 334, kuremo/Shutterstock; 335 (LE), Satoshi-K/Getty Images; 335 (RT), galitskaya/Adobe Stock; 336–7, Lucas Vallecillos/Alamy Stock Photo; 338, Alain Schroeder/REA/Redux; 339, zatletic/Adobe Stock.

Index

About the Author

Andrew Nelson is an author, writer, and educator with an interest in destinations of all sorts. His articles and stories have been published in various outlets including the *Wall Street Journal*, *National Geographic*, and *San Francisco Magazine*. Nelson's work has been recognized for its descriptive power and humor, earning him numerous accolades including two Lowell Thomas Awards for travel writing. He served as the director of editorial projects for *National Geographic Traveler* magazine in Washington, D.C. He has also lived and worked in San Francisco, New York, London, and the Big Bend region of Texas, where he restored an old adobe house. In addition to his travel writing, Nelson is an expert on the doomed steamship R.M.S. *Titanic*. He created and wrote an early best-selling computer game about the ship, *Titanic: Adventure Out of Time*, which won industry awards for its creativity and vision.

A passionate educator, Nelson served as a visiting professor in the mass communications program at Loyola University New Orleans' College of Music and Media for five years. He currently teaches classes on narrative and placemaking at the College of Charleston in South Carolina. Nelson is a graduate of Syracuse University in New York and holds a master's degree in journalism from the University of Missouri at Columbia. He splits his time between Charleston, South Carolina, and New Orleans.

Since 1888, the National Geographic Society has funded more than 14,000 research, conservation, education, and storytelling projects around the world. National Geographic Partners distributes a portion of the funds it receives from your purchase to National Geographic Society to support programs including the conservation of animals and their habitats.

National Geographic Partners, LLC
1145 17th Street NW
Washington, DC 20036-4688 USA

Get closer to National Geographic Explorers and photographers, and connect with our global community. Join us today at nationalgeographic.org/joinus

For rights or permissions inquiries, please contact National Geographic Books Subsidiary Rights: bookrights@natgeo.com

ISBN: 978-1-4262-2258-0

Printed in South Korea

23/ISK/1

The information in this book has been carefully checked and to the best of our knowledge is accurate. However, details are subject to change, and the publisher cannot be responsible for such changes, or for errors or omissions. Assessments of sites, hotels, and restaurants are based on the author's subjective opinions, which do not necessarily reflect the publisher's opinion.